The Imperial Dynasty

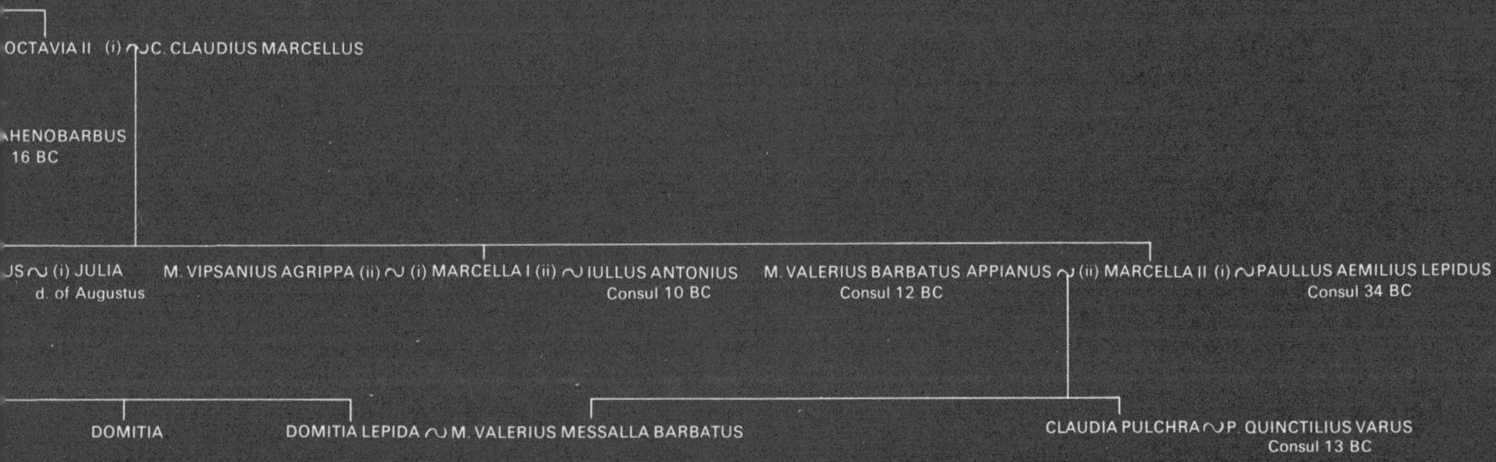

The Age of Augustus

Donald Earl

Photographs by Mario Carrieri and others

Exeter Books
NEW YORK

for Catharine,
Caroline
and Victoria

This edition published in USA 1980
by Exeter Books
Distributed by Bookthrift, Inc
New York, New York

ISBN 0-89673-044-1
LC 79-92323

Printed in Hong Kong
by South China Printing Co.

Contents

Preface

The Age of Augustus, the period between the death of Julius Caesar on 15 March 44 B.C. and the death of Augustus himself on 19 August A.D. 14, was of crucial importance for the history of Europe. At the beginning of the period the Roman world stood on the brink of disintegration; at its end Rome, Italy and the empire had received, for the first time in Rome's history as a Mediterranean power, an adequate and effective system of government which was to endure for three centuries. The Roman empire shaped western Europe and it was Augustus, more than any other single man, who created the Roman empire and the imperial system. It is this conception which has conditioned my treatment of the subject. The chief bias is biographical, the main framework political, constitutional and administrative, as they must be, partly because of the nature of the ancient sources, but, above all, because of the nature of the Augustan achievement, without which the past history and present state of western Europe would be vastly different from what it is. Into the main framework I have attempted to integrate economic and social developments, in particular that of the expansion of the Roman ruling class. The main theme is how Augustus' ambition for personal power and survival in the enjoyment of it led to the establishment of peace and stability in the Roman world, the proper administration of the empire, the integration of all classes of society in the business of government.

Just as economic and social developments, literature and architecture, thought and religion are considered not as discreet phenomena but as integral parts of a single whole, so the illustrations have been conceived not as decoration but as documenting and expanding the text. My thanks are due to all those who were concerned in the collection and supply of the photographs and especially to Miss Judith Farmer for her patient and courteous stimulation of my natural dilatoriness.

To attempt an exhaustive bibliography of the subject would be presumptuous were it not impossible. The Bibliography and Notes have two purposes only, to acknowledge the sources of information I have used in writing the text and to direct the interested reader to fuller discussions of the various topics treated. One work requires special acknowledgement, *The Roman Revolution* by Sir Ronald Syme. My debt to this book, which has revolutionized the study of the Augustan Principate, will be apparent on every page which follows.

I wish to thank my colleagues at Leeds University Dr A. R. Birley, Mr E. L. Harrison and Mr K. R. Rowe for their suggestions and their help.

Leeds April 1968 Donald Earl

List of Plates

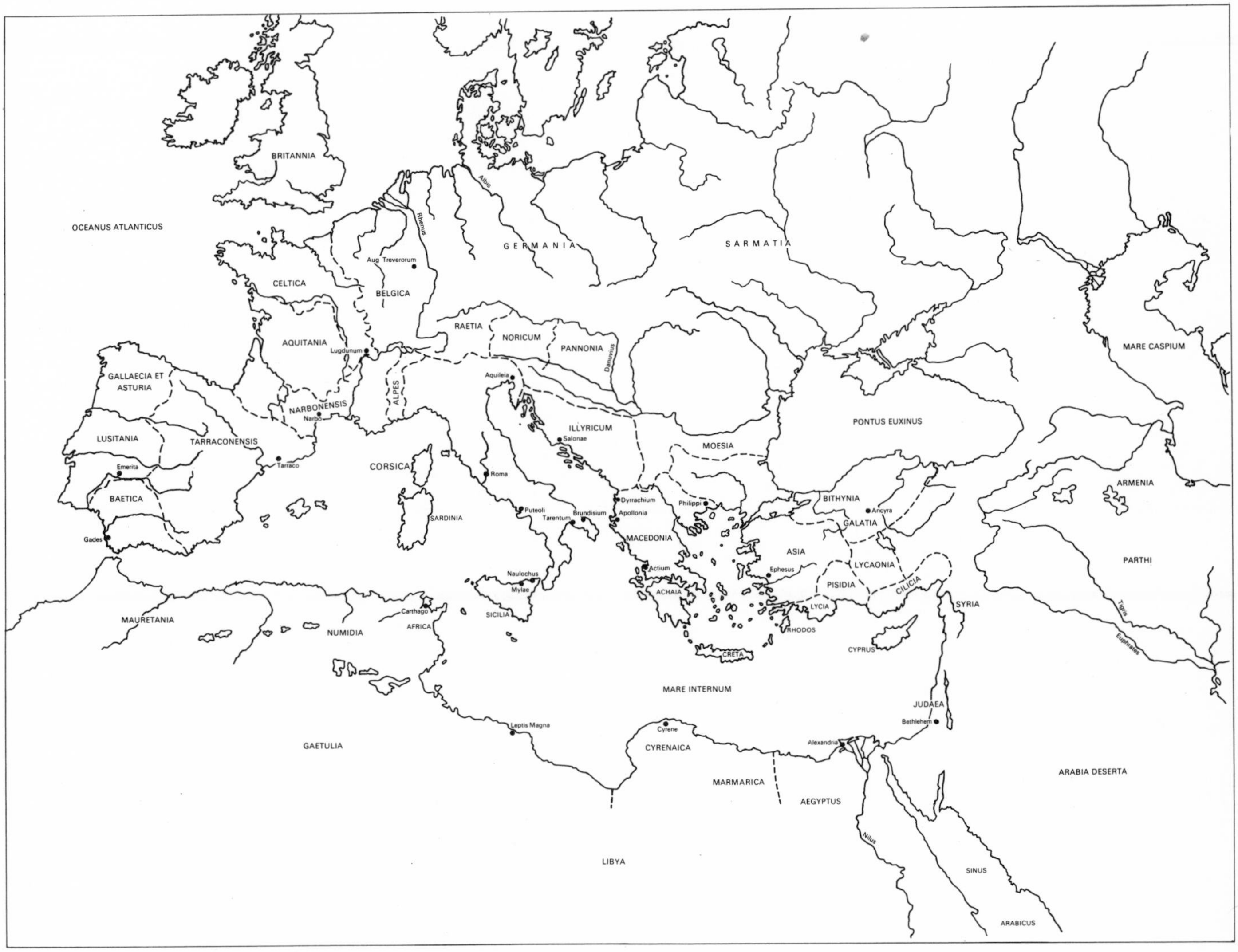

I The Roman World.

II Italy showing road networks.

Background and Antecedents

1

When in 44 B.C. C. Octavius (cf. plate 8) by posthumous adoption by his uncle became C. Iulius Caesar Octavianus, it may be supposed that his inheritance from the Dictator Caesar outweighed his birth and origin as an Octavius; and when, on 13 January 27 B.C., C. Iulius Caesar Octavianus, victorious over all rivals and master of the Roman world, transformed himself into the Princeps Augustus, a clean break with the Caesarian and Triumviral past might have been expected and was, indeed, announced and celebrated for Rome and her empire by poets and propagandists. Yet a man, raised through whatever vicissitudes to whatever eminence of power and fortune, does not easily slough off all trace of his origin. Consideration of the family and class into which C. Octavius was born may illuminate not a few of the attitudes and actions of the emperor Augustus (cf. plates 1, 30, 37).

Octavii had featured in Roman public life since the later years of the third century B.C., acquiring through the years considerable political success and connection with mighty political factions. Generation after generation they supported the Republic, the senatorial oligarchy and their own advancement. With this family propagandists, seeking a respectable ancestry for Augustus, sought to connect him. The attempt, although it imposed itself on later credulity, is not convincing. Augustus' forebears were not even Romans of Rome; they came from Velitrae (cf. map II, page 10, now called Velletri) in the Alban hills on the borders of Latium. Occupying an important strategic position dominating the approaches to the Alban hills from the south, the town had a complicated early history. The name itself is Etruscan and there is a large cemetery of Villanovan culture on the site. Velitrae, like Rome itself, seems to have been a community of Latin stock which was developed and urbanized by the Etruscans in the later seventh century B.C. When the Volsci began to push northwards into Latium, Velitrae became a border town between two expansionist powers and changed hands many times. In the final settlement of the Latin peoples in 338 B.C. after the revolt of the Latin league, the town was severely punished. The walls were thrown down and the local senate deported to live on the other side of the river Tiber. New colonists were sent to occupy the land confiscated from the exiled senators. The punishment of Velitrae, destruction of the walls and exile of disloyal senators, became Rome's customary method of dealing with the revolt of contumaciously refractory states. After 338 Velitrae slips from notice. Volscian influence remained strong. A bronze inscription in the Volscian language records officials called *meddices*, the usual title of the chief magistrate of Oscan communities, which suggests that for some time the full Roman citizens of Velitrae lived closely with men of lesser rights.

Later propaganda or family pride invented for the Octavii a glorious and fabulous history. The truth was more prosaic. The Roman Octavii first came into notice during the war with Hannibal. As for Augustus' family its connection with the Octavii of Rome is uncertain and for long years it dwelt quietly and obscurely at Velitrae; the Princeps himself admitted it. A C. Octavius was military tribune in 205 B.C., but the family's first Roman senator was Augustus' father, praetor in 61. Its first consulate came only with C. Iulius Caesar Octavianus, the future Augustus himself, in 43 B.C. Yet the family lived not entirely without importance in wider affairs. A street in Velitrae was named after the Octavii and there stood an altar dedicated by a certain Octavius who had been a general in a war between Velitrae and a neighbouring town. As he was sacrificing to Mars, the enemy was reported to be making a sudden attack. Seizing the entrails from the fire he offered them half-raw and then marched out to battle and victory. A decree of the people of Velitrae was on record ordering that in future the entrails should always be offered to Mars in this way and that the other parts of the victims should be handed over to the Octavii. For all the frauds of propaganda, the inventions of family pride and the prominence in Roman politics of the other homonymous clan, the class to which the Octavii belonged is patent; they came from, were possibly the leading family in, the local aristocracy of Velitrae.

At Rome political power and social position centred on the senatorial nobility. In the last age of the Republic the word *nobilitas* approached the status of a technical term, restricted to those families of which one member at least, either in the past or in the present, had attained the consulship. The first man in a family to reach the consulate became *nobilis* himself and, theoretically, ennobled his family forever. Not all members of the Senate, not even a majority of members, were noble in this sense and not all members of the nobility disposed of equal power and influence. Within the nobility itself there existed an oligarchy of some twenty or fewer families who possessed the reality of power and who by commanding armies, governing the provinces and directing the policy of the Senate shaped the destiny of Rome and of the western world.

The power of this oligarchy, indeed of the governing class as a whole, rested not on any legal or constitutional foundation but merely on its ability to control the votes of the Roman People. Before the law the *nobiles*, with the exception of the Patricians who retained from an earlier age a few, largely decorative, privileges, were in no different position from the other members of the Roman citizen body. Exactly how the nobility maintained its control over the Roman People, especially over the electoral assemblies which generation after generation returned members of the same few families to office and power, is frankly mysterious. Prestige and authority commanding respect and deference played their parts; so did bribery, direct and indirect. And, at the basis of the political power of the nobility lay the institution of clientship, *clientela*, by which the lower orders of society were closely bound to the various noble families in a relationship of mutual benefit. A noble patron helped and protected his client in various ways, thus creating reciprocal obligations, the chief of which was for the client to support his patron in his political career. Through a complicated network of personal and extra-constitutional relationships of this type the Roman nobility controlled not only the people of Rome but the whole of Italy by its ties of clientship and friendship with the leading men of the Italian communities. In the second century B.C. and later the concept was exported overseas and provincial *clientelae* came to be used, first for display and to enhance the prestige of the individual noble and then for direct and menacing influence on the political struggles of the capital. An informal arrangement of this kind can have succeeded only with the acquiescence of the Roman People at large. Regarding government as a service, the Roman People was content to leave politics to the politicians so long as the individual noble protected his clients and the government assured stability for the citizens. At no time, not even when the Republic was perishing amid civil war and chaos impended, can anything like a sustained popular movement be detected among the Roman People. Discontents existed in all ages, but they influenced political life only when used by the politicians for their own ends. The ordinary Roman desired only stability and freedom from interference, and a dictatorship of the type established by Caesar, if accompanied by these benefits, suited him as well as any amount of Republican liberty. It was because the Republican nobility failed in the end to provide these benefits that it failed to interest the ordinary Roman in its survival.

Assured of the uninterrupted enjoyment of political power, the Republican nobility was consumed within itself by a fierce and incessant competition for position. The basic political unit was the family group. Noble families formed alliances with each other the better to further the ambitions of their members or to attack their enemies. Such factions, with the ties of mutual interest frequently cemented by those of marriage, were usually *ad hoc* arrangements, but in the course of time certain lines of alliance became traditional, although always liable to modification by reason of personal ambition, antipathy or opportunism. Sometimes even the interest of the state entered the calculation and very occasionally the competing factions of the nobility would close ranks to face some quite exceptional crisis. But to the Roman noble the pursuit of power and glory, position and prestige was paramount. It was this that he equated with liberty and the Roman Republic.

The maintenance of the power of the Roman nobility depended precisely on the conservation of the existing status. By the second century B.C. Roman politics, though a ceaseless struggle for position and power by the leading men, had achieved a fair degree of equilibrium, the preservation of which was a major concern of every faction in the noble oligarchy. Every individual and every faction aspired to a position of pre-eminence and predominance, which every other individual and faction conspired to prevent—and aimed at for themselves. Just as the power of the senatorial oligarchy as a whole depended on its ability to control the voters at large, so within the oligarchy the power of each faction rested ultimately on its ability to control a specific section of the voters, its own clients. By their votes its members obtained the offices of state from which all prestige and position flowed. Hence the nobility's persistent resistance to reform. Given the existing political conditions, any reform of importance, by conferring an exceptional benefit on part of the populace, was likely to attract an increase of prestige and *clientela* to its sponsors and thus to upset the delicate political balance. Nor was it merely that the nobility had a vested interest in maintaining the present state; its whole power and position were founded only on custom and precedent. In the same way, while the Senate itself had emerged as the controlling and directing organ in the government of Rome, technically it remained a private and unofficial body, the council of the magistrates, particularly of the consuls. Very few indeed of its powers and prerogatives were sanctioned by law. The Roman revolution began when a faction of the nobility, prosecuting the incessant internal struggle of the oligarchy, exposed, in the tribunate of Tiberius Gracchus, the lack of any solid constitutional foundation to the power of the Senate and the control of public life by the aristocracy.

Fig. 1 Coin: Denarius; head of Julius Caesar. *London, British Museum. (Actual size).*

Under these circumstances the Roman nobility might have been expected to have hardened into a rigidly exclusive caste. It is true that hostile propaganda spoke of the arrogant exclusiveness of the nobility and of their guarding the consulship so jealously as to consider it polluted if held by a new man. It is true that a new man might in a moment of personal vainglory speak of storming the citadel of the nobility, exaggerating to enhance his achievement the barriers that were placed in his way. In fact, between one in six and one in eight of the consuls in the century and half which followed the defeat of Hannibal came from new families. These are minimum figures, based on the appearance of new names in the consular lists, and they demonstrate clearly that the Roman aristocracy was not rigorously exclusive of all new men at all costs, not even from the highest office of state. On the contrary, the nobility was in a state of continuous recruitment and regeneration. Many of the new men, promoted for personal talent or the convenience of their noble patrons, remained isolated examples; their descendants, though sometimes to be detected in the lower ranks of the Senate, lapse from eminence. Others, however, founded powerful political families which took their places only little inferior to aristocratic houses of fabulous antiquity. Very few, if any, of such new men, whatever their propaganda might claim, were honest sons of toil or boys fresh from the plough. They came, in the main, from the leading families of the Roman townships of Italy. Conditions in the communities from which these men came may be described as feudal, at least in the vulgar sense of that word, with a small number of families monopolizing social position and political power. Controlling the mass of their populations, they formed the essential link between the government at Rome and the ordinary people of Italy and from them the Roman nobility, always on the look-out for young men of talent and promise who might be introduced into the public life of the capital, took its

Fig. 2 Coin: Aureus, struck in Sicily by Sextus Pompey: reverse showing the heads of Pompey the Great and his son Gnaeus. *London, British Museum.* (*Actual size*).

recruits. As a result by the middle of the first century B.C. the Roman nobility was an heterogeneous body. Families of great antiquity vied with others of much more recent origin. The most extreme and efficient faction of the oligarchy was led and animated by the younger M. Porcius Cato. His great-grandfather had been a farmer in the Sabine country, introduced to Rome by the Patrician L. Valerius Flaccus.

Such new men succeeded at Rome because they accepted the standards of the capital and, even more important, because they were admitted and promoted by members of the established oligarchy. It was not from their ranks that the revolutionaries of the last age of the Roman Republic came. On the contrary, the new men tended to be the most ardent supporters of the authority of the Senate and of the Republic, that is, of the privileges and prerogatives of the class to which they had won admittance. Italian origin might be paraded for reasons of sentiment, interest or profit; essentially the outlook and standards of such men were those of Rome. A member of the nobility would make play with the mighty deeds of his ancestors and the standards of antiquity. To a new man this avenue was closed; he was, by definition, without ancestors in the special sense of the Roman political tradition. But he was not without resource. Cato the Censor, for instance, countered the ancestral claims of the aristocrat with his own youth spent in frugality and hard labour in the Sabine country. The appeal to the stern morality of the remoter parts of Italy to balance the noble's parade of a long line of ancestors and generations spent in the service of the state became traditional. Yet although the noble and the new man used different propaganda themes, their aims tended to be identical. No less than the noble, the new man strove at Rome for political glory and political power. The new man desired parity with and recognition by the nobles, not to supersede them.

In the last age of the Republic the effects of the enfranchisement of Italy began to make themselves felt and the emerging monarchic faction leaders, first Sulla and then Pompey (cf. figure 2, above) and Caesar, offered wider opportunities for advancement. But the real revolutionaries were not the new men, nor were they members of the ordinary nobility. Ap. Claudius Pulcher, the leader of the faction of Tiberius Gracchus, L. Cornelius Sulla and M. Aemilius Lepidus, L. Sergius Catilana and C. Iulius Caesar—all these men came from the most ancient and revered section of the nobility, the Patriciate. In strong contrast was Pompey whose family, although noble for three generations, was despised and hated by the good men of the ruling oligarchy. His youth was spent in prosecuting through illegality and fraud, through treachery and bloodshed, the interests of Sulla and his own advancement. His maturity was consumed by a struggle to win recognition of his pre-eminence and acceptance by Sulla's oligarchy and its successors. Returning from the east in 61 B.C. he ostentatiously refused to imitate Sulla and sought accommodation and connection with the younger Cato. Cato's rebuff drove him into uneasy alliance with Caesar from which he almost immediately tried to extricate himself. In the end it was the threat of civil war which drove Cato and his faction, whose pretentions Pompey had overshadowed, whose relatives he had murdered and whose alliance he had desired, to accept and use him. It was their fault that the accommodation was so late. Ambitious and bloodthirsty, untrustworthy and devious, Pompey was yet no revolutionary. He never crossed a Rubicon in his life.

The Roman Republic was destroyed by the ruinous lust for power and position of the class which had traditionally identified itself most closely with the *respublica*—the *nobiles*. Social and economic change there certainly was, rapid and relentless, but such developments merely provided the weapons for aristocratic ambition. The ideal of the Republican nobility had laid it down that only by doing good to the state could a man win prestige and glory, that the title to power was concern for the public good. When this ideal was destroyed, when personal power and domination were sought at the expense and ultimately to the ruin of the commonwealth, then the Republic itself was destroyed. Every generation in the history of the Roman Republic could show examples of oppression abroad and arrogance at home, of neglect of duty and self-regarding ambition. Yet for long years the defects of individuals were contained by the strength of the tradition. As late as the early decades of the second century B.C. the demands of the aristocratic ideal could be felt as imperative. The great Scipio Africanus, the conqueror of Hannibal, assailed by his enemies despite, or rather because of his services to the state, was yet not prepared to defend his position by subverting the whole aristocratic way of politics: he bowed to the storm and departed into exile. But not much more than thirty years later we have documented in the events of the Spanish wars clear evidence of a profound change in attitude. In these wars, which began in 154 B.C., the Roman armies were constantly defeated, the noble commanders proved themselves incorrigibly incompetent, treacherous and brutal, the Senate as a body was quite unable to impose its will and policy on the individual generals. That was bad enough, but what was entirely novel and portentous was that over an extended period of time the military needs of Rome and the demands of the provinces were consistently subordinated by all sections of the nobility to factional self-interest. It is not the least of the melancholy attractions of the study of the decline of the Roman Republic to observe how, as Rome's power and empire grew, everything became more and more subordinated to the factional struggles of the ruling oligarchy. Rome and the politics of the city came to be all that mattered.

Before the wars in Spain were over the mould of second-century politics was irreparably shattered when a powerful faction of the nobility, which included the leader of the Senate, Ap. Claudius Pulcher, and the tribune Tiberius Gracchus, attempted to exploit Rome's difficulties to upset the political balance in their own favour. Chief among Rome's difficulties had been that of finding sufficient recruits for the army. C. Marius, when he ignored the property qualification hitherto demanded for military service in raising his troops for the war with Jugurtha, solved the problem. He looked to win by his own efforts and by the political influence of his grateful veterans the prestige and authority which far-flung hereditary *clientelae* conferred on the nobles and a position in the Senate commensurate with his achievements. The senatorial oligarchy saw only an over-powerful outsider who had to be cut down to size. Hence the refusal to accept responsibility for settling the veterans of the Jugurthine and Cimbric wars, for if Marius were unable to redeem his promises to his discharged veterans, his clients, then his following and influence based on these clients could be expected to melt away. The result, however, was that the Senate lost control over the new type of army. For in the revolt of the Italian allies in 91 B.C., which was provoked by the persistent refusal of Roman politicians to treat the Italians and their claims as anything but pawns in the factional struggles of the capital, the soldiers became accustomed to civil war on Italian soil and to fighting not for their country against a recognizable foreign enemy but at the command of their generals against old comrades in arms. The developing professional army changed inevitably into a client army attached to its commander as its patron.

It was Sulla who crowned the process by his treasonable compact with Mithridates and his invasion of Italy. To secure personal position and power, to assert one's own prestige, what the Roman politicians called *dignitas*, any degree of force or fraud became legitimate. Catiline and Caesar document the ruin of the Republic. Catiline raised his revolution in the hope of preserving the remnants of his prestige, because despite his efforts he had not received the position due to his *dignitas* and saw unworthy men preferred to him. With Caesar the assertion and defence of his *dignitas* was a life-long obsession. It was in its defence that he finally crossed the Rubicon and marched on Rome. He himself admitted it. Well might Cicero exclaim, 'Are we talking about a general of the Roman People or Hannibal?'

In this revolutionary age the significance of Italian origin for any particular individual is undeniably difficult to determine. It is impossible, however, to over-estimate the importance of the leading men in the towns of Italy. Not many would reach the consulship at Rome; there is nothing surprising or sinister about that: the consulate conferred the highest power and formed the title to nobility—and there were only two consuls a year. But by the middle of the first century B.C. men of Italian origin may already have approached half the membership of the Senate, as they certainly did in the Senate as enlarged by Caesar. Most of them came, as would be expected, from communities near to Rome which had possessed the Roman citizenship for many generations. Yet before Caesar's death P. Vatinius was consul, in 47 B.C. He was of the Marsi, enfranchised only after the Italian rebellion. Then came P. Ventidius, consul in 43 B.C. He was phenomenal. He came from Asculum (cf. map II, page 10, now called Ascoli Piceno), the stronghold of the Italian rebellion, and as an infant had been captured when the fortress was taken and led in the triumph which Cn. Pompeius Strabo celebrated. C. Asinius Pollio, consul in 40, came from Teate. His grandfather, Herius Asinius, only fifty years before, had led the Marrucini against Rome and had died fighting for *Italia*. Such men were prophetic. Before long the men of Italy were to establish first equality with and then superiority over the nobility in the government of Rome.

Nor were they merely soldiers and politicians who came from Italy. The Italian communities gave to Rome many of the most famous names in Roman literature: Cicero (cf. plate 70) from Arpinum (Arpino), the home town of Marius, and M. Terentius Varro, the most learned man of his age, from Sabine Reate (Rieti); Sallust from Amiternum, also a Sabine community, and Asinius Pollio from Teate; Propertius from Assisium (Assisi) in Umbria, Ovid from Paelignian Sulmo (Sulmona), Horace from Venusia on the border of Apulia and Lucania; and from outside Italy proper, from Cisalpine Gaul, a notable triad: Catullus from Verona, Livy from Patavium, Virgil (cf. plate 24) from Andes near Mantua (cf. map II, page 10). Such names highlight the problem of Italian origin. What did it signify? Pollio might detect provincialism in Livy, yet Ovid's shallow sophistication is thoroughly metropolitan.

Many motives not scrutable to us might impel a young man from Italy to embark on the perilous course of a public career at Rome. In the case of the father of Augustus, the connection with Julius Caesar must have been decisive. His father, Augustus' grandfather, had been content with the quiet business of amassing a fortune by banking in Velitrae. But the son married Atia, daughter of M. Atius Balbus from nearby Aricia (Ariccia), a respectable and expected marriage uniting the leading families of two neighbouring towns. There must have been many such throughout Italy. But Atia's mother was no local woman, however wealthy and important; she was Julia, sister of Julius Caesar. The marriages of Caesar's family form an instructive study. The Iulii Caesares belonged to the most ancient and exclusive section of the Roman aristocracy, the Patriciate. They claimed descent from the goddess Venus, no less. Yet for all their fabulous antiquity the Iulii had in the later Republic fallen on hard times, and had become impoverished and politically obscure. Of Caesar's grandfather we know no more than that he married a woman called Marcia; that his great-grandfather was the brother of Sextus Iulius Caesar, consul in 157 B.C., and thus connected with the more successful line of the clan is the merest hypothesis. In their obscurity Caesar's family was far from unique. The history of the Patriciate after the closing of the Struggle of the Orders was one of rapid and continuous decline. Overtaken in the political aristocracy by the Plebeian nobles, many Patrician families died out altogether. A few, such as the Claudii Pulchri and the Cornelii Scipiones, retained the fullness of prestige and power. Many lived on in obscurity with little but an ancient name to comfort them in their loss of wealth and influence. Sulla came from one such family, Catiline from another. An ancient name and long obscurity could be as powerful a stimulus to revolutionary ambition as the energy and determination of a new man. And ambition, the re-assertion of ancient claims, the rehabilitation of a name long absent from the annals of Rome took precedence over considerations of dignity and the exclusiveness of class.

In their marriage alliances the Iulii of Caesar's branch were clearly on the lookout for wealth or political influence, not mere social distinction. Caesar's aunt was the wife of Marius, a new man from Arpinum. In the next generation one of Caesar's sisters married M. Atius Balbus, the other appears to have been the wife first of a Pinarius and then of a

Pedius and Caesar himself was betrothed to a girl called Cossutia before he was forced to marry Cinna's daughter, Cornelia. Not, at first sight, good marriages in the social sense. The Pinarii, it is true, were a Patrician clan with an ancestry as ancient and distinguished as that of the Iulii. But it is clear that not every man called Pinarius in this age could make good the claim to Patrician descent. M. Atius Balbus, for all the efforts of Augustan adulation to transform him into a Roman senator, belonged to the Italian gentry. As for the Pedii and the Cossutii, their fortunes were sustained by the process of trade. But what these families possessed was what the depressed Patrician most lacked and most needed—money. There were, of course, other advantages and connection with the gentry of Italy would not be without political profit. But the central question was that of money.

Politics at Rome were a fantastically expensive business. Cash was constantly required, for show and ostentation, for bribery, to subsidize friends and allies. Crassus remarked that nobody could be considered rich who could not support an army on his income. In 55 B.C., before he left for his ill-fated invasion of Parthia, he sacrificed a tenth of his estate to the god Hercules, gave a banquet to the whole population of Rome, furnished every citizen with enough to live on for three months—and was still able proudly to report that he had 7,000 talents left. His fortune before this display must have been over 8,000 talents; that is, roughly the same as Rome's total revenue from the provinces before Pompey's conquest of the East. Not that Crassus was the richest man in Rome. Pompey could have bought him out at any time. At the end of his Asian campaign Pompey had distributed to his soldiers, who had already received prize money and a great deal of booty, no less than 16,000 talents. What his own profit must have been we can only imagine. To succeed in this sort of company a Roman politician had to be or become extremely rich. Yet the senator, precluded by law and the sentiment of his class from direct involvement in trade, if he possessed a fortune, tended to have it in property and land or lent out at interest through agents and it might not, for many reasons of sentiment or economics, be desirable or possible to realize it. Hence the political importance of the business and commercial classes to provide cash for the landed noble and the ambitious but impoverished aspirant to political power. The senator affected to despise the business man, considering even one as cultured and acceptable as Cicero's friend Atticus inferior to the meanest member of his own order. It was a matter of *dignitas*, that peculiar prestige which was held to be the attribute only of senators and the importance of which to a senator was paramount. But he did not, could not afford to hesitate to enjoy the company, borrow the money and marry the daughters of business men. With money available to gratify senatorial ambition and with senators and aspiring senators deeply in his debt the business man disposed of real power.

Ambition and mutual advantage united the Patrician Iulii with the Italian Atii and Octavii. Iulii and Octavii shared another common interest: both were ancient sacerdotal families. An exact knowledge of religious ritual was an accomplishment proper to a Patrician and useful to any Roman politician. The Romans had no notion of the separation of Church and State, the state religion being considered an aspect of the government of the Republic not much different from other branches of domestic affairs, and consequently the chief priesthoods were occupied by the leading politicians. With few exceptions sacerdotal office did not disbar from an active political career. On the contrary, it increased prestige, authority and influence and bestowed real power which could be applied for political ends. Being almost entirely formalistic and, at the same time, closely woven into the fabric of public life, the Roman state religion offered endless opportunity for political manipulation. Before every piece of public business sacrifice was made and the will of the gods determined by inspection of the victim's entrails or some other method of divination. Even when this initial barrier had been safely crossed, disruption and postponement of business could be engineered by deliberate observation of the heavens for untoward meteorological phenomena or the report of such unlooked for events as the squeak of a mouse or a case of epilepsy. An aspiring politician could not afford to neglect his religious education. As rich a field for political manipulation was offered by the Republican constitution—if we may dignify with such a name the chaotic result of a series of *ad hoc* concessions to forestall internal revolution mingled with archaic survivals and preserved by an excessive and interested conservatism to produce a number of ill-defined, overlapping and potentially conflicting sources of power and authority. Caesar was an expert in both and not in the state religion only. Local or private cults with ancient deities and archaic rituals announced attitudes proper for a gentleman, advertised social position and conferred prestige. As a clan the Iulii worshipped the archaic and enigmatic deity Vediovis at Bovillae on the site of Rome's destroyed parent city Alba Longa (Albano), founded by Iulus, son of Aeneas, from whom the Iulii traced their descent. Similarly, Augustus' branch of the Octavii occupied a special position in the worship of Mars at Velitrae.

Connection with Caesar brought C. Octavius, abandoning his father's safe and lucrative profession of banker at Velitrae, to the uncertainties of politics at Rome, to honour and advancement. The praetorship of 61 B.C. was followed by the governorship of Macedonia (cf. map I, page 9), with military successes against some fugitive slaves on his way to his province and as governor against the Bessi and other Thracian tribes. He was a certainty for the consulship, but died before he could enter his candidature. The ancient sources praise his character with remarkable and suspicious unanimity. But at least some of the praise may have been merited, not prompted by natural adulation of his son. Cicero wrote to his variously unsatisfactory brother Quintus, who was then serving as governor of Asia (cf. map I, page 9) with no great credit, that he should imitate his neighbour Octavius. On his death Octavius left a widow and three children, two daughters and a son. Atia, by reason of her Julian descent a valuable resource of dynastic politics, was at once married to L. Marcius Philippus, consul in 56 B.C., and a member of a family whose talent for survival in the enjoyment of place and power was remarkable even among the Roman aristocracy. Her son, C. Octavius, born in Rome on September 23, 63 B.C., the year of Cicero's consulship and the conspiracy of Catiline, was taken up by Caesar.

Octavius' later fortune magnified his birth and his boyhood. Myth abounds, duly recorded by Suetonius; hard facts are in short supply: a funeral oration precociously delivered at the age of twelve before the Roman People in honour of his grandmother Julia; assumption of the toga of manhood on October 18, 48 B.C. and the receipt at the age of sixteen of military prizes at Caesar's African triumph; enrolment among the Patricians by Caesar, with whom he was in Spain for some time in 45 B.C. At the end of his life Caesar was planning an expedition against Parthia, to avenge a signal disgrace, to win military glory and to escape from Rome. Part of the army was mustered at the great military base at Apollonia in northern Greece. Thither C. Octavius was sent to study at the university and to make himself known to the soldiers. The decisive event in the young man's life happened on December 13, 45 B.C. On that day Caesar remade his will, naming Octavius as his chief heir. At the very end of the will he adopted him into his family and gave him his name.

Caesar's Heir

2

Inordinate personal ambition and total lack of concern for the interests of Rome and her empire were the marks of the leading politicians of the last age of the Republic. There was no hint of true revolution, of the replacement of the Republican system by another better suited to Rome's position as mistress of the Mediterranean world, no hint, either, of reform within the existing system. Reform came and revolution too, by which the Roman state was transformed, but they came slowly and haphazardly, without foresight or intention, the accidental by-products of the satisfaction of personal ambition. It was for the possession of power that men like Pompey and Cato, Caesar and Crassus struggled, not so that they could use it to implement some far-reaching political programme, but so that they, emerging stronger than their peers, might rule the Roman world according to their own desires and for their own profit. They did not even notice that in the process the Republic was destroyed. Caesar, outmanoeuvred and baffled by his enemies, turned his army against the government and won by civil war power such as no Roman had ever possessed. The result was ruthlessly to expose the limitations of his class and of himself. It has often been remarked that the measures of Caesar's dictatorship show no comprehension of Rome's problems and no ability to solve them. But, given time and civil peace, traditional remedies might in the end have alleviated traditional difficulties. But Caesar could not give Rome time. Sheer political incompetence, which caused his murder and a further thirteen years of civil war, is the heaviest count in the indictment against him. That he had no novel solutions to offer for Rome's difficulties is venial. What condemns him is his own perplexity, that he did not know and did not care to learn what was possible in Roman politics. Caesar condemned Sulla as a political illiterate because he resigned his power; the remark reveals the deficiency of Caesar, not of Sulla. Sulla, unlike Caesar, did not confuse the reality of power with titles and outward show and he died in his bed. If the Roman Republic meant anything, it meant the free traffic of power and office among the members of the ruling oligarchy. If an individual or faction, establishing by force or excess of prestige a temporary predominance, prevented this traffic, that was tyranny. Caesar ruled as a tyrant, not caring to disguise his position and power. Yet by an ostentatious parade of clemency, itself a tyrannical attribute, he pardoned his enemies. They accepted his clemency, recognized it for what it was and, on the Ides of March 44 B.C., murdered him.

The Conspirators destroyed a tyrant and restored liberty and the free Republic. But the liberty they acted to restore was the freedom of the *nobiles* to scramble for office and power and by the Republic they meant the rule of the aristocratic oligarchy. They had not learned that their style of politics was out of date, that their Republic was already dead, destroyed by a century of ruinous assertion of noble power and prestige and by the slow political and social revolution, the more irreversible for being unintended, that it had caused. The Ides of March were followed not by the rebirth of Republican liberty but by chaos and proscription, the devastation of Italy and civil war until Octavian emerged superior against all odds over all his rivals as master of the Roman world.

Money and, above all, soldiers were necessary for success and the Conspirators had neither in sufficient quantity. Caesar's murder faced them suddenly with their own impotence and the unreality of their aims. A day or two after the Ides of March Decimus Brutus wrote to Marcus Brutus and Cassius, 'We must give place to fortune; I think we must leave Italy and go to Rhodes or somewhere else. If the best happens we shall return to Rome; if ordinary fortune, we shall live in exile; if the worst, we shall employ the last resort. It will occur to some of your party at this point to ask why we wait for extremity rather than do something now. Because we have no support except Sextus Pompey and Caecilius Bassus'. Such were the resources of the Republic, the fugitive son of Pompey the Great and a bandit.

Overwhelmingly the advantage was with the Caesarians, for the money was Caesar's and the soldiers too. Whoever controlled Caesar's army would control the Roman state. Among Caesar's associates two men were peculiarly well placed, M. Aemilius Lepidus, Caesar's *magister equitum* (cf. plate 9), and Mark Antony (cf. plate 7), Caesar's colleague in the consulship of 44. Antony's portraits disclose a man of action, bull-necked and powerful, and in the chaotic days after Caesar's death he moved to control the situation and to establish his own position. The Senate had scattered in terror and the Conspirators, astonished that the people of Rome did not share their enthusiasm for the removal of the popular tyrant, fled to the Capitol. Antony first secured the support of Lepidus, in return for which he had Lepidus illegally appointed *Pontifex Maximus*, and then persuaded Calpurnia, Caesar's widow, to hand over her husband's private papers and private fortune. At a meeting of the Senate on March 17 he caused resolutions to be passed forbidding any inquiry into Caesar's assassination, proclaiming a general amnesty and ratifying Caesar's acts, not merely those which had already been carried out or published but anything which it could be shown the Dictator had intended. Since Antony was already in possession of Caesar's private papers, it would be rash, especially in view of what was to happen in the next few months, to assume that piety was the sole motive for this last decree. By his politic acceptance of the present situation, which he emphasized by entertaining the Conspirators to dinner and by acquiescing in Dolabella's assumption of the consulship left vacant by Caesar's death, Antony secured time to assess the possibilities for Rome and for himself. But this demonstration of concord, the more remarkable since Antony himself had, during Caesar's life, declared invalid Dolabella's election to the consulate that Caesar would vacate on leaving for Parthia, was but a prelude. Three days later Antony felt sufficiently in command to take positive action.

Fig. 3 Coin: Aureus; obverse of fig. 2 showing the head of Sextus Pompey. *London, British Museum.* (*Actual size*).

The ordinary people of Rome and the rank and file of the army had adored Caesar. The speech which Antony delivered at Caesar's funeral on March 20 was deliberately inflammatory. The houses of the Conspirators were attacked by mobs. Antony did nothing to repress the passions he had aroused and within a month of Caesar's death Brutus, Cassius and others had been driven from Rome in fear of their lives. The Conspirators, indeed, lacking any sort of power, had nothing to contribute to a settlement and a man who claimed to be the heir to Caesar's influence with the People and the army could hardly look favourably upon Caesar's murderers. To Antony and to Rome Brutus, Cassius and their associates were an embarrassment and a nuisance, but this was not true of the main bulk of the senators who were ready as ever to acquiesce in any solution which would avoid civil war. Their support was valuable, if only because it might confer that appearance of legitimacy necessary to even the most revolutionary Roman politician. Consequently early in April Antony proposed and the Senate decreed that the office and title of Dictator should be abolished forever, that Lepidus should offer terms to Sextus Pompey (cf. figure 3, above) by which Sextus would receive compensation for the estate of his father, confiscated after his death, and that no further decrees of Caesar should be published. In addition Antony secured the province of Macedonia and Dolabella that of Syria for the following year.

But the real bases of power were now remote from the Senate and constitutional forms. The Roman People and, above all, the legions would finally decide the issue. To secure their support would be expensive. Antony had begun by obtaining Caesar's fortune and by inciting the Roman mob. If we may believe Cicero, whose violent enmity with Antony found frequent expression in the sentiment that he should have been killed with Caesar, Antony used every opportunity to raise money and collect dependable followers. He seized the public treasury in the temple of Ops and sold privileges and immunities to individuals and provincial communities. In this latter activity he was merely following what had become established practice in the last age of the Republic to obtain at one stroke money and the support of provincials and client kings. But, again according to Cicero, he went further. Ignoring the recent senatorial decree, he pretended Caesar's intentions as reason and excuse for his actions and, worse, co-operated with Faberius, Caesar's secretary, in inserting forged documents among Caesar's papers. The Roman People and the provincials were useful, but it was the army which was the key to the situation. Antony and Dolabella together passed a law providing allotments of land and founding colonies for Caesar's discharged soldiers. Towards the end of April Antony left Rome for Campania to superintend the assignments and to assert his control over the veterans. He travelled through Campania urging them to rise in defence of Caesar's acts and by the middle of May he had raised a force of six thousand men.

Antony had demonstrated a firm grasp of the realities of the situation and he was now master of events; there was no one to oppose him. The Conspirators had fled—they would have to be dealt with eventually—but Antony had time to build up his force for a crushing blow. Cicero's continual laments for the Republic and the deep depression of his letters serve to emphasize the impotence of the main body of senators. Dolabella, pursuing his own ambitions, was a nuisance, but nothing more and Antony had his measure. Sextus Pompey, who by now had raised an army in Spain, inspired fear of civil war in Cicero. And then while Antony was in Campania, the situation was radically altered. The young C. Octavius arrived in Rome.

The news of Caesar's death took almost two weeks to reach Apollonia. It was not until the end of March that Octavius received a letter from his mother informing him that Caesar had been murdered and asking her son to join her in Italy. His friends, appealed to for counsel, were divided. Some urged immediate invasion of Italy with the Macedonian legions, others that Octavius should proceed with caution. Octavius decided on the latter course and to return to Italy and there to make his plans in accordance with a personal assessment of the situation. Brundisium (Brindisi, cf. map II, page 10), the normal port in Italy for voyages to and from Greece, he avoided since he was uncertain of the attitude of the garrison. Instead he landed a few miles to the south and at the small town of Lupiae learned the provisions of Caesar's will and what had happened at Rome since the Ides of March. Then, reassured as to the temper of the troops in the town, he moved to Brundisium where the soldiers turned out to welcome him. There he found letters from his mother and his step-father, both of whom advised him to decline Caesar's legacy and adoption as Caesar's heir. Octavius' mind, however, was already made. He wrote to Philippus that he intended to accept Caesar's legacy in all its implications, to punish his murderers and to succeed to his power. A lesser man would have listened to those hot-heads who pressed Octavius to appeal to Caesar's veterans in the colonies and march on Rome. But now, as in Macedonia, Octavius revealed wisdom and maturity beyond his years. He wanted not the spectacular gesture followed immediately by uncertainty and insecurity, but the solid reality of enduring power. He travelled to Puteoli near Naples (cf. map II, page 10) where his step-father was staying and thence to Rome. Octavius' progress from Brundisium was followed by Cicero with intense excitement. Octavius for his part treated Cicero in these early days with studied deference. His support with his powerful oratory, his extensive circle of friends and his influence among the senators, which now at last approached what he had always considered his due, would be well worth having. But Cicero foresaw trouble with Antony over Caesar's legacy and Caesar's heir could never be reconciled with Caesar's murderers. At Rome Octavius, even if he himself had no thought of a *coup d'état*, must inevitably be drawn to the enemies of the Conspirators.

Welcomed and attended by Caesar's veterans Octavius travelled from Puteoli to Rome, which he entered at about the beginning of May. The day after his arrival he presented himself in the Forum (cf. map III, page 98) and formally announced to the praetor C. Antonius, a brother of the absent Mark Antony, his acceptance of his adoption by Caesar. Then one of the plebeian tribunes, L. Antonius, produced Octavius at a public meeting in the Forum and allowed him to address the People. Cicero disliked the tone of the speech and, even more, Octavius' intention to celebrate at his own expense the games which Caesar had instituted to commemorate his victory at Thapsus and which officials dared not give for fear of disturbance from the supporters of the Conspirators. More powerful men than Cicero were worried. Before May 21 Antony had hurried back from Campania.

To Antony, Octavian—as we may now conveniently style C. Octavius who had become by acceptance of his adoption by Caesar, C. Iulius Caesar Octavianus—was an unfortunate but hardly a serious complication. To Cicero and the enemies of Antony he was a useful tool. So long as Antony and the Caesarians monopolized the allegiance of the army and the veterans and the favour of the Roman populace they commanded events. But Octavian, who was Caesar's heir and who now bore Caesar's name, might be used to break this monopoly and to provide the enemies of Antony with the military and popular support they needed. Cicero was said to have remarked, and he did not deny it, that Octavian was a young man to be praised, honoured and discarded. Both Antony and Antony's enemies fatally miscalculated the ruthless ambition of Octavian. Neither side saw that, far from their using and then discarding him, he would use them all in the relentless pursuit of the programme he had already announced to his step-father, to punish Caesar's murderers and to succeed to Caesar's power. The miscalculation was not entirely their fault. 'The boy', as Cicero perpetually described Octavian, was only eighteen years old.

That Octavian had already laid his hands on the levers of power, the Roman People, Caesar's veterans and money (he had already at Brundisium sent to Asia for the treasure deposited by Caesar for his Parthian campaign) Antony could not ignore. But with his vast superiority in age, experience, position and authority he imagined that Octavian could easily be reduced to size. When Octavian visited him, Antony kept the young man waiting in an antechamber and when Octavian was finally admitted to the consul's presence, he complained that Antony had not yet punished the Conspirators and demanded the money left to him in Caesar's will. Antony, who had already absorbed Caesar's fortune, refused and, further, managed to delay the formal ratification of Octavian's posthumous adoption. Antony felt secure and on June 1 proceeded to put his security beyond doubt. On that day a tribune carried a law prolonging the provincial commands of the consuls Antony and Dolabella for five years and giving Antony control of Cisalpine and Transalpine Gaul instead of Macedonia. He was to retain the Macedonian legions. The history of the previous fifty years had decisively demonstrated the importance of the Gallic provinces, especially the Cisalpina, the wealthy and populous valley of the Po, one of the chief recruiting grounds of the Roman army, from which close watch could be kept on Italy and intervention could be speedy. Caesar in 59 B.C. had shown that he had learned the lesson and Antony now emulated his old commander. As Pompey had once claimed of Caesar, he would hold Italy in subjection with his Gallic army.

Cisalpine Gaul, however, already had a legitimate governor, the conspirator Decimus Brutus, and Antony would have to fight for his province. Therefore his rear had first to be secured. In particular, the loyalty of the discharged veterans and of the Roman proletariat had to be assured against tampering by Octavian or some other enemy and Brutus and Cassius, potential centres of disaffection, had to be removed from Italy. Early in April the Senate had decreed an end to the resurrection of measures intended or alleged to have been intended by Caesar. This decree Antony had ignored as it suited him and had persuaded the Senate to modify by a further decree empowering the consuls, acting on the advice of a commission, to decide the truth about Caesar's intentions. In the first week of May Antony promulgated a law which he contrived to be voted into effect by importing veterans from Campania: under its terms the commission to advise the consuls was to consist of—the consuls. Dolabella, after a display of independence during Antony's absence in Campania, had been safely bought with a share of the treasure from the temple of Ops. Thus the powerful support of the name of the dead Caesar was obtained for Antony's measures. In the course of June Antony and Dolabella together secured the passage of a law distributing all remaining public land in Italy among the veterans and the urban poor. The distribution was to be supervised by a commission under the presidency of L. Antonius and including both Antony and Dolabella among its members. As for Brutus and Cassius, while they had to be removed from Italy, they had equally to be prevented from establishing themselves in a province of strategic or military importance. On June 5 the Senate decreed that provinces should be allotted them in the future and that meanwhile Brutus was to oversee the corn supply from Asia, Cassius that from Sicily. Cicero in a letter to Atticus records a meeting at Antium on June 8 at which there were present, besides Brutus, Cassius and Cicero himself, those two powerful political ladies Servilia, the mother of Brutus and mistress of Caesar, and Brutus' wife Porcia. The proposed appointments were discussed and both Brutus and Cassius vehemently denied that they would ever accept them. Cassius threatened to go to Greece, Brutus to Rome. Eventually Servilia undertook to have the senatorial decree altered and, in fact, some time later Brutus received Crete and Cassius Cyrene. Whether the alterations were accomplished by Servilia or not, Antony had no reason for complaint. Both provinces were militarily and financially insignificant, remote from any area of struggle that could be foreseen.

Octavian, however, was not to be shrugged off. Antony, in refusing to hand over Caesar's fortune, had hoped to make it impossible for Octavian to pay Caesar's legacies to the Roman People. Octavian, however, raised the money by selling the real property he had acquired under the will, Pedius and Pinarius resigned to him the bequests they were to receive and at a public meeting in the Forum Octavian requested in return the support of the People. When Brutus, although not daring to come to Rome himself, celebrated the Ludi Apollinares as urban praetor at vast expense, Octavian stole the limelight by paying Caesar's bequest to the People and then, soon afterwards, himself gave the games in honour of Caesar's victory at Thapsus. The effect of the games was much enhanced by the appearance on the last seven days of the festival of a comet, which the credulous or inspired affected to believe was the soul of Caesar. Octavian as usual seized his opportunity: he had a statue of Caesar with the star above its head placed in Caesar's temple of Venus Genetrix.

Antony, therefore, had reason for alarm and worse was to follow. When he denounced Octavian to the People, the officers of his bodyguard complained that he was unfair to the young man. To lose the favour of the Roman People was bad enough; to lose the support of the troops would be fatal. Desperate measures were demanded and under the watchful eyes of Caesar's veterans a formal reconciliation was arranged. But like all such gestures made under duress against the real wishes or interests of the principals, the reconciliation was short-lived. The soldiers who had surrounded Antony escorted Octavian home and Antony recognized that he had suffered a defeat. But when Octavian attempted to stand for election to a place in the tribunician college left vacant by death, Antony as consul forbade his candidature on the ground that it was illegal since Octavian was a Patrician and threatened punishment if he persisted. The result was a popular demonstration in Octavian's favour. Antony considered it politic to suspend the election. Soon afterwards, on October 5 or 6, he made a startling disclosure. Octavian, he said, had bribed some of the veterans in his bodyguard to assassinate him. The truth of the accusation was never established. It will never now be known whether it was a serious attempt by Octavian or, as the Roman populace believed, the charge was trumped up by Antony to discredit or remove his opponent who was now beginning to emerge as a real danger. All that can be said is that on balance it was more to Antony's advantage to pretend the assassination than to Octavian's actually to attempt it. It was by no means certain that Antony's soldiers, with whom he was popular, would transfer their allegiance to Octavian if he had their leader murdered. Octavian was playing the long game. It would be uncharacteristic for him to grasp theatrically at a short-term advantage at the cost of introducing an element of uncertainty which might wreck his long-term plans.

At all events, on October 9 Antony began his preparations to oust Decimus Brutus and to claim the provinces of Cisalpine and Transalpine Gaul. On that day he left Rome with his wife Fulvia for Brundisium to take command of the legions from Macedonia. This was the signal for the beginning of the second stage of Octavian's rise to power. So far he had survived: Antony had not been able to shrug him off. He had paraded Caesar's name and had damaged Antony's claim to be the true heir of the Dictator. He was popular with the city mob and the soldiers had shouted for him. He had cultivated connection with certain eminent senators, whose influence might be useful but about whose motives he can have been in no doubt. But he had hardly begun to acquire the really solid basis of power that he needed. The mob was notoriously fickle; the soldiers might shout but if pressed to a decision would not abandon the well-tried Antony; the senators would use 'the boy' and discard him. Antony, once at the head of a proper army, could crush him. This above all had to be prevented. Octavian's survival demanded firm military backing and formal recognition of his position. Caesar's name and the hostility of leading senators to Antony could be used to obtain both.

Fig. 4 Coin: Aureus; reverse showing the head of Agrippa wearing a combined mural and rostral crown in honour of his victories by land and sea. The obverse has the head of Augustus and the issue commemorates the life-long friendship of Augustus and Agrippa. *London, British Museum. (Actual size)*.

Octavian took counsel with his closest advisers, M. Vipsanius Agrippa (cf. figure 4, left), with whom he had been at school and who had accompanied him to Apollonia, C. Maecenas and others. Trusty agents were sent ahead of Antony to Brundisium to win over the legions and Octavian himself went to Campania to raise a force of veterans from the colonies founded by Caesar. Even Cicero was constrained to admit the enthusiasm with which he was greeted. From Calatia and Casilinum, for instance, three thousand veterans joined Octavian and when Antony arrived at Brundisium he found Octavian's agents had been no less successful. Only three legions had arrived and they shouted at Antony for still not having hunted down the murderers of Caesar. Antony replied that they should count themselves lucky to have been brought back to Italy instead of being sent to Parthia. He then informed them that they were to go to Cisalpine Gaul and promised each man a donative of four hundred sesterces. The soldiers laughed at him: Octavian had already given five times as much. Antony's summary execution of the leaders of the ensuing riot only inflamed the soldiers more and Octavian's agents played on their feelings by distributing leaflets contrasting the liberality of Octavian with Antony's meanness and cruelty. Antony was hard put to it to establish control. In the end the three legions consented to march to Ariminum (Rimini); the fourth was to follow under his brother Lucius when it arrived. Antony himself set out for Rome with a bodyguard.

At the same time Octavian was in urgent correspondence with Cicero at Puteoli. Antony was marching on Rome, he wrote, with the Gallic legion *Alaudae*. What did Cicero advise? Should Octavian bring his private army to Rome, should he join the Macedonian legions and hope to detach them from Antony or should he confront Antony himself at Capua? Cicero hesitated to give advice, even more to meet Octavian at Rome. He did not trust him and he was right not to. Cicero was about to be taught a lesson in the realities of politics. Octavian, however, came to Rome, where on November 10 he delivered a speech praising Caesar, denigrating Antony and, at last, offering openly to fight him. It was one of Octavian's rare miscalculations. The veterans were disillusioned with Antony and attracted by Octavian. But many of them had served under Antony and were not ready to fight against him. Octavian quickly recognized his mistake, allowed those who wished to return to their homes and withdrew from Rome northwards up the Via Cassia (cf. map II, page 10), levying fresh troops in Etruria (Tuscany) as he went.

1 Bronze bust of Augustus showing him at the age of 30. Found in Syria; *London, British Museum. Height* 42.5 cm.

Antony then arrived at Rome, left the bulk of his troops at Tibur (Tivoli) and himself entered the city surrounded by armed soldiers. To Octavian's recent speech he replied with pamphlets of traditional obscenity, alleging, among much else, that Octavian had

2

purchased adoption by Caesar only by the prostitution of his body, and ordered the Senate to meet on November 24 to denounce Octavian as a public enemy. But on November 24 Antony failed to appear in the Senate. Cicero said that he was too drunk to attend, but Antony's problems were, in reality, somewhat different. One of the three Macedonian legions, the *Martia*, had deserted the march northwards and gone to Alba Longa, intending to join Octavian. Antony dashed to Tibur to confirm the loyalty of the troops there and returned to Rome for a meeting of the Senate on November 28. The motion condemning Octavian was duly produced, but before it could be put to the vote Antony learned that another of his legions, the Fourth, and some of his auxiliary troops had deserted to Octavian. Again Antony dashed from Rome, this time to Alba in the hope of recovering the Martian legion. His answer there was a shower of arrows from the walls. Therefore, visiting Rome only to be present in the Senate for a redistribution of provincial commands, in which, Cicero hinted, the lots were fixed to suit Antony's friends, he decided to cut his losses in Italy and make for Cisalpine Gaul and the inevitable war with Decimus Brutus. Further delay in Italy would have undermined the morale of more of his troops: the best way to assure their loyalty was to get them into action. Reinforcements would come from L. Antonius and the remaining legion from Macedonia and from P. Ventidius who was raising and training recruits for Antony. Lepidus, the governor of Gallia Narbonensis (cf. map I, page 9) and Hispania Citerior (Nearer Spain), would probably assist him. L. Munatius Plancus, the governor of the Transalpine province, was due to hand his command to Antony. He was known as a nice judge of political situation. Antony had only to succeed against Decimus Brutus to convince Plancus of the right course of action. In Hispania Ulterior with three legions was C. Asinius Pollio, independent and enigmatic. But Lepidus lay between him and Antony. When Antony arrived in Cisalpine Gaul, Decimus Brutus refused battle. Rejecting Antony's demand that he should hand over his province, Brutus shut himself up in Mutina (Modena) and prepared to withstand a siege.

Cicero, meanwhile, had finally arrived in Rome and in the last weeks of December 44 B.C. and the early weeks of January 43 he delivered in the Senate and before the People a series of speeches hysterical alike in their denunciation of Antony and in their adulation of Octavian. But Antony still had his supporters in the Senate and Cicero could not obtain the decree he desired, the condemnation of Antony as a public enemy. His praise of Octavian, whom he compared to Scipio Africanus, the conqueror of Hannibal, and to Alexander the Great, although Octavian had not yet fought a single battle, reveals only the impotence of Antony's enemies. They included military men of ability, for instance the consuls of 43 B.C., A. Hirtius and C. Vibius Pansa, but what was needed was a personality and a name. The state's impotence was Octavian's opportunity. On January 3, 43 B.C. he was appointed to command with the *imperium* of a propraetor together with the consuls and made a member of the Senate. The donative promised to the two legions who had deserted Antony was to be paid by the state. Both they and the other troops raised by Octavian were to be exempted from further military service when the campaign was over and were to be given land as a gratuity. More extravagantly, L. Marcius Philippus proposed that a gilded statue of Octavian should be set up and Servilius Vatia suggested that he should be allowed to stand for the consulship ten years before the legal age. With regard to Antony, Octavian's friends in the Senate were, on the whole, not unsuccessful. Envoys were sent to order him not to attack Decimus Brutus, to raise the siege of Mutina, not to advance within 200 miles of Rome and to obey the authority of the Senate and the Roman People. Ser. Sulpicius Rufus, L. Calpurnius Piso and L. Marcius Philippus were entrusted with the mission but Sulpicius died before they reached Antony and the other two were not allowed to interview Decimus Brutus as they had been charged. They returned to Rome on February 1 or 2, 43, bringing not Antony's submission but a series of defiant demands. The consul Pansa convened the Senate and a state of war was declared.

The other consul, Hirtius, and Octavian had already arrived in Cisalpine Gaul to find

2 General view of the Forum of Augustus, Rome, showing the boundary wall of Gabine stone and the temple of Mars Ultor, consecrated in 2 B.C.

the province, with the exceptions of the towns of Bononia (Bologna), Regium Lepidum (Reggio) and Parma which had gone over to Antony, inclined to support them or, at least, to await the outcome in cautious neutrality. The campaign, if it can be dignified with such a name, of Mutina is confusing. Lepidus, Pollio and Plancus refused to make any decisive move until it became clear which side would win (Plancus in particular coupled inaction in his province with fervent protestations of loyalty to Cicero and the Senate) and Octavian seems never to have had any serious intention of fighting Antony. The troops which had recently deserted Antony might prove unwilling to fight their old comrades. Moreover, the defeat of Antony would place Octavian at the mercy of those whom we may loosely, but conveniently term the Republicans. With the armies of Decimus Brutus and the consuls joined by those of Lepidus and Plancus and, probably, Pollio as well, the stage would be set for the discarding of Octavian. And Octavian, as he himself said when Cicero's assessment of his usefulness was reported to him, had no intention of being discarded. What Octavian could not have foreseen was that the battles of Forum Gallorum (Castellfranco) on April 14 and of Mutina on April 21, in both of which Antony was defeated, would result in the deaths of the consuls Hirtius and Pansa, thus presenting him with the command of both their armies, and that the receipt of the news of the two victories at Rome would betray the Senate into a premature display of overconfidence which publicly revealed its intentions for Octavian. The first battle was long and hard fought. The issue was settled by the intervention of Hirtius late in the day. In the honours and celebrations at Rome, including a public thanksgiving to last fifty days, no distinction was made between the commanders. Cicero, writing to Marcus Brutus, was strong in Octavian's praise. But the second battle, which forced Antony to raise the siege of Mutina, was held to be decisive. Immediately the news reached Rome on April 26 Antony and his associates were at last declared public enemies. The Senate decreed a triumph for Decimus Brutus, who was placed in sole command of the war. When Cicero proposed an ovation, a minor form of triumph, for Octavian, friends of Marcus Brutus objected and the motion was defeated. More than this, the donatives promised to Octavian's troops were reduced; the legions he had taken over from the dead consuls were to be transferred to Decimus Brutus. Nor was Decimus Brutus the only man exalted above him. Others of the enemies and murderers of Caesar were honoured. Sextus Pompey was appointed admiral in charge of the fleet; Marcus Brutus and Cassius were confirmed in the provinces of Macedonia and Syria which they had seized.

Antony could not afford another defeat. He had to act quickly before Lepidus, Plancus and Pollio decided against him. The day after the battle of Mutina he began a masterly retreat westwards to join Lepidus, with whom, as he had written to Hirtius and Octavian in March, he had an understanding. Indeed, even in April Pollio could write to Cicero that Lepidus was writing to everyone that he was on Antony's side. But sides change rapidly in civil war. Decimus Brutus was unable to pursue Antony. His army had been reduced in numbers by losses in action and in effectiveness by the rigours of the siege. He had no cavalry and few baggage animals: they had been killed and eaten. He therefore called on Octavian to assist but Octavian flatly refused to cross the Apennines. Caesar's son could not co-operate with one of Caesar's murderers. The Fourth and Martian legions, Caesar's old troops, refused to serve under Decimus and Octavian kept tight hold on the legions of Pansa. Nevertheless, Decimus started after Antony. Antony, however, had a long lead and easily evaded him. On May 3 he was joined by Ventidius who brought three legions of new recruits and on about the fifteenth of the same month passed safely into Lepidus' province. Lepidus had already reached agreement with Plancus, ostensibly to attack Antony. On May 12 Plancus and his army had crossed the Isère near Grenoble and had sent 4,000 cavalry to meet Antony's advance guard under L. Antonius which had already reached Forum Iulii (Fréjus). Lepidus, however, moving from his base near Avignon, ordered Plancus to hold back. He himself could finish the campaign. And so he could, though not in the way that Plancus understood. The two armies met in the middle of May near Forum Voconii. Lepidus was encamped on the west bank of the river Argens, Antony and Ventidius separately on the east. Plancus had followed and was less than forty miles away. Then, so the story goes, the soldiers of Lepidus and Antony fraternized. Lepidus' troops announced that they would not fight Antony and their commander condoned the mutiny. Antony was welcomed in the camp of his nominal enemies and on May 29 he and Lepidus joined forces. The balance of power was decisively altered. Immediately Plancus broke away across the Isère to his own province, there to await Decimus Brutus who joined him early in June. Together they believed they could hold the Isère against Antony.

Fig. 5 Coin: Aureus; reverse showing head of Octavia, issued in the East in 38–37 B.C. by Antony, whose portrait is on the obverse. *London, British Museum. (Actual size).*

Cicero still clung to the pathetic notion that he could control Octavian despite the many letters in which Marcus Brutus tried to recall him to a sense of reality. Plancus repeatedly urged Octavian to join him and Decimus. Octavian repeatedly replied that he was coming—and made not a move in their direction. His intentions were directed elsewhere. Late in June he demanded election to one of the vacant consulships. The Senate offered him candidature for the praetorship, which would have left him inferior to whoever were elected consuls and he could not trust that they would be his friends. He sent a deputation of centurions to Rome to insist that only the consulship would do. They returned rebuffed. Octavian's reaction was swift and grim. With his whole army, eight legions, cavalry and auxiliaries, he marched not on Antony but on Rome. The city was defended by a single legion of recruits raised and left behind by Pansa. The Senate in panic gave Octavian permission to stand for the consulship in absence and decreed payment of the long withheld donative to his troops. But when it was reported that the legions earlier summoned from Africa had arrived, the Senate annulled its decrees. As far as was possible the city was put in a posture of defence. But it was useless. Octavian occupied a suburb beyond the Quirinal hill and there the population of Rome flocked to welcome him. The next day he entered the city with his bodyguard. Atia, Octavia (cf. figure 5) and the Vestal Virgins formally received him; the soldiers in the city, in defiance of their officers, went over to him; Cicero, hoping even now to save something of power and influence from the wreck of his schemes, had an interview with him. Octavian observed sourly that Cicero was the last of his friends to welcome him. The accuracy of Octavian's judgement was soon revealed. The rumour got about that the Fourth and Martian legions had deserted Octavian. It was eagerly believed by some senators who sent to Picenum to raise troops and flocked to the Senate House where Cicero received them. The rumour was false and Cicero fled. Nothing the senators could do could now disturb Octavian. He seized the public treasury, paid an instalment of the donative to each of his soldiers and then withdrew outside the city to await the inevitable result of the consular elections. On August 19 Octavian and his kinsman Q. Pedius were elected consuls. Octavian's adoption by Caesar was confirmed by a law of the Roman People and Q. Pedius passed a law setting up a judicial commission to try Caesar's murderers. Most of them were already abroad and the rest fled from Rome. The commission condemned them all to outlawry.

Barely fifteen months before Octavian had entered Rome with nothing but Caesar's name and his own ruthless determination. In a short time he had given Rome and its politicians a sharp lesson in the harsh realities of politics. No one could shrug him off, no one use him now. But he had still only just begun. The final defeat of Antony and the final entrance on the fullness of his inheritance from Caesar had still to be worked for. For the present, he could capture Rome, rouse the populace and cow the Senate. But he was no match for the combined armies of Antony and Lepidus. The next step was inevitable: to join them, to gain recognition as their equal and with their help to crush the murderers of his adoptive father. Octavian, as usual, played the game long. He could afford to. He was not yet twenty years old.

Octavian started northwards to Cisalpine Gaul. Q. Pedius at Rome persuaded the Senate to rescind the decree of outlawry against Antony and Lepidus. C. Asinius Pollio with two of his three legions left Corduba, complaining of lack of support from the Senate, and when he reached the Rhône he not only himself joined Antony but persuaded

Plancus to do so as well. Decimus Brutus was left without support. Condemned under Pedius' law as an assassin of Caesar, he decided to break out and reach Marcus Brutus in Macedonia but Octavian advancing from the south interdicted the direct route. Decimus therefore made for the Rhine. His troops gradually deserted him. He had only ten horsemen left when he was captured by a Gallic chieftain, who, on Antony's orders, put him to death.

Antony, Lepidus, Pollio and Plancus were in experience and number of troops vastly superior to Octavian. But he was consul in office and Caesar's son. His popularity had been clearly demonstrated, his hold on his soldiers placed beyond question. The armies which faced him were, like his own, largely composed of Caesar's soldiers. His opponents had no more freedom of action than he. A conference lasting two days was held between Octavian, Antony and Lepidus on an island in the river Lavino near Bononia. It was decided that the three of them should have themselves appointed as a commission for the establishment of the Republic, as *Triumviri rei publicae constituendae*, with consular power for five years, and Octavian was to resign the consulship he presently held in favour of P. Ventidius. The provincial arrangements, however, demonstrated Octavian's junior position. Antony was to continue in the provinces of Transalpine and Cisalpine Gaul. Lepidus added the Spains to Gallia Narbonensis, but was allowed to govern these provinces through legates while he himself from Rome assured the security of Italy and Antony and Octavian went East to deal at last with Brutus and Cassius. Octavian received Africa, Sardinia and Sicily (cf. map I, page 9), a portion which in no way compared with those of his two associates. Moreover, Sicily was in the hands of Sextus Pompey, who, since he controlled the sea, could make it difficult for Octavian to assert his claim to Africa and Sardinia as well. If Octavian wished really to control his provinces he would have to fight for them and, having fought for them, was not likely to find them, with the possible exception of Sicily, much use in the struggle for power at Rome. Eighteen of the richest Italian cities were marked down for allotment to the troops when the campaign against Brutus and Cassius was over. But before Antony and Octavian could leave for the East, two further provisions had to be made. Opponents had to be removed, so that the campaign would not be distracted by unrest in Rome and Italy, and money had to be found for the war. The public treasury was almost empty, credit at Rome had collapsed and the revenues from the East, by which the whole Roman empire was financed, had been intercepted and diverted by Brutus, Cassius and Dolabella. The Triumvirs decided to achieve both ends at one stroke and to emulate the examples of Marius and Sulla by declaring a proscription, whereby lists were published of men who could be killed with impunity and whose estates were confiscated. To cement the compact Octavian, although already betrothed to Servilia, daughter of P. Servilius Isauricus, was to marry Claudia, the daughter of Antony's wife Fulvia by her marriage to P. Clodius. Fulvia, we are told, wrecked the marriage before it was consummated.

Fig. 6 Coin: Aureus issued in 39 B.C.; obverse with head of Mark Antony inscribed III VIR R.P.C. Reverse: Mars, the common reverse for this Triumviral issue. The complementary coins of Octavian and Lepidus are shown in plates 8 and 9. *London, British Museum. (Actual size).*

The Triumvirs journeyed to Rome, where on November 27, 43 B.C. the compact of Bononia was given legal effect by a law carried by a tribune, P. Titius. Antony, Lepidus and Octavian were appointed *Triumviri rei publicae constituendae* for five years and that night the lists of the proscribed were published. The proscription is a subject much obscured no less in antiquity than in modern times by emotion and propaganda. The sources tend to exculpate Octavian, excusing him on the grounds of his youth and the grim experience of his older colleagues. We need not believe them. Augustus wrote his own biography; the historical sources mirror Augustan propaganda; nobody survives to speak for Antony and Lepidus. Suetonius was perhaps near the truth when he wrote that Octavian held out against a proscription for some time, but when it was decided and begun pursued it more ruthlessly than either of his colleagues. It accords with all we know of him: slow and careful to decide, but relentless in the execution of his decision. At least 130 senators and a large number of the business and commercial men were marked down, according to Livy. Appian gives 200 senators and 2,000 business men. The exact numbers are uncertain, inflated, no doubt, by horror, the pursuit of private vengeance and later self-excuse. We know nearly a hundred names of men who are said to have been proscribed. The proscription was an act of considered policy; its object not blood or the settling of private feuds. We know of many who escaped. Only one consular perished, Cicero, trapped more by his own indecision than the cruelty of the Triumvirs. The object was by terror to drive from Italy those men who might cause trouble while the campaign against Brutus and Cassius was being fought. Cicero clearly must have come near the head of any such list, yet even he could have escaped. He had had, with the other proscribed, plenty of warning. But although the proscribed could escape with their lives, they could not take their estates and property with them.

The proscription was as much an instrument of economics as of politics—more, perhaps, since the bulk of the lists must have been composed of the names of men distinguished not for partisan zeal but for wealth, obscure senators and men who had preferred the certainties of business to the hazards of political life. Such men too could save their lives by the abandonment of their estates and a discreet withdrawal from Italy for a period. Some indeed managed even to avoid leaving Italy and Cicero's friend Atticus, one of the wealthiest men in Rome, was not even proscribed. He had protected Fulvia when Antony was declared a public enemy and his financial expertise would be useful. Atticus knew how to survive. His protection extended to the mother of Marcus Brutus, a valuable insurance. His daughter was to marry the greatest of Octavian's marshals, M. Vipsanius Agrippa. The removal of their political opponents and the raising of funds were two of the Triumvirs' purposes. There was a third which goes to the root of their power. Individually and collectively the Triumvirs were powerful only because of their legions. They would retain control of their legions only so long as they satisfied the soldiers' demands for donatives during service and for land afterwards. Enemies and malcontents might have been removed by means other than proscription, money for the impending war might have been otherwise raised, but land for the troops could be obtained only by expropriation.

Now began the social revolution which culminated after Octavian's victory at Actium. The proletariat of Italy in the persons of the legionaries revenged themselves for their long exploitation by seizing what they regarded as their rights. A curious reversal had taken place. Rome had grown great and the game of Roman politics had been financed by the wealth of the provinces. The Roman citizens of Italy were subject to no taxation, direct or indirect, but now Rome and Italy had to pay for civil war. The experience was painful; indeed, as a fund raising venture the proscription was a failure, for few purchasers were found for the estates of the proscribed. Land was not a good investment in a revolutionary epoch and money was hoarded, became scarce and soared in value. Then the Triumvirs took their most courageous action. They made an edict which ordered 1,400 rich women to declare the value of their property and to contribute to their exchequer whatever proportion might be demanded. A storm of indignant protest arose. The mother of Antony and Octavian's sister interceded for the ladies and were rebuffed by Fulvia. No man would take their case. A great Republican matron, Hortensia, the daughter of the orator Hortensius, Cicero's early rival, headed a deputation to the Triumvirs in the Forum and delivered an indignant speech. The Triumvirs ordered their removal, while the crowd shouted for the ladies. Prudence postponed the matter to the following day, when the number of those required to pay was reduced to 400. Other novel taxes were imposed. Every man who owned property worth more than 400,000 sesterces was to contribute one year's income towards the cost of the war. Then at the beginning of 42 B.C. a new proscription list was published, confiscating real estate only.

The new year began with the Triumvir M. Aemilius Lepidus and L. Munatius Plancus, also gaining the reward of his prudence, as consuls. On January 1 the Senate and the magistrates, led by the Triumvirs, solemnly swore to maintain the acts of Caesar. The oath was to be renewed annually. Moreover, the Senate and the Roman People obediently enrolled the Dictator among the gods of the Roman state. A temple was to be erected in the Forum to the new deity, *Divus Iulius*, and provision was made to establish the cult throughout Italy. To his nomenclature Octavian could now add *Divi filius*, son of the Deified.

It was time, finally, to deal with Brutus and Cassius. The Triumvirs commanded a total of forty-three legions plus cavalry and auxiliary troops. It was decided to employ twenty-eight legions against the Republicans and of these eight under C. Norbanus Flaccus and L. Decidius Saxa had already crossed the Adriatic and established themselves in a favourable position east of Philippi. But before Antony and Octavian could follow there were distractions. L. Staius Murcus, an old Caesarian but now with Cassius, descended on Brundisium with sixty galleys, and seized the islands off the harbour entrance with the aim of preventing Antony's heavy transports from getting out. Antony had to send for Octavian, who was attempting to assert his claim to Sicily against Sextus Pompey. Sextus, hearing of the formation of the Triumvirate and the inclusion of his own name in the list of the proscribed, had sailed to Sicily and called on the governor to surrender to him. The governor refused but soon found it prudent to accept Sextus as a colleague. Sextus obtained considerable support not only from pirates and fugitives from the proscription, but also from the inhabitants of the towns in Sicily which the Triumvirs had marked down for their soldiers after the defeat of Brutus and Cassius. Octavian despatched a fleet against Sextus under Q. Salvidienus Rufus. Salvidienus was defeated, lack of ships prevented a proper invasion of the island and Octavian was constrained to promise that Rhegium and Vibo should be removed from the list of towns to be handed over to the troops. The arrival of Octavian at Brundisium was sufficient to cause Murcus' withdrawal and the Triumviral fleet sailed. Their safe arrival in northern Greece was lucky, however, since Cn. Domitius Ahenobarbus with a large part of the fleet of Brutus and Cassius joined Murcus, established complete control of the Adriatic and inflicted damage on the supply ships which were following the troop transports. As a result the communications of the Triumviral army with Italy were completely cut, so that a swift decision against Brutus and Cassius was now essential.

Marcus Brutus had left Italy in July 44 B.C. and had gone not to his province of Crete but to Athens where he was joined with enthusiasm by Roman youths studying at the university, among them Horace and Cicero's son. He then moved north into Illyricum (cf. map I, page 9). The acting governor of Macedonia, Q. Hortensius Hortalus, brother of the courageous and eloquent Hortensia, had placed himself at Brutus' disposal and P. Vatinius, an old legate of Caesar and governor of Illyricum, handed over his army. Money was supplied by the quaestors of Asia and Sicily. Early in January 43 B.C. C. Antonius had landed at Dyrrachium (Durrės, cf. map I, page 9), to take over the province of Macedonia. Brutus expelled him from the town and drove him southwards to Apollonia. Early in February of the same year the Senate had recognized Brutus as governor of Macedonia.

Cassius had stayed in Italy somewhat longer than Brutus. He seems to have left some time in October 44 and like Brutus had not gone to the province assigned him. He had gone to Syria, strategically an excellent choice, for that wealthy province was the hinge on which Roman defence of the East turned. Syria, however, was the province of P. Cornelius Dolabella, who early in January 43 entered the province Asia on his way to his own province. Asia was under C. Trebonius, one of the Conspirators of whom Cicero said that the only crime he had ever committed was that he detained Antony outside the meeting of the Senate on the Ides of March and thus prevented his being killed with Caesar. Trebonius kept a wary eye on Dolabella's troops as they passed through Asia, but Dolabella tricked him, stormed Smyrna, captured Trebonius, and had him decapitated. If we may believe Appian, his head was used as a football by Dolabella's soldiers. The Senate received the news with incredulous horror and, on the motion of Cicero, confirmed Cassius as governor of Syria. By way of reply Dolabella seized all the money he could from the province Asia, hired warships from Rhodes, Lycia and elsewhere and marched through Cilicia to Syria. Cassius, however, was too strong for him in men and money. Dolabella was forced into Laodicea (Denizli) and besieged by land and sea. When Cassius bribed officers of the garrison to open the gates, Dolabella committed suicide and his soldiers swore allegiance to Cassius. Towards the end of 43 Cassius went to Smyrna where he conferred with Brutus who, after Antony's defeat in the battle of Mutina, had campaigned in Thrace where he had won money and the loyalty of the native chieftains.

The two men now controlled the whole of the Roman East, with the exceptions of Egypt, whose queen Cleopatra had sent help to Dolabella, Rhodes and the cities of Lycia. The early months of the year 42 B.C. were spent in gaining control of Rhodes and Lycia. The fleets of these regions were added to the ships of Brutus and Cassius and their cities were plundered for treasure and money, both public and private. The communities of Asia were ordered to pay ten years' tribute at once. Not that there can have been much hope of raising the actual sum demanded: Dolabella had already pillaged these cities. But an exorbitant demand backed by force and the threat of terror can often produce startling results and Asia was very wealthy. Brutus and Cassius met again at Ephesus and from there they moved to the Hellespont, which the armies, some nineteen legions with contingents from the client kings of the East, reached in September 42. They were in a strong position. Backed by all the resources of the East they could, when ready, emulate the strategy of Sulla, which Pompey had hoped to use against Caesar, and invade Italy. Even when Octavian and Antony had arrived in northern Greece, the chance of war inclined to the side of Brutus and Cassius, if only their legions, the best of which were Caesar's veterans, would stand and fight against the name of Caesar. Brutus and Cassius commanded the sea. All they had to do was to avoid battle and prolong the campaign into winter, when lack of supplies would cause the army of Octavian and Antony to break up. Macedonia was a desolate and impoverished country.

Fig. 7 Coin: Denarius, issued in the East by M. Brutus, 43–42 B.C., to commemorate the murder of Caesar; obverse with head of Brutus, reverse with the Cap of Liberty between two daggers, inscribed EID MART. (The Ides of March). *London, British Museum.* (*Actual size*).

Antony and Octavian, on the other hand, had to press for a quick decision. Brutus and Cassius marched westwards and outmanoeuvred and defeated Norbanus and Decidius Saxa. They then established themselves in a strong position across the Via Egnatia near Philippi. Their northern flank was protected by mountains, the southern by a marsh and the western front, from which they expected attack, was fortified by a wall across the road. Antony, leaving Octavian who was ill at Dyrrachium, marched eastwards to Amphipolis (Neochevi) where he established his base. Then with his troops he encamped in the plain north of the marsh, less than a mile from the wall erected by Brutus and Cassius. Octavian at last joined him. Ill though he was and constitutionally averse from personal involvement in fighting, he had to be there; he could not allow Antony to monopolize the credit and the prestige of victory. Eventually, after occasional preliminary skirmishing and much engineering work designed by Antony to turn the enemy's fortifications, battle was joined on October 23, 42 B.C. Antony broke Cassius' line and swept on to capture and plunder his camp. Cassius committed suicide. His despair was, however, premature. On the right flank Brutus had routed the troops of Octavian and captured his camp, but Octavian was not there. In his autobiography he wrote that he left his tent in obedience to a warning dream which had visited his favourite doctor. The rumour got about that he had spent the first battle of Philippi skulking in a marsh and even Agrippa and Maecenas did not deny it.

The battle seemed to have settled nothing. Indeed, the situation of the Triumvirs had worsened, for on the day of the battle the combined squadrons of Staius Murcus and Domitius Ahenobarbus had destroyed the fleet of Domitius Calvinus which was transporting two legions of reinforcements across the Adriatic. Winter was approaching and supplies were nearly exhausted. If Brutus could have held off, the victory would have been his. But he was not a soldier like Cassius. He was unable to impose his will on his officers and men, who were constantly provoked to battle by the taunts of their opponents. He was afraid that his Caesarian veterans would desert; his native levies, untrustworthy as always, were already slipping away. At last he yielded and late in the afternoon on about November 16, 42 B.C. he led out his troops. The struggle was desperate and bloody, but eventually Brutus' front rank was broken, the second and third gave way and defeat became a rout. Octavian's army captured the camp and blocked its entrances. Antony's cavalry pursued the beaten army, some to the sea, some to the mountains. Brutus himself got away to the mountains with four legions, but escape was impossible. At dawn on the next day he persuaded a friend to kill him.

Antony treated the corpse of Brutus with honour, covering it with his own purple cloak. They had been friends and belonged to the same class and type. Brutus had seen it. Antony, he had said, had given clear proof of insanity, for, when he could have been numbered among men like Brutus, Cassius and Cato, he had handed himself over to Octavian and even if he were not defeated with Octavian, he would have to fight him in the end. When the leading survivors of the Republican army were led before the victorious generals, they saluted Antony as *imperator*, Octavian they foully abused. Some were executed. Of those who got away from the battle, a party of nobles, including L. Calpurnius Bibulus and M. Valerius Messalla, took refuge on the island of Thasos and negotiated surrender to Antony; the rest made their various ways to Staius Murcus, Domitius Ahenobarbus or Sextus Pompey.

The victory of Philippi was Antony's and the immediate dispositions declared it. Antony was to stay in the East to settle its affairs and to raise the money necessary to satisfy the demands of the armies, while Octavian was to return to Italy to superintend the settlement of the veterans. He retained his province of Africa, Sardinia and Sicily and Antony added Gallia Narbonensis to the Transalpine province, giving up the Cisalpina which was, at last, to become part of Italy. Lepidus was also deprived of Spain; it was alleged that he had been in treacherous communication with Sextus Pompey. The truth is beyond discovery, nor does it matter. Lepidus had not been at Philippi. He had lost his hold on the legions.

Octavian arrived at Brundisium so ill that it was rumoured that he was dead, but the joy which many felt was misplaced. The Senate, instead, had to order a thanksgiving in honour of Philippi. Antony's partisans at Rome were shown a copy of the agreement reached after the battle and to Lepidus Octavian ceded the province of Africa. The task which faced Octavian would have broken any ordinary man. The veterans, remnants of twenty-eight legions, insisted that their demands be met in full, that the eighteen towns already marked down should be assigned to them, but the towns protested. The burden of satisfying the soldiers, they said, should be spread over the whole country. This merely increased alarm and despondency as more cities joined the agitation to protect themselves. Landowners crowded into Rome with their families and the Roman mob, eager as ever for a good riot, cheerfully supported their demonstrations. Proposals made by Octavian in the Senate to alleviate the situation only made the soldiers suspect that they were to be cheated. Lepidus, his colleague in the Triumvirate, and P. Servilius, the consul, gave Octavian no help. The other consul, Antony's brother Lucius, was a positive hindrance. He and Fulvia represented to the soldiers that it was Octavian's fault that they had not yet received their lands and that they should leave the decision to Antony. To those who were to be dispossessed L. Antonius and Fulvia equally blamed Octavian and urged that Antony would be more equitable, with the result that Octavian divorced Claudia, Fulvia's daughter.

As the year 41 B.C. went on, all order in Italy collapsed. The agents of L. Antonius encouraged the soldiers to plunder as they pleased; agriculture was neglected; Rome was threatened with famine; Sextus Pompey intercepted the corn fleets; pirates of various sorts raided southern Italy; theft and violence were everywhere and war was coming. L. Antonius retired to Praeneste (Palestrina) and from there he marched on Rome, easily defeating Lepidus. Despite his welcome by the People and the Senate he did not stay long. He marched away northwards, hoping to join his brother's generals in the Gallic provinces. Here lay Octavian's greatest danger. In Gallia Cisalpina was Pollio with seven legions; in the Transalpine province Calenus and Ventidius with a large force. Octavian had four veteran legions at Capua. He had already recalled Q. Salvidi-

3 The theatre of Marcellus, Rome, dedicated in 13 or 11 B.C.

4 Inscription in honour of L. Caesar dating from 2 B.C. from Porticus Gai et Luci, Rome.

3

4

L·CAESARI·AVG F·DIVI·N
PRINCIPI·IVVENTV COS·DESIG
CVM SSET·ANN·N·N T·XIIII·AVG
SENATVS

enus Rufus who was marching to Spain with six legions and when Salvidienus turned back Ventidius and Pollio came after him. Agrippa, in command of part of Octavian's army, occupied Sutrium (Sutri) in southern Etruria in an attempt to divert L. Antonius, who, ignoring Salvidienus for the moment, tried to join Pollio and Ventidius further north. Salvidienus and Agrippa, however, joined forces and outmanoeuvred him. Antonius then returned into Perusia (Perugia), where he was besieged by Octavian, Agrippa and Salvidienus. Octavian surrounded the town with an elaborate system of fortifications and then marched with Agrippa to confront Ventidius and Pollio. They refused battle and retired across the Apennines, Ventidius to Ariminum, Pollio to Ravenna. Nor did help come to L. Antonius from the south. Plancus had been put in charge of a private army of veterans raised by the indefatigable Fulvia. He waited at Spoletium, careful as ever not to commit himself until the issue was decided. Through the winter the siege of Perusia continued and on January 1, 40 B.C. Antonius tried to cut his way out but was beaten back. Later Ventidius and Pollio decided to try to join Plancus and relieve the town. Salvidienus and Agrippa met them less than twenty miles from Perusia. Ventidius and Pollio were ready to fight; the cautious Plancus dissuaded them. They separated and, once more, retired, for there was no trust or confidence between the three men and their hearts were not in the fight, nor were those of their soldiers. They would not get their gratuities of land from a victorious L. Antonius supported by the landowners of Italy. Perusia was left to its fate. After a last desperate attempt to break out had been defeated, L. Antonius capitulated, probably late in February 40 B.C. Antonius himself was received honourably by Octavian as the brother of his colleague in the Triumvirate and sent away to Spain and the veterans who had served with Antony were pardoned. The city itself was to be turned over to Octavian's troops, but they were thwarted of their plunder. A prominent citizen committed suicide in despair and his ostentatious funeral pyre started a blaze which engulfed the whole town. Octavian had already learned the value of terror judiciously applied. The whole town council of Perusia—with the single exception of one L. Aemilius who had been a member of the commission which had condemned Caesar's assassins—Roman senators, including Ti. Cannutius who had presented Octavian to the People when he first marched on Rome, and business men were put to death. To those who begged for mercy Octavian returned one implacable and inevitable answer: 'You must die'. The story was spread that three hundred Roman senators and business men were ritually slaughtered at an altar dedicated to *Divus Iulius* on the Ides of March 40 B.C.

The motives of L. Antonius baffle comprehension. He ended by preaching Republican doctrines, but appears an unlikely convert. Perhaps Fulvia, knowing that her husband would never go back on his agreement with Octavian, intended to force on Antony a return to power in Italy by destroying or discrediting Octavian. As for Mark Antony himself, the ancient sources, baffled by his failure to intervene, found an easy answer; he was sunk in torpor induced by drink and the charms of Cleopatra. In sober truth Antony could not intervene. Octavian was carrying out the joint policy of both the Triumvirs. Land had to be found for the discharged troops whatever the cost and Antony's interest was as great as Octavian's. No doubt Antony would not have been displeased overmuch if Octavian had been destroyed; he would have been rid of a dangerous rival and would have gained sole credit for the ensuing distribution of land. But while Octavian survived Antony could not move against him without destroying his own credit with the veterans.

Octavian had not merely survived. By his own ruthlessness and the skill of his generals, Agrippa and Salvidienus, he had emerged as master of Italy. He had defeated L. Antonius and, more important and impressive, the three most experienced generals in the West had given way before him. But Octavian needed all his strength and prestige, for troubles were everywhere. The seas were controlled by Sextus Pompey, who had captured Sardinia, and Domitius Ahenobarbus. Octavian's general in Hispania Ulterior, C. Carrinas, faced an invasion by a Moorish prince incited by L. Antonius and Fulvia and Africa was torn by confused warfare. The death of Calenus in Gaul offered

5 Pyramid of C. Cestius, Rome.

solitary but welcome comfort. His son was persuaded to surrender to Octavian all Gaul and eleven legions. Octavian went north to receive this unexpected addition to his strength. He placed Salvidienus in charge of Gaul and returned to find Antony himself besieging Brundisium. More than that, Domitius Ahenobarbus and Sextus Pompey were now openly allied with him.

War seemed likely and if it came there could be little doubt of the result. Octavian, his legions starving and unreliable and his enemies in total command of the sea, would be caught and crushed between Antony in the south and the armies in the north. This was how Q. Salvidienus Rufus read the situation. With Ventidius and Agrippa one of the most remarkable generals of the Roman revolution, and hitherto a faithful adherent of Octavian, he began negotiations with Antony. But war did not come, for the soldiers of Octavian and Antony refused to fight. Antony as a gesture of goodwill sent away Domitius Ahenobarbus, a convicted and proscribed assassin of Caesar, to govern Bithynia. Negotiations between the principals were begun, conducted by Maecenas for Octavian, Pollio for Antony, with L. Cocceius Nerva acceptable to both parties. The expected recriminations were paraded and a new settlement reached. Italy was to be a common recruiting ground for both Octavian and Antony. For the rest, Octavian was to rule Dalmatia, Sardinia, Spain and all Gaul, Antony all the provinces from Macedonia and the Ionian sea to the Euphrates. Lepidus was to retain Africa and Sextus Pompey was, for the present, to be left in possession of Sicily. The compact was sealed by a marriage. The incorrigible Fulvia having opportunely died in Greece, Antony married Octavia, the sister of Octavian, left a widow by the no less opportune death of her husband C. Marcellus. Antony and Octavian travelled together to Rome. Domitius had already left for Bithynia; Plancus soon followed to take up the command in Asia; Pollio perhaps went to Macedonia at about the same time. At last Antony revealed Salvidienus' intended treachery. He was arraigned before the Senate and executed or committed suicide.

Such was the treaty of Brundisium, advertising openly for the first time that Rome's empire was not one, but two and that between them there was no necessary connection. Octavian emerged with his power apparently much enhanced, but it would be superficial to hail him as the victor. Events since Philippi had demonstrated that if Octavian was to force through the settlement of the veterans, then he had to be strong enough to deal not merely with general unrest in Italy, but also with any military adventurer who tried to turn the unrest to his own advantage. The settlement of the veterans was Antony's policy as much as Octavian's and its success also affected him vitally. For the sake of its success he could not afford a repetition of the actions of L. Antonius, Ventidius, Pollio and Plancus. If Octavian were really to control Italy, he must also control Gaul. Further, Antony was already contemplating a wholesale reorganization of the East and war with Parthia. Antony was a serious man in the best tradition of the Roman aristocracy. Settlement of the Eastern provinces and client kingdoms was in Rome's interest as well as his own, but if he were to pursue his aims seriously, he could not afford constantly to be distracted by disturbance in the West. On this ground, too, Octavian must be built up to full control. From the East, Antony doubtless hoped, increased revenues and the reports of glorious victories would endear him to the people of Rome and Italy. Octavian, on the spot and carrying through an unpopular policy, would take any odium that arose. There was also Sextus Pompey. He would have to be dealt with. If a politic surrender of liabilities disguised as assets is a victory, Antony won one at Brundisium.

But Sextus Pompey was displeased. He had expected to become an equal member of an enlarged Triumvirate. There were rumours of a secret agreement between Octavian and Antony to attack him. His general, the Greek freedman Menas, ravaged the coast of Etruria and made a descent on Sardinia. Italy was blockaded and faced with famine and as a result the Roman plebs rioted. Octavian was wounded by a stone and Antony turned his troops on the mob. Military operations against Sextus, with the plebs openly disaffected and Sextus in command of the sea, were impossible, and so there was no alternative to negotiation. On Sextus' side Menas was for pressing their advantage home: the pressure of famine would soon compel the Triumvirs to offer better terms. Staius Murcus, however, was for peace. Sextus had Murcus assassinated—and negotiated. The talks, however, were at first unfruitful, and Sextus was disappointed in his expectation that he would succeed Lepidus. The conference was renewed in the pleasant resort of Puteoli in the summer of 39 B.C. and agreement finally reached. Sextus was to withdraw his troops from Italy and make no further raids. Above all, he was to guarantee Rome's corn supply from Sardinia and Sicily, of which he was recognized as the ruler. In addition he was to receive the Peloponnese, election to the college of augurs and the consulship of 38. All the exiles in his army, with the exception of the condemned assassins of Caesar, were to be restored to their civic rights; the proscribed who had fled to him were to receive back a quarter of their property; slaves serving with him were to be freed and his free soldiers to be rewarded at the end of their service on the same terms as the veterans of the Triumvirs. The agreement was duly signed and sealed and delivered to the Vestal Virgins for safe custody. The next day Sextus entertained Antony and Octavian on his flag-ship. For a few hours he had the masters of the world at his mercy. Menas urged him to kill his guests. Sextus replied with a proud assertion of the good faith of a Roman aristocrat. Naturally marriage solemnized the compact: Sextus' daughter was betrothed to Marcellus, son of Octavia by her late husband and now step-son of Antony. Finally, before Antony left for the East consuls were nominated for the period 35 to 31 B.C., among them Domitius Ahenobarbus, the consuls for the years 39 to 36 having already been decided, to provide for Antony's Parthian expedition and to reward adherents of the Triumvirs.

At Rome great rejoicing greeted the Peace of Puteoli. It was premature because by the beginning of 38 Octavian and Sextus Pompey were again in conflict. Sextus alleged that the Triumvirs had not carried out the agreement with regard to the Peloponnese. In fact, Caesar's heir could not allow the survival of the son of the great Pompey, a rallying point for malcontents. If Octavian was to destroy Antony, he had first to obtain undisputed control of his own domain and the seas. Menas shrewdly assessed the probable outcome. He deserted to Octavian, handing over the island of Sardinia. Octavian summoned Antony to conference at Brundisium and Antony, true to his compact, came. But Octavian was not there and Antony immediately returned to the East, pleading as reasons for his haste the pressure of Eastern affairs and the Parthian war. He wrote to Octavian urging him to respect the agreement with Sextus; but Octavian prepared for war.

He began by divorcing Scribonia, claiming that he was fed up with her shrewish disposition and advertising his breach with Sextus. Scribonia was the aunt of Sextus' wife. With indecent haste on January 17, 38 B.C. he then married Livia Drusilla (cf. plate 25), whom he loved and esteemed for the rest of his life without rival. This marriage was perhaps the most important single event in all the long rise of Octavian to supreme power. Livia was already married, had borne her husband one son and was pregnant with another. No impediment, however, in high politics. She came from the very heart of the senatorial oligarchy of the last age of the Republic. Her father, who had died with so many of his class at Philippi, was by birth a Claudius and had been adopted as a child by the tribune of 91 B.C., M. Livius Drusus. Drusus' sister was by her two marriages the mother of the great Servilia, whose son was Marcus Brutus, Caesar's assassin, of another Servilia, who became the second wife of L. Licinius Lucullus, of Porcia, who married L. Domitius Ahenobarbus, and of M. Porcius Cato himself, who led the oligarchy in its last struggle against Caesar. Livia Drusilla had married a kinsman, Ti. Claudius Nero who had fought for Caesar against Pompey, for L. Antonius against Octavian, and with his wife and child had taken refuge with Sextus Pompey after Perusia. This formidable connection was vitally important for Octavian. It marked the point when his cause first began to attract ambitious aristocrats. They joined him not from sentiment but because at last they judged that he might become the equal, even the superior of Antony and carry them to power.

Hitherto few aristocrats and few men of senatorial family could be found among Octavian's adherents. The 'best men' preferred to be with their own kind, with Brutus and Cassius, with Sextus Pompey, with Antony. Octavian's earliest and closest associates had been men like himself: M. Vipsanius Agrippa, whose father nobody knew and whose origin no one could discover, Q. Salvidienus Rufus, of non-Latin name, and the rich and voluptuous C. Maecenas. These three were the foundation members of Octavian's faction. Salvidienus and Agrippa were with him already in Caesar's camp at Apollonia. A few other names are recorded, chiefly of military men; a few were of respectable but modest senatorial family, but the others were either the first members of their families to reach the Senate, through Caesar or the Triumvirs, or non-senators. As for the most important class in the Senate, the ex-consuls, Octavian at the time of the treaty of Brundisium could count on only two: C. Carrinas, whose family had been proscribed by Sulla but who had been advanced by Caesar; and a solitary noble, Cn. Domitius Calvinus, consul as long ago as 53 B.C. Calvinus is an enigma. Caesar, who had intended him to be his deputy in the Dictatorship, had set out from his house for the fatal meeting of the Senate on the Ides of March. We hear nothing more of him until he attempted to reinforce Octavian and Antony in the campaign of Philippi. Then he again disappears from record until he gained a second consulship in 40 B.C. and the governorship of Spain for Octavian in 39.

But now a change took place. For instance, in the war between Octavian and Sextus Pompey we find on Octavian's side significant names, four new and three old in the history of Rome; of Q. Laronius, suffect consul in 33 B.C., nothing is known except his service against Sextus and his consulate. He perhaps came from Vibo in Bruttium (Calabria) in the far south of Italy. Equally obscure is L. Cornificius, consul in 35. But C. Calvisius Sabinus, consul in 39 B.C., had been an officer of Caesar, who had admitted him to the Senate. After Caesar's death his allegiance had lain naturally with Antony. In due, but unknown, season he had deserted him for Octavian. Calvisius promoted the career of T. Statilius Taurus, suffect consul in 37, who came from Lucania (Basilicata) and who was soon to rival the great Agrippa. These were men of the same type, though of more distinction, as those to whom Octavian had appealed from the beginning. But with them were Ap. Claudius Pulcher, consul in 38, Paullus Aemilius Lepidus, consul in 34, and M. Valerius Messalla Corvinus, consul in 31. All were noble, all Patrician. The career of Caesar's heir had reached its turning point.

The first operations of the war against Sextus Pompey were disastrous. Octavian's plan was to invade Sicily, but Menas and Calvisius Sabinus were defeated, though not decisively, by Sextus' fleet in the bay of Naples. As Octavian with his fleet passed the straits of Messana on his way from Tarentum to join them, Sextus himself fell on him and destroyed many of his ships. The destruction was completed by a storm which arose in the night and which also damaged Calvisius' fleet. To secure Italy from invasion by Sextus Octavian was thrown back on the defensive. Meanwhile at Rome the populace rioted and Octavian's failure was emphasized by the triumph celebrated by the Antonian, P. Ventidius, for victory over the Parthians. The diplomatic Maecenas was sent to Greece to ask help of Antony. Under the supervision of Agrippa, who had lately returned from Gaul, money was raised, a new fleet was built and crews trained for it. To accommodate it a huge artificial harbour was built at the Lucrine Lake on the bay of Naples.

In early spring 37 B.C. Antony arrived at Tarentum with a powerful fleet. He was bitter and resentful. Once more his obligation to Octavian had interrupted his work in the East. It was not, however, merely obligation that made him come. He needed troops and Octavian controlled recruitment in Italy. Octavian went to meet him and with him went Maecenas and L. Cocceius Nerva and three poets, Virgil, Horace and L. Varius Rufus. Even Maecenas could not soothe or reassure the angry Antony. In the end

6 Bust of Julius Caesar found originally at Tusculum in 1825; *Turin, Museo di Antichità.*

7 Bust of Mark Antony; *Narbonne, Palais des Archévêques. Height* 36 cm, *width* 22 cm.

8 Golden Aureus, showing the head of Octavian, minted during the triumvirate and inscribed C. CAESAR III VIR R.P.C.; *London, British Museum. Diameter* 2.1 cm.

9 Golden Aureus, showing the head of Lepidus minted while he was one of the triumvirs, and inscribed M. LEPIDUS III VIR R.P.C.; *London, British Museum. Diameter* 2.1 cm.

10 Bronze statue of a youth; perhaps Gaius or Lucius Caesar; *New York, The Metropolitan Museum of Art.*

7

8

9

10

Octavia intervened and arranged a settlement between her husband and her brother. Antony resigned to Octavian 120 ships and admirals to command them. In return Octavian promised to send 20,000 legionaries to fight the Parthians. They were never sent. All Antony got were 1,000 men detached from Octavian's bodyguard in return for ten more ships. Technically Octavian and Antony were now without legal or constitutional standing, for the Triumvirate had lapsed at the end of 38. Not that it mattered. The Triumvirate was now prolonged for another five years, to expire on the last day of 33. Octavian had got what he needed. What he did not want was for Antony to share in the glory and prestige of defeating Sextus. All offers of further assistance were declined and Antony left for Syria. Octavia went with him, but no further than Corcyra. In late summer 37 Antony sent her back from there to Italy.

Meanwhile preparations for the war against Sextus pressed on. There was to be no mistake this time. The rest of 37 passed and half of 36. Then on July 1, 36 the campaign opened. The strategy was Agrippa's: to invade Sicily from three directions at once, Octavian from Puteoli, Statilius Taurus from Tarentum and from the south Lepidus with the fourteen legions of the army of Africa. Lepidus, weathering a storm, successfully established a foothold on the island; Statilius, when the same storm broke on him, put about and safely regained Tarentum; Agrippa was successful in an action off Mylae (Milazzo); but Octavian was defeated in a great battle in the straits to the great mirth of Antony who knew well Octavian's unsoldierly nature. Octavian escaped to the mainland in despair, but his generals and Lepidus gradually overran Sicily until Sextus was forced to risk everything in a desperate sea battle. On September 3, 36 B.C. the battle of Naulochus was won by Agrippa for Octavian. Sextus fled to Messana and then to the East, where his father had been powerful. In Asia he raised a private army of three legions, but was slowly hunted down by Antony's generals until M. Titius, whose life Sextus had saved some years before, captured and killed him. Titius deserted Antony at the right time, before Actium, but when he presided at games in the theatre of Pompey the Great the Roman populace remembered his treatment of Pompey's son and drove him from the place in indignation.

Lepidus had not joined Octavian through affection. A member of the Triumvirate only because Antony needed his army after Mutina, he had been continually humiliated, his power constantly diminished. Once Sextus was destroyed, Octavian would inevitably turn next against him. That had to be provided against. Lepidus, therefore, attempted to seize Sicily, which he had done much to conquer. But he, too, miscalculated the audacity of his adversary. Octavian with a few attendants entered Lepidus' camp and with Caesar's name won away his soldiers. Lepidus' humiliation was complete and he begged for mercy abjectly and publicly. Octavian stripped him of his Triumviral powers, allowed him to retain the office of *Pontifex Maximus* and sent him away to Circeii, where he lived on for another twenty-four years. In fact, Octavian had been in no danger. Lepidus' troops had already been carefully worked upon. Only Lepidus could have been in any doubt as to the outcome. It was a stroke brilliant in its economy, and it saved Octavian a whole civil war and much odium.

A victor in civil war inherits obligations to his enemy's as well as to his own troops. Octavian now had some forty legions to provide for, all of them demanding land and gratuities. The legionaries who had already served at Mutina and Philippi, some 20,000 men, were demobilized and settled, some in Campania and some in southern Gaul. In addition all the troops received a gratuity of 100 denarii each. The money was exacted from the communities of Sicily. Sextus' troops were easier to deal with. Many of them were slaves and could, therefore, be crucified or returned to their former masters. Certain of Sextus' associates, some of them Roman senators, were also put to death.

Octavian returned to Rome a hero. His rule had secured peace in Italy, despite minor disturbances, for four years since the treaty of Brundisium. To this he had now added freedom of the seas and the liberation of Rome from famine. It was enough for most Romans. Senators and citizens flocked to greet him and to escort him to the temples and

11 Marble relief showing an Italian hill town from Lago Fucino, mid-first century A.D.; *Avezzano, Villa Torlonia.*

12 Brick building on the Palatine, sometimes identified with the Temple of Augustus begun by Tiberius and Livia after Augustus' death and reconstructed by Domitian after a fire in A.D. 69. It may, however, be the entrance hall built by Domitian for the Imperial Palace, the Domus Tiberiana.

13 The Temple of Mars in the Forum of Augustus, Rome.

14 Caryatid from the attic storey of the portico of the Forum of Augustus, Rome.

to his house. The next day he spoke to the Senate and to the People, recounting the acts of his administration. Honours were heaped on him: the personal inviolability or sacrosanctity enjoyed by the tribunes of the plebs; the right, which had also been granted to Caesar, of wearing a laurel wreath on all occasions; annual religious ceremonies in honour of his victory; a golden statue erected in the Forum with an inscription announcing that peace had been restored on land and sea after prolonged disturbances. Not merely at Rome was he honoured: the various towns of Italy enrolled him among their tutelar deities and placed his statue in their temples. Agrippa, the greatest of the admirals in the war and the true architect of victory, received an extraordinary distinction: a golden crown to be worn on the occasion of triumphs.

Now, at long last, Octavian could begin to think of disposing of Antony. He commenced at once to prepare the ground. As soon as Antony returned from the Parthian war, he declared, the Republic would be restored. This declaration and the inscription on the golden statue already contain the essence of Octavian's later propaganda. But before he faced Antony, much had to be done. Octavian had to put beyond challenge his control of Rome, Italy and the West. Above all, he must stand before the legions as the equal of his tried and tested adversary. Philippi had been Antony's victory; L. Antonius and Sextus Pompey had been defeated by Agrippa and the other marshals. It was not merely Octavian's grasp of strategy and tactics which was suspect: there were persistent rumours about his personal courage. About Antony there was no doubt. He had learned the military art with Caesar and Philippi had confirmed his quality and enhanced his glory. His generals celebrated triumphs from the East and kept his name and military reputation before the soldiers of the West.

Octavian's solution illustrates once again his brilliant grasp of the essentials of a situation and his passion for economy. Not for him an easy but remote victory, spectacular with booty. He would safeguard Italy itself, fighting in a hard country against a stubborn enemy. In one war he would secure his own northern frontier, prove his courage, confer an immense benefit on the peoples of Italy and commend himself to the legions. Illyricum (cf. map I, page 9) had long been a Roman province, or, rather, a *provincia*, an area in which Roman commanders exercised or claimed to exercise power. Despite its strategic position commanding the eastern frontier between the Alps and Macedonia and the passes over the Julian Alps, Illyricum had never been properly conquered and had in recent years fallen into chronic unrest. To the conquest of this vital area Octavian devoted the years 35 and 34 B.C. The campaign opened in the north. In the first year he defeated the Iapodes, capturing their fortress of Metulum, and then invaded Pannonia (cf. map I, page 9) with the immediate object of seizing Siscia at the confluence of the Kulpa and the Save. Siscia fell before the end of 35. Octavian returned to Rome for the winter and in the spring of 34 started south from Siscia along the coast of Dalmatia. He had secured all his objectives. The north-eastern frontier of Italy was closed to invasion by an enemy foreign or Roman and he would obtain no support along the coast of Dalmatia. More than that, Octavian had been with the army throughout, often risking his own person and receiving honourable wounds.

Octavian impressed his achievement on Rome. The colonnade near the Flaminian Circus, built more than a century before by the Cn. Octavius who had commanded the fleet against Perseus, was rebuilt from the booty of the Illyrian war and the standards lost by an earlier Roman army and recovered by Octavian were laid up there. For himself Octavian postponed the triumph decreed by the Senate. The assistance of Agrippa and Statilius Taurus received no public commemoration; Illyricum was to be Octavian's victory. But the achievements of his generals elsewhere were duly celebrated. In 34 B.C. Statilius Taurus triumphed from Africa and C. Norbanus from Spain. The following year saw another triumph from Africa, that of L. Cornificius, and two more from Spain by L. Marcius Philippus and Ap. Claudius Pulcher. The display of military success was deliberate and pointed. Antony's much advertised Parthian campaign had ended in defeat and heavy losses. The triumphs of Octavian's generals were perpetuated in public buildings. Cn. Domitius Calvinus followed his Spanish triumph in 36 B.C. by rebuilding the Regia in the Forum. Statilius Taurus on his return from Africa began to erect a theatre. Paullus Aemilius Lepidus completed the Basilica Aemilia. L. Marcius Philippus repaired a temple of Hercules. These were for show and enjoyment; meanwhile Agrippa, typically, built for utility and the common people of Rome. In 34 B.C. before the end of the Illyrian campaign he had repaired at his own expense the Marcian aqueduct from which Rome obtained her purest water. In 33, although an ex-consul and second man in the West to Octavian, he became aedile, commissioner for public works, and began a vast programme of building and repair. Roads and public buildings were put in order. The sewers and drains were cleaned and repaired. It is characteristic that Agrippa insisted on personal inspection, rowing down the most ancient of the three main sewers of Rome into the Tiber. A new aqueduct was built, named the Aqua Iulia (cf. plate 61), for Octavian. Free baths for both sexes were provided and lavish distributions of oil and salt. Tickets dropped among the poorer spectators in the theatre entitled them to free gifts of money and clothing. Magnificent games were celebrated. To the common people of Rome and Italy, both civilians and soldiers, Octavian had consistently appealed. He had reason now to feel strong in their support. He was ready for Antony.

Fig. 8 Coin: Denarius, 32–31 B.C.: obverse showing head of Antony. The inscription commemorates his conquest of Armenia; reverse showing the head of Cleopatra who is described as 'The Queen of Kings'. This issue was struck by Antony as a declaration of solidarity with Cleopatra in the face of Octavian's charges and the declaration of war by the Senate. *London, British Museum. (Actual size).*

In 33 B.C. Octavian was consul for the second time. Early in the year, before he resigned the office, he delivered a speech in the Senate criticizing Antony's Eastern acts. Antony in reply charged Octavian with breach of their compact. He had been prevented, he said, from recruiting troops in Italy, his own soldiers had been excluded from the allotments of land, Octavian had arbitrarily and illegally deposed Lepidus. If Octavian wished to talk about the restoration of the Republic, Antony too was ready. Antony's charges were well founded, but reason and appeal to legality were useless. Octavian was determined to manoeuvre Antony into a false position and Antony himself had already provided the means: his relations with Cleopatra. Octavian exploited the topic with cool unscrupulousness, the success of which has not yet passed away. 'The triple pillar of the world transform'd into a strumpet's fool' was Octavian's creation. Study of the tradition and historical fact reveals a different picture. Roman political invective was obsessed with moral, above all with sexual issues. If Octavian accused Antony of being lost in lust for Cleopatra, that was only to be expected and Antony could reply in vigorous kind. 'What's made you change?' he wrote to Octavian, 'Because I get up the queen? She's my wife. Have I just begun it or hasn't it been going on for nine years? Do you only get up Drusilla? Good luck to you, if when you read this you haven't been up Tertulla or Terentilla or Rufilla or Salvia Titisiena or the whole lot at once. Does it matter to you where or in what woman you get stiff?' Sexual freedom was a prerogative of the ruling class at Rome. Antony took his pleasures eagerly and where he could. He did not allow them to distract him from serious business. Antony had known Cleopatra before Philippi, in Egypt and at Rome as Caesar's mistress. In 41 B.C. he had summoned her to Cilicia and had passed the winter with her at Alexandria. Then he had not seen her again for nearly four years, despite twin children, Alexander Helios and Cleopatra Selene, born after his departure. In 37 B.C. he summoned her again, this time to Syria. Cleopatra was not merely a fascinating woman. She was queen of Egypt, the last of the great successor kingdoms to the empire of Alexander, and heiress to generations of statecraft stretching back to the first Ptolemy who had legitimized his seizure of Egypt by the theft of Alexander's corpse. She was not driven from her political senses by her affair with Antony, nor he from his.

What Cleopatra wanted from Antony was the renascence of the Ptolemaic empire. In recent years Egypt had been feeble, its rulers ridiculous. Antony gave Cleopatra the central Phoenician coast and the tetrarchy of Calchis, the island of Cyprus and some cities in Cilicia Aspera. It was not a large donation of territory, though exceedingly rich, especially when the balsam groves of Jericho and the monopoly of bitumen from the Dead Sea were included. It did not satisfy the queen of Egypt. She wanted the whole kingdom of Herod of Judaea to extend her empire to the borders of Syria. The demand was repeated; so was Antony's refusal. He was not thinking of the kingdom of the Ptolemies but Rome's eastern empire. To him Egypt was a link in a chain of client kingdoms stretching north to Pontus and west to Thrace which protected the Roman provinces of Syria, Bithynia, Asia and Macedonia. For his eastern wars Egypt could provide him with money and supplies, ships and bases. All this Octavian seized on and perverted. Antony's besotted lust and Cleopatra's oriental depravity were paraded; slighted family honour, in Antony's rejection of Octavia, and criminal diminution of the Roman empire in Antony's gifts to Cleopatra. Above all, the existence of Cleopatra allowed Octavian to disguise the true nature of the war he was about to fight. Antony was no danger to Rome; Cleopatra could be built up as such. From a civil war forced on an unwilling adversary by an unscrupulous military adventurer it became a foreign war against a foreign enemy who threatened the whole Roman way of life, a crusade in which the civilized West faced the corrupt and debased East.

At the end of 33 B.C. the Triumviral powers lapsed. The consuls for the year 32 were two Antonians, Cn. Domitius Ahenobarbus and C. Sosius. To them in the previous year Antony had entrusted a written statement of his Eastern dispositions and a demand for their ratification. This document they were to read to the Senate after they had taken office. It was never read, whether because Domitius and Sosius had formed some agreement with Octavian or because they feared the formal disclosure of certain provisions, such as the titles and gifts bestowed on Cleopatra and her children, is unknown. Instead Sosius delivered a speech praising Antony and denouncing Octavian, whom he even attempted to have condemned by decree of the Senate but was prevented by a tribune's veto. Octavian had already withdrawn from Rome. Although technically without power or position he mustered his supporters from the towns of Italy, entered Rome and summoned the Senate. And the Senate came to his bidding. He had prestige and force enough to dispense with the constitution. Sitting between the two consuls he attacked Antony and Sosius. Not a single senator, not even Sosius himself, dared reply. Octavian then dismissed the Senate, fixing a day for the next meeting at which, he said, he would support his accusations with documentary proof. The consuls, however, fled to Antony and with them went more than 300 senators. Octavian was left in an uncharacteristically exposed situation. The monarchic faction leaders of the long Roman revolution, prepared though they were to destroy the Republic in pursuit of their ambition, were reluctant to act without an army, an emotional plea and a semblance of legality. The last Octavian totally lacked. The consuls were with Antony as well as 300 senators. Octavian stood revealed as the aggressor. Nor had he the documentary evidence he had promised the Senate and which would make his propaganda effective.

But the flight of the consuls and the senators was not a complete loss to Octavian. As Pompey the Great had learned in the civil war with Caesar, to have the leading men in the Senate on one's side could bring divided counsel, interference and military ineffectualness. The Republican nobility did not lay aside its ambition when it went to Pompey or Antony. Further, Antony's following had become through the years steadily more heterogeneous. To his early Caesarian supporters he had added Republicans and Pompeians. United only by their allegiance to Antony and disunited even in their motives for that, between many of his leading men there was no trust or confidence, but rivalry and open enmity. In the war of Perusia this had operated to Octavian's advantage: it did so again now. Antony was at Ephesus with an army of thirty legions. Cn. Domitius Ahenobarbus urged him to dismiss Cleopatra; the Caesarian P. Canidius Crassus, on the other hand, pointed to the men, money and ships Cleopatra had provided. Domitius was right. Cleopatra's presence obscured the real nature of the war and allowed Octavian to develop his emotional plea. But Antony, who had just finally divorced Octavia, listened to Canidius. Domitius stayed with Antony, but not L. Munatius Plancus and his nephew Titius, who deserted and fled to Rome. It was a momentous desertion. The cautious and politic Plancus had since Caesar's death been a true mirror, alike in his hesitations as in his actions, of the sway of the balance of power.

When Plancus chose Octavian, men's minds must have been powerfully impressed. Nor did Plancus and Titius come empty-handed. They knew where Octavian could find Antony's will, which they themselves had witnessed and sealed and the contents of which they knew. This was the documentary evidence which Octavian so desperately needed. He demanded that the Vestal Virgins, in whose charge it was, should surrender it. They refused. He went and took it. He read it first to the Senate and then to the Roman People. In it Antony repeated his declaration that Cleopatra's child Caesarion was the son of Julius Caesar, bequeathed large legacies to his own children by Cleopatra and directed that, when he died, he should be buried beside her. Sober men regretted the violence done to the Vestals and the attempt to discredit Antony in his lifetime with information which should have remained hidden until his death. They might with advantage have reflected on the possibility of forgery. Octavian's discovery of the will was suspiciously opportune and he alone had first sight of it. Among the lower orders of society the effect of the disclosure of the will was enhanced by wild rumours: that Antony intended to make Cleopatra queen of Rome; that the capital of the empire was to be transferred to Alexandria; that Roman soldiers had the name of Cleopatra emblazoned on their shields; that Antony, dressed as an oriental, followed her litter among her eunuchs; that his bust and hers as Osiris and Isis were displayed side by side; that he had been sent out of his mind by witchcraft. Against unreason reason is powerless. Antony's friends were baffled and unable to defend him.

Octavian had his emotional plea and the evidence to back it. He now proceeded to arrange the show of legality. He invoked that last resource of tyranny, the will of the people. Beyond the Senate and the magistrates, beyond the law he appealed to the peoples of Italy and the West. 'The whole of Italy,' he wrote in the *Res Gestae* (cf. plates 83, 84) 'spontaneously swore an oath of allegiance to me and demanded me as its general in the war which I won at Actium. The same oath was sworn by the Gallic provinces, the Spains, Africa, Sicily, Sardinia.' That all Italy, all the West rose as one man without prompting to swear the oath cannot be believed. Neither can it be believed that the oath was extorted from a wholly unwilling populace by military intimidation. That would have left Octavian's rear insecure when he went to meet Antony. Some communities, chief among them the colonies of veterans, particular supporters of Octavian, no doubt eagerly embraced the oath; others, perhaps, had to be coerced, although Bononia, which had especial ties with Antony, was ostentatiously exempted. But for the most part, we may suppose, the system of *clientelae*, damaged and changed but not destroyed by civil war, was employed. Many areas were under the control of Octavian's partisans. Maecenas would deliver the unanimous voice of the people of Arretium, for example, and Agrippa and Statilius Taurus those of their native regions. Elsewhere the local notables would be approached and persuaded and they would persuade in turn their local populations. The oath was not an act of state, but private and personal. By it all the individuals and communities of Italy enrolled themselves, civilians and soldiers, as clients of Octavian. It remained through all the subsequent shifting of titles and pretended powers the firm basis of his authority.

Thus fortified Octavian had Antony stripped of his powers and the consulship to which he had been designated for the following year. War was finally declared, with Octavian in person performing the solemn rites in the temple of Bellona. But it was declared on Cleopatra alone. Octavian was to lead the people of Rome and Italy in a foreign war against a foreign enemy. If Antony chose to stand by Cleopatra, he would stand self-condemned as an enemy of Rome. Not that Octavian had any doubt. He knew Antony's loyalty to his given word: he himself had experienced and exploited it many times in the past.

Early in 31 B.C., after a winter spent in preparation, the forces of Octavian, with Agrippa as usual leading the way, crossed the Ionian sea not for Apollonia or Dyrrachium, but for the promontory of Actium on the north shore of the gulf of Ambracia (cf. map I, page 9). Antony's forces were strung out to protect the western coast of Greece from Epirus in the north to the south of the Peloponnese. The campaign of Actium is badly reported, the course and purpose of the final battle obscure. The operations were lengthy: the battle itself was not fought until September 2. We hear of isolated skirmishes and a great naval battle in which C. Sosius was defeated by Agrippa. We hear too of famine and disease in Antony's camp and of dissension. Client princes began to desert and Romans too, M. Iunius Silanus, Q. Dellius and Cn. Domitius Ahenobarbus himself. Whether Antony, already defeated by sea and baffled on land, fought the battle of Actium for victory or escape to Egypt is unknown. C. Sosius, through error or treachery, allowed himself to be drawn off station into the open sea where Octavian's ships were superior. A large part of Antony's fleet either refused to fight or was defeated and driven back into the harbour. Cleopatra broke away for Egypt and Antony followed with forty ships. Canidius, in command of Antony's land forces, tried to persuade the troops to march away through Macedonia, but they refused and bargained for terms with Octavian.

Octavian had won a victory shabby but complete. Antony and Cleopatra could be dealt with at leisure. Meanwhile some settlement of the East was necessary; demobilization and reward of the soldiers pressing. Agrippa was sent to Italy to superintend the latter, Octavian himself saw to the former. He had gone no further than Samos when urgent letters from Agrippa demanded his return to Italy. The disbanded soldiers were mutinous. Octavian returned, satisfied their demands and after about a month set sail once more for Asia. Cleopatra and Antony sent envoys to Octavian in Rhodes. She received promises, he was ignored. Then Octavian moved to Egypt. Antony, deserted by his fleet and cavalry, was defeated. On August 1, 30 B.C. Alexandria surrendered. Antony at once killed himself. Cleopatra survived for a few days to be interviewed by Octavian before she succumbed to the bite of the asp.

Octavian, who knew well the use of terror, knew also the value of mercy in due season. Actium and Alexandria were not followed by widespread massacre of Antonians. Following the example of his adoptive father after Pharsalus, he made a studied display of clemency. In the *Res Gestae* he claimed to have spared all Roman citizens who asked for pardon. He could afford to: there was no one left to terrorize. We know the names of some who were executed, but C. Sosius and M. Aemilius Scaurus, half-brother of Sextus Pompey, were among those pardoned. Of Cleopatra's children Caesarion was killed. He was the legitimate heir to the throne of Egypt and believed to be the son of Caesar: on both grounds a rival to Octavian. As the sapient Arius of Alexandria observed to Octavian, 'a plurality of Caesars is no good thing'. Alexander Helios and Cleopatra Selene were sent to Rome to appear in Octavian's triumph. The boy is not heard of again, but the girl was married eventually to the scholarly Juba, king of Mauretania. She and Antony's children by Fulvia were brought up at Rome by Octavia. From Octavia's own two daughters by Antony were descended the emperors Caligula, Claudius and Nero.

Egypt Octavian took as his own possession. Elsewhere in the East he confirmed Antony's arrangements, for that in essence was the truth behind his much advertised reconquest of the East for Rome. Then in the summer of 29 B.C. he returned to Italy. On August 13 he entered Rome and on that day and the two following celebrated three triumphs for his campaigns in Illyricum, for the victory at Actium and for the war of Alexandria. Caesar's heir had gained his inheritance.

The Republic Restored

3

Octavian was now endowed with all the problems of the whole empire. Most urgent was the problem of the armies of Rome, a greater threat to her security and stability than any foreign army. Octavian had become responsible for close on seventy legions, his enemy's and his own. His own survival no less than the security of Rome demanded effective and stable demobilization. The problem was a nice one, which abode with the Roman emperors until the fall of the empire: how to reduce the army to a size which threatened neither the solvency of the treasury nor the safety of the ruler without making it too weak properly to defend the frontiers and ensure internal peace. Octavian decided that twenty-eight legions would suffice. The remainder were disbanded and settled in colonies in Italy and the provinces oversea. Land was taken from towns and individuals who had supported Antony, the Italians thus dispossessed being settled elsewhere. But there was no widespread confiscation as after Philippi, no proscription. For Octavian with the problems of the empire had also inherited its resources. He now had access to the wealth of the East, especially of Egypt. From there came the money to buy land. And not merely to buy land. Every discharged soldier received a gratuity of 1,000 sesterces; every Roman citizen a gift of 400 sesterces. Arrears of taxes were remitted and when each of the thirty-five tribes presented Octavian with 1,000 pounds of gold, he returned the gift.

After the depressed economic conditions of the last thirteen years, money was suddenly plentiful, property secure. Real property in Italy mounted in value and the rate of interest fell from twelve to four per cent. At Rome a new Senate House, begun in the first year of the Triumvirate and named after Julius Caesar, was dedicated. In it was placed a statue of Victory adorned with the spoils of Egypt. A temple to Caesar was also dedicated to the accompaniment of chariot races, gladiatorial shows and the sportive slaughter of outlandish beasts never before seen at Rome, the hippopotamus and the rhinoceros. Octavian, however, was absent from the dedication and the spectacles for he was, as often, ill. He had not yet recovered when early in 28 B.C. Agrippa presided at the first of the quinquennial games in honour of the victory at Actium. The public party continued. The temple of Apollo, decreed after the victory at Naulochus, was consecrated on the Palatine; records of arrears of taxation were burned; the corn-dole to the proletariat of Rome was increased four-fold; eighty-two temples which had fallen into decay were repaired at the expense of the descendants of their founders and of Octavian himself.

The celebration of victory and the festive enjoyment of its fruits could not permanently be prolonged. Nor could Octavian's present position. Since 31 B.C. he had held the consulship every year. This office gave no recognition or support to the immense power he possessed from his control of the army, the support of the people and the conquest of the Roman world. What was tolerable in an emergency and post-war reconstruction would form an uncertain basis for permanent power. Two events, similar in kind, but, so far as we know, unconnected in origin or intention, pointed the problem and may, perhaps, have influenced decision. The year 28 B.C. saw a blaze of triumphs by Octavian's generals but there was one notable absentee. M. Licinius Crassus, proconsul of Macedonia, had pacified Thrace, defeated the Bastarnae and earned a triumph. But since he had killed the enemy chieftain with his own hand in single combat, he demanded the wholly exceptional honour of the *spolia opima*, awarded to only two Romans since Romulus. Octavian rejected the claim: Crassus had fought merely as proconsul and, therefore, not under his own auspices; only to a general fighting under his own auspices, that is, in this case, to a consul in office, could the *spolia opima* be granted. The rejection was backed by documentary evidence, the discovery of which is as suspiciously opportune as that of Antony's will. According to the historian Livy, no less an authority than Augustus himself told him that he had seen in the temple of Jupiter Feretrius the linen corselet worn by Cornelius Cossus, the last man to win the *spolia opima* four centuries before, and that this relic, miraculously preserved, described Cossus as consul and, therefore, fighting under his own auspices although all historians before Livy and his august source agreed that Cossus had been merely a subordinate military tribune. Crassus not only lost the *spolia opima*. Octavian would not even allow him the title of *imperator*, which other proconsuls since Actium had enjoyed. Instead he took the title from Crassus and added it to his own total of imperatorial salutations. It was not until July 27 B.C. that Crassus was even allowed his triumph. Thereafter we hear no more of him. Crassus knew bitter and arbitrary humiliation. C. Cornelius Gallus governed Egypt for Octavian as its first prefect; his fall was also sudden and dramatic and Suetonius ranked it with the fall of Salvidienus Rufus. Octavian broke off friendship with him. Prosecution for treason followed and condemnation by the Senate, then Gallus committed suicide in 27 B.C. The cause and offence are mysterious: Suetonius wrote of Gallus' ingratitude and envy; Cassius Dio of Gallus erecting statues of himself and defacing the pyramids with boastful inscriptions. Chance has preserved an inscription of Gallus from Philae. In it he recorded his military successes and claimed to have led his army beyond the cataract of the Nile to a region which no army of the Roman People or king of Egypt had ever penetrated.

M. Licinius Crassus was a great noble, the grandson of the triumvir Crassus, the associate of Caesar and Pompey. C. Cornelius Gallus was a new man from Fréjus in Narbonese Gaul, the descendant not of a Roman or Italian immigrant but of a native dynastic family. Severally and together, intentionally or unintentionally, they struck at the basis of Octavian's power and exposed the weakness of his standing in public law. His power rested on conquest and control of the legions. To maintain it he had to assert a monopoly of military glory. Other generals might win victories and be permitted to triumph, although this was soon to end, but they did so only to the greater glory and by permission of Octavian himself. Octavian had learned too well the lesson of military usurpation not to know the menace of the armed and self-assertive provincial governor. Tacitus was later to condemn envy of a subject's military glory as characteristic of bad emperors. In truth it was inherent in the nature of the imperial system under good emperors as under bad. Military glory in a subject was dangerous because, although politics could be stifled and civil affairs controlled, the army made and unmade emperors. The army had raised Octavian; it could undo him. It was time for a new dispensation to alleviate the danger of the armed proconsuls and to regularize the despotism of Octavian.

'In my sixth and seventh consulships, after I had extinguished the civil wars, having acquired by general consent supreme and absolute power, I transferred the *respublica* from my own control to the disposal of the Senate and the Roman People.' Thus Augustus himself in the *Res Gestae* described the new settlement. It is a sentence of consummate political art. Octavian's supreme power over the whole state and the whole empire before 27 B.C. is not disguised but openly paraded. The document was not written until A.D. 14, not published until Augustus' death. Emphasis of the supremacy of his position over forty-one years before made its renunciation the more magnanimous. But as the foundation for this position Augustus could claim no legal enactment. He had to pass beyond the forms of the constitution to the universal consent of public opinion. Completely lacking is any detailed account of the exact form of the transference of power, although a long sentence follows which lists various honours conferred on Augustus by the Senate.

The transference of power, Augustus claimed, was not a sudden or a single event, but extended over part, at least, of his sixth and seventh consulships, the years 28 and 27 B.C.

15 View of the Decumanus Maximus from the theatre, Ostia.

16 View of the Decumanus Maximus, Ostia.

17 Mosaic from the so-called Villa of Cicero at Pompeii – either a copy of an original by Dioscorides, or the original itself; *Naples, Museo Nazionale*. 47.5 cm × 45.75 cm.

18 Detail of a fresco from Herculaneum showing Hercules recognizing Telephus; *Naples, Museo Nazionale*. 219.75 cm × 185.5 cm.

19 Fresco depicting the Rape of Europa from Pompeii; *Naples, Museo Nazionale*. 124.5 cm × 119.4 cm.

20 Detail of a mosaic from Pompeii; *Naples, Museo Nazionale*. 333 cm × 63 cm.

17

18

19

20

21

23

LATINI
LATINUS
HAEC EFFATUS EQUOS NUMERO PATER ELIGIT OMNI·
STABANT TER CENTUM NITIDI IN PRAESEPIBUS ALTIS·
OMNIBUS EXTEMPLO TEUCRIS IUBET ORDINE DUCI·
INSTRATOS OSTRO ALIPEDES·PICTISQUE TAPETIS·
AUREA PECTORIB· DEMISSA MONILIA PENDENT
TECTI AURO·FULVUM MANDUNT SUB DENTIB· AURUM
ABSENTI AENEAE CURRUM GEMINOSQUE IUGALIS·

In 28 B.C. Octavian was consul with Agrippa. For the first time since 41 B.C. the ordinary consuls held office for the whole year and for the first time for twenty years they both remained in Rome for the whole term of their office. It was a striking return to Republican practice. In addition to their powers as consuls Octavian and Agrippa received a special grant of censorial power, armed with which they conducted a revision of the Senate. Easy advance under the Triumvirs had grossly enlarged the Senate to over 1,000 members. Caesar, it had been said, admitted into the Senate centurions and soldiers, scribes and the sons of freedmen and, ultimate disgrace, Gauls who knew neither the Latin language nor the whereabouts of the Senate House and who were more at home in barbarian trousers than the Roman tunic. The allegations were libellous, in a traditional way. Only one centurion can be detected among Caesar's new senators and the Gauls, it may be assumed, came from the anomalous and Romanized province of Cisalpine Gaul, the home of Catullus, Livy and Virgil. The majority of the new senators came from the local municipal gentry, men of a class largely represented in the Senate ever since the time of Sulla. Caesar's policy was an intensification of that of the nobility at large and he preserved necessary and proper distinctions. The really discreditable accretions came with the Triumvirs, under whom a certain Barbarius Philippus, an escaped slave, became not merely a senator but praetor. There was a sharper reason, however, for purging the Senate than the purification of that body of foreigners and men of low origin, infamous pursuits or financial inability to maintain the dignity appropriate to their station. In 32 B.C. over 300 senators had chosen Antony. Not that all Antonians were discarded; some rose to high office, but some 200 senators lost their places. Fifty or sixty were persuaded to depart voluntarily; 140 were formally expelled by Octavian and Agrippa and their degradation publicly recorded. Complementary to the purge of the Senate was a full-scale census of the Roman People conducted by Octavian and Agrippa in 28 B.C., the first for forty-one years. The Roman census included both the enumeration and registration of the Roman citizens (on this occasion 4,063,000 were registered) and a ritual purification of the whole Roman People gathered in the Campus Martius, in which a sow, a sheep and a bull, after being driven thrice around the multitude, were sacrificed to Mars while a prayer was offered for the safety of the state and increase of empire. The first stage of the new settlement concluded with an edict of Octavian annulling the illegal and arbitrary acts of the Triumvirate. Not all Triumviral acts were, surely, to be condemned. The effect of the edict as a gesture can readily be imagined as can its place in the advertisement of the return to order and legality.

It remained to order the position and powers of Octavian himself. On January 13, 27 B.C., when consul for the seventh time with Agrippa again as his colleague, he appeared before the Senate and resigned all his powers and all his provinces to the disposal of the Senate and the Roman People. The senators vociferously urged him not to abandon the *respublica* which he had saved. At length Octavian, with ostensible reluctance, consented to assume the command of a large *provincia* consisting of Spain, Gaul and Syria for a period of ten years. Three days later the Senate met again to vote exceptional honours to the saviour of the state. A wreath of laurel was to be placed on Octavian's doorposts and oak on his lintel because he had saved the lives of Roman citizens. A golden shield, inscribed with his virtues (cf. plate 38), was set up in the Senate House. Now or later copies were widely disseminated in Italy and the provinces. To mark the new dispensation Octavian took a new name. On the proposal of the pliant L. Munatius Plancus he became, by decree of the Senate, Augustus. The month Sextilis was also so renamed, just as Quinctilis had earlier become July in honour of Julius Caesar.

Thus Augustus 'restored the Republic'. It was not the sudden or spontaneous gesture that propaganda pretended. Every action and reaction had been carefully weighed and provided for, the leading men of his faction consulted. How much of Agrippa was in the settlement is unknown. The ancient sources, piously based on propaganda, concentrate on the magnanimity of Augustus. We do know that Augustus was eager for the name of Romulus but this would not have been a wise choice. By the convolutions of centuries of

21 The Porta Palatina, Turin. A gate of the Augustan colony of Augusta Taurinorum founded in 28 B.C.

22 The theatre at Orange, Provence.

23 Fresco from Pompeii showing Daedalus and Icarus; *Naples, Museo Nazionale.* 35 cm × 36.25 cm.

24 A page from a fourth-century manuscript of Virgil's *Aeneid; Biblioteca Apostolica Vaticana,* Codex Vaticanus Latinus 3225, page 63.

legend and propaganda the first founder of Rome had become an equivocal figure. He had killed his brother and, so one version ran, had himself been killed by Roman senators for aspiring to tyranny, hardly a good omen for Rome's second founder. Who dissuaded Augustus we do not know, the practical and utilitarian Agrippa or the subtle and agile Maecenas. The name finally decided on was a brilliant choice. Suetonius summarized what it conveyed to Romans: 'Sacred places and all those in which anything is ritually consecrated are called august . . . as Ennius also tells us when he writes, "when by august ritual glorious Rome had been founded".' A sacerdotal term implying formal consecration by due observance of augural ritual, the name of Augustus was ideally suited to proclaim the re-establishment of legitimate government under the favour of the gods.

But in what sense was the Republic restored? Augustus' settlement had been variously seen as a blatant fraud and as a genuine attempt to share power with the Senate, to establish a dyarchy. It was, in fact, neither. The real power of Augustus no law of the Roman People, no decree of the Senate, no settlement however far-reaching and comprehensive could affect either by addition or by diminution. The Roman world was his by right of conquest and his power was personal, resting on the enrolment of the population of Rome, of Italy, of the provinces in his private *clientela*. The oath of allegiance before Actium, not the settlement of 27 B.C., was the foundation charter of the Augustan Principate. Yet the restoration of the Republic was not an idle or unnecessary act, nor was it a hollow pretence. Neither the modern connotations of the word Republic nor the special definition imposed on the Latin term *respublica* by the nobility of the Late Republic are helpful. *Respublica* did not denote first and foremost a specific structure of government or distribution of power. Nor did it necessarily imply the freedom of the leading men to scramble for office and power, to govern the Roman world in their own interest and for their own profit. At Rome, naturally, it implied the continued existence of the traditional organs of government, the magistrates, the Senate and the assemblies of the Roman People. But elsewhere different criteria applied. *Respublica* was less an intellectual concept, less a description of a specific form of government than an emotion and a pledge of a purpose of government. The restoration of the Republic, *respublica restituta,* stood for the re-establishment of legitimate government, the restoration of the rule of law, the reaffirmation of the rights and liberties of the citizens. Augustus' restoration of the Republic was not fraudulent because he did not claim to have restored a particular form of government or a specific distribution of power. His claim was that the lawless anarchy of the Triumviral period was ended, that military usurpation and the rule of force had given place to legitimate government and the rule of law.

Not the rule of law only. The inseparability of law and order is a very English concept: the sole guarantee of ordered social life is an effectively enforced system of law, which, as social structure increases in complexity, itself becomes ever more complex and pervasive. It is not the only possible system. In China, for instance, the effective guarantee of order in the Confucian system was not law but social conformity enforced by a clearly defined hierarchy of moral authority. At Rome both systems operated. Over against law stood custom and habit; the health and stability of society was assured by good laws and good habits together. To legislate men into virtue may seem to us a useless occupation but not so to the Romans. The more a society lost its moral bearings, the less assured became its discipline; the less assured its discipline, the more certain the collapse of internal stability and with the collapse of internal stability went loss of empire. Thus the Romans explained the failure of the Republic. A long and ineffective tale of laws in the last two centuries of the Republic condemned and forbade every conceivable form of vice and luxury. If men were not moral by nature, they could be coerced into morality by law, for if the individual citizen were corrupt then the whole empire was in danger. The restoration of the Republic included, therefore, not merely the regularization of Augustus' position and the reaffirmation of the rule of law. It involved also the consolidation of the traditional morality. The poet Horace summarized the Roman attitude when he addressed Augustus as the man who 'alone bears the weight of all public affairs, guards the state of Italy in war, adorns her with morals, reforms her with laws'. Care for morality was as important as administrative ability, military quality or legislative activity.

In 19, 18 and 11 B.C. Augustus was pressed by the Senate and the People to accept a general oversight of morals and laws with supreme power. He seems to have accepted censorial power for a period of five years; then in 18 B.C. he presented in person to the Roman People a body of legislation designed to stabilize and encourage marriage and childbirth. An abortive attempt appears to have been made ten years earlier as part of the original restoration of the Republic, but the laws, if they were ever formally promulgated, were withdrawn in the face of protest and opposition. Now came the *lex Iulia de adulteriis coercendis* and the *lex Iulia de maritandis ordinibus*. The former for the first time made adultery a public crime, the latter liberalized the Roman law of marriage by recognizing the validity of unions between free-born citizens and men and women freed from slavery, although senators were expressly forbidden to marry freedwomen. The law assumed that marriage and parenthood were the natural state of men between the ages of twenty-five and sixty and of women between the ages of twenty and fifty. It therefore imposed disabilities on those who abstained from marriage or childbirth. On the other hand, husbands and fathers who entered public life were rewarded by more rapid promotion. The number of a man's children gave him precedence when he stood for office and he could stand as many years before the legal minimum age as he had children. In A.D. 9 the law was modified by the *lex Papia Poppaea*, which increased the distinction between the merely and, possibly, unwillingly childless and those who contumaciously refused even to marry. It also allowed women who had been divorced or widowed a longer period in which to remarry before they incurred the legal penalties.

How successful this legislation was in its ostensible object it is impossible to determine. It was maliciously observed that neither of the consuls who carried the *lex Papia Poppaea* was married or a father. But practical effect was, perhaps, not the most important purpose. Just as the constitutional arrangements of 27 B.C. and subsequent settlements regularized and legitimized Augustus' position without affecting his real power, so the moral legislation proclaimed a return to traditional moral standards, the flagrant abandonment of which among the nobles of the Late Republic had been held to have been the cause of the Republic's ruin. It was an essential part of the restoration of the *respublica*.

For what Augustus' restored Republic meant to contemporaries we have the impressive testimony of the poets Virgil and Horace. At one level Virgil's *Aeneid* (cf. plate 24) expounds the ideal of the new order which had replaced the self-seeking chaos that had gone before. The nobles of the Late Republic by pursuing glory at the expense of the state had destroyed the *respublica*. All that they had meant by glory Virgil showed to be false and disruptive. True glory attended the foundation of a secure society, based not on war but on the rule of law and extending its civilizing influence over the whole world. To Aeneas himself, although he was amply qualified by his honourable birth and his fame which had mounted to heaven, Virgil nowhere ascribed nobility or glory. These attributes, as recently interpreted, were anachronisms. Aeneas' great quality, emphasized and invoked at every turn of the poem, is *pietas*. It meant nothing else than doing his duty to his gods, his country and his family. This duty Virgil's Aeneas pursued against his own will, in violation of his passionate desire for rest and tranquillity, with growing steadfastness and deepening understanding of his destiny. Early in the poem he is characterized: 'Our king was Aeneas, than whom none was more just or greater in sense of duty and war'. Sense of duty and justice, *pietas* and *iustitia*, went together. *Pietas* left no room for the pursuit of personal glory and prestige; by *iustitia* those who arrogantly asserted their power to the enslavement of others were tamed and made into a civilized nation. If they refused to submit, it was Rome's duty, ordained by heaven, to destroy them in war. Horace agreed with Virgil that there was no room in the new order for the pursuit of that glory which had ruined the Republic. In the *Carmen Saeculare* he listed the key-notes of the new dispensation: 'Faith and Peace and Honour and ancient Modesty and neglected Virtue dare to return and blessed Plenty with her full horn appears.' The establishment of peace and security in Rome and Rome's empire, that was the important task. Like Aeneas the politicians of the new Republic were not to be heroes in the vulgar sense: the world had suffered enough from such heroics. Aeneas' aim was not personal domination, but to unify and reconcile Rome and Italy on the basis of law, not conquest. Again and again Horace insisted that it was Augustus who had saved the Roman world from ruin and that it was Augustus alone who prevented the return of chaos. The cynical may dismiss it as propaganda. But Virgil and Horace were not hypocrites—and they were right. It was not Augustus nor any of the other monarchic faction leaders who remarked that civil war was worse than monarchy; it was M. Favonius, the fanatical adherent of the younger Cato who was Caesar's great enemy and the staunchest defender of the Republic and the power of the noble oligarchy. The propaganda of Augustus succeeded precisely because, unlike the polemic of the factional strife of the last age of the Republic, it was founded ultimately on real issues. Before Actium the unity of Italy was a real aspiration and the division of the empire into East and West aroused real fear. After the restoration of the Republic order, security and the *Pax Augusta* answered men's prayers. For them liberty and the Republic, as they had lately existed, were well lost. The Roman People understood; they wanted Augustus to assume more power, not less, and to assume it more openly.

The regularization and self-legitimization of absolute power won by conquest is a delicate business. In the middle of the year 27 B.C. Augustus left Rome to attend the war in Spain, still not completely conquered after two centuries. He was absent for three years, returning about the middle of the year 24 exhausted and ill. In his absence he had been elected consul year after year. This series of consulships was certainly an integral part of the settlement of 27 B.C., but we do not know that it was publicly announced at the time. Not only did Augustus thus annually remove one of the consulships from competition: there were no suffects and his colleague in each year was a loyal adherent attached to his cause by past service, interest or marriage. Augustus had, therefore, placed himself in a position which could scarcely be called Republican. Moreover, his possession of the consulship nullified the ostensible purpose of the settlement of 27 B.C., a return to legitimate government in which Augustus resigned his powers to the Senate and the People and received in return a defined sphere of duty. For the consuls had power over all provinces and all proconsuls and by virtue of his consular power Augustus could interfere in the supposedly senatorial provinces no less than in his own. This we know he did. A decree of Augustus and Agrippa in 27 B.C. ordered the restitution of sacred property in the provinces. The inscription also contains a consequential judgement of the proconsul of Asia, a province nominally in the control of the Senate, which refers to 'the order of Augustus Caesar'. Matters were not improved by the ostentatious parade of Augustus' nephew M. Marcellus as his heir.

Augustus had dangerously exposed the reality behind the settlement of 27 B.C. In 23 B.C. came the reckoning. That year, it has been said, might well have been the last, and was certainly the most critical in all the long Principate of Augustus. Late in 24 or early in 23 B.C. M. Primus, proconsul of Macedonia, was arraigned on a charge of treason in that he had made war on the Thracian Odrysae without the authorization of the Senate and the Roman People. Primus, defended by A. Terentius Varro Murena, Augustus' colleague in the consulship of 23, claimed that he had been carrying out the orders of Augustus and Marcellus. Augustus appeared in court and denied the allegation on oath, whereupon Murena asked him why in that case he had come into court. Murena, in fact, used his defence of Primus to issue a direct challenge to Augustus. He could not at the same time claim to have restored the Republic and constitutional government and still continue to exercise arbitrary and extra-constitutional power. If the settlement of 27 B.C. was not a hollow sham, why should Augustus order about a senatorial proconsul? As for Marcellus, he had no legal right to instruct Primus to do anything. Any authority he might have derived solely from his relationship with Augustus and was, therefore, private and personal, without constitutional foundation. Primus was duly condemned, but worse followed. A conspiracy was discovered, its author the mysterious Fannius Caepio. Varro Murena was implicated. The conspirators were condemned in absence, captured and killed. Fannius was no loss to the new order. He was a 'bad man', Republican in family and sentiment. But Murena was a Caesarian and brother of Terentia, wife of the all-powerful Maecenas, of the inner circle of Augustus' party. More, he was consul in office. The trial of Primus and the conspiracy and executions of Fannius and Murena cast a glaring and unwelcome light on the real nature of Augustus' new Republic. They were not the only casualties of this year. No less a personage than Maecenas made a fatal mistake when he told Terentia of her brother's danger. The breach of confidence was never forgiven. After 23 B.C. Maecenas declined in importance and influence with Augustus. The strain proved too much for Augustus' health. Never robust, it had been undermined in Spain and had grown steadily worse. Now he was close to death. He handed his signet ring to Agrippa, certain state papers to Cn. Calpurnius Piso, whom he had appointed (there was no question of an election) to the consulate vacant on Murena's death, but gave no indication of his intentions for the empire.

Augustus, however, recovered, saved by a drastic regimen of cold baths prescribed by his doctor Antonius Musa. On July 1 he resigned the consulship. In his place there was appointed L. Sestius, an open admirer of Marcus Brutus whose quaestor he had been. The suffect consuls of 23 B.C., Calpurnius and Sestius, attest the readiness of old Republicans to support the new order and of Augustus to use them for his own purposes. In twenty years Augustus had held eleven consulships, the last nine of them in succession. In the remaining thirty-six years of his reign he held the office only twice, in 5 and 2 B.C. To compensate for the loss of the powers of the supreme magistracy, the power he exercised in his *provincia* was modified in two ways: it was not to lapse when he entered the city of Rome, as did the *imperium* of an ordinary proconsul, and it was to be superior to that of all other proconsuls. In this way Augustus was placed with regard to the provinces in much the same position as he had had as consul. If anything his position was strengthened, for he could now exercise control over the other provincial governors by virtue of powers expressly granted and formally defined, instead of relying on the vague, undefined and challengeable powers of the consulship. But in Rome and Italy Augustus now lacked legal standing. A proconsul possessed his *imperium* until he entered the city of Rome, when it automatically lapsed, but without special authorization from the Senate or the People he could exercise it only in the sphere of duty, the *provincia*, assigned him by the Senate. To provide Augustus with a modest position in Rome the Senate and, no doubt, the Roman People voted that he should possess tribunician power for life. In 36 B.C. he had received the personal inviolability, the sacrosanctity of a tribune and six years later a general power of pardon in all cases under the criminal laws, that is, not merely an extended form of the traditional power of the tribune to defend the liberty of Roman citizens against the arbitrary exercise of magisterial power, but also the Roman People's own prerogative of mercy even in cases where no appeal had hitherto lain. Not that he appears to have used these powers. Now in 23 B.C. he acquired with the full tribunician power the right of veto over the acts of all magistrates, the right of summoning and transacting business with the Plebeian Assembly and the right of consulting the Senate.

It was a modest position indeed. The plebeian tribunate lacked the trappings of power that attended the consul, occupied a humble and inessential place in the career of office and enjoyed a very low priority in summoning and consulting the Senate. True, the negative powers of the tribune were enormous. One tribune could by his veto paralyse the whole machinery of state. There is no evidence that Augustus used it. Nor did he much employ the milder positive powers. Some of his social and moral legislation he put through by virtue of his tribunician power and duly recorded the fact in the *Res Gestae*. But the majority of his major social laws and other legislation was proposed by consuls. Consuls also moved all the existing decrees of the Senate of Augustus' reign. Of the actual powers of the tribunate Augustus had no need. Formal veto was unnecessary where mere hint of displeasure would suffice. Personal action or intervention was not called for when there were members of the government in high office to act for him. If it were called for in an exceptional crisis, then Augustus would act by virtue of his immense extra-constitutional powers.

The attraction of the tribunate lay elsewhere. It was essentially a civilian office. A tribune could not command armies and his competence was restricted to the city of Rome. Created in the early years of the Republic to protect the Plebeians from Patrician oppression, the traditional function of the office was the defence of the liberties of the citizens. In the factional struggles of the last century, Republican propaganda had made great play with the liberties of the People and the rights of the tribunes. In every sense it was a popular office. To the whole of this popular tradition, from the early defenders of the Plebeians to more recent heroes such as the Gracchi, Augustus now laid formal claim. The events of the early months of the year 23 B.C. had shown the difficulty of satisfying the politicians. Against them Augustus appealed to his faithful clients, the common people of Rome, whom he pledged himself, by his assumption of tribunician power, not to desert.

Fig. 9 Coin: Aureus; reverse showing the altar of Fortuna Redux. *London, British Museum.* (*Actual size*).

The People responded. The winter of 23–22 B.C. brought floods, famine and plague. The People rioted and pressed Augustus to assume a dictatorship, an annual and perpetual consulship or the censorship. The offers were declined, but Augustus did assume control of the corn supply and had censors elected. In the course of 22 B.C. the corn supply was transferred to a pair of curators of praetorian rank. Augustus departed to the East. In his absence the People insisted on electing him consul for 21 and, when he refused the election, refused in turn to fill the vacancy with another. The second consul was elected only in 21 itself and it took the return of Agrippa to achieve it. Agrippa also arranged the consular elections for the next year and then left for Gaul and Spain. Whereupon, at the elections for 19 B.C. the People once more insisted on reserving one consulship for Augustus. By the summer of 19 the situation was so serious that the Senate passed its 'last decree' calling on the one consul in office and the other magistrates to see that the State took no harm and the consul begged Augustus to return. He arrived on October 12 to the Senate's great relief. A special delegation of senators went to Campania to meet him and the Senate decreed the erection of an altar to Fortuna Redux (cf. figure 9).

Augustus and the Roman People had taught dissident politicians a sharp lesson. Spontaneous demonstrations of popular enthusiasm for any regime are rightly suspect in any age, but the agitation would scarcely have been so sustained had it not been founded on genuine popular sentiment. Augustus' propaganda—the defence of Rome and Italy against the corrupt forces of the East, the victory at Actium and the clemency which followed it, the restoration of the Republic—had been highly successful. To the ordinary Roman Augustus was indeed the great leader of his country. More than that, the ordinary Roman had grasped the essential truth that only the person and power of Augustus stood between Rome and the return of factional strife. The Roman People wanted order and security, not the anarchy of the Late Republic. Beside that constitutional niceties were irrelevant luxuries.

Augustus could now recover the ground he had lost in 23 B.C. Exactly what form the arrangements of 19 and 18 B.C. took is difficult to determine. Augustus makes no mention of them in the *Res Gestae*, but there is much of importance which that document omits. It would appear that his *imperium*, now merely proconsular, was upgraded to make it equal to that of the consuls. Certainly we find Augustus once more exercising powers and performing functions normally reserved to holders of full consular power. He commanded troops, the praetorian cohorts in Italian towns and the three urban cohorts and the *Vigiles* in Rome itself. He raised soldiers by conscription in Rome and Italy. He exercised a criminal and civil jurisdiction and a power of summary punishment, as when he relegated by edict the poet Ovid to Tomis. In the latter part of his reign he received, concurrently with the consuls, formal declarations of candidature for the consular and praetorian elections. In 8 B.C. and A.D. 14 he conducted censuses in Italy by virtue of consular power. Most significantly, he appointed Prefects of the City to govern Rome when he was absent and delegated *imperium* within the city to them. Thus Augustus' legal power was again released from the territorial limitations imposed on it in 23 B.C. and from late in the year 19 B.C. he exercised it not merely in his own and, when necessary, in the senatorial provinces, but also in Rome and Italy.

Thus Augustus arrived at a final regularization of his constitutional position. Behind all the constitutional shifts, however, lay a sharp and urgent problem: how was he to ensure his personal survival? The nobles who had joined him against Antony did so for their own interest and their own power. Their chance and Augustus' danger came with the defeat of Antony. Then they might have decided to restore their notion of the Republic by removing Augustus. After Actium, despite the purge of the Senate, the political class at Rome included men of many sympathies, not all of them devoted to the new order and the preservation of its founder. The events of the decade after Actium, therefore, constitute the education of this class in political responsibility by Augustus and the leading men of his party, chief among them Agrippa. Those who remained unconvinced had to learn what the ordinary Roman already knew: that Augustus alone was the guarantee of peace, order and prosperity, that the insane pursuit of personal power and personal position which had ruined the Republic was an anachronism. Augustus and his closest associates had a lesson to learn too: how best to deploy the immense power he had acquired.

In this respect the various constitutional adjustments were in the last resort irrelevant to the realities of Augustus' position. The power of the leading men of the Republican oligarchy, the *principes*, had rested on the system of clientship which pervaded the society of Rome and Italy, the provinces and the client kingdoms. When Augustus emerged as sole Princeps he gathered to himself all the privileges and prerogatives shared and competed for by the many *principes* of the Republic. All the inhabitants of the Roman world were his clients. The army and the Roman People were the twin pillars of his power and his hold over them was personal and beyond the constitution. Not merely clientship became the monopoly of one man, but all glory, dignity and that particular form of prestige which had attached to the leading men of the Republic, *auctoritas*. The term denoted the moral influence and authority, not sanctioned by law, possessed by a man who was an instigator and originator of public policy, an *auctor publici consilii*. It belonged in the Republic to that small group of senior senators who controlled the business and decisions of the Senate and thus governed the Roman world according to their own wishes. After Actium it belonged to Augustus alone. This, too, the constitutional adjustments could not touch. As he himself wrote in the *Res Gestae*, 'After that time (28–27 B.C.) I was superior to all in *auctoritas*, but I had no more legal power than the other men who were my colleagues in each magistracy'. With pre-eminent *auctoritas* there was no need of excessive legal powers.

The position reached in 19 B.C. endured with minor adjustments until Augustus' death thirty-three years later. In 19 the long and difficult process of restoring the Republic in the sense of the re-establishment of law and order, peace and stability, was almost completed. In 18 B.C. came the moral and social legislation proposed by Augustus in person and another purge of the Senate which by a complicated procedure reduced the size of that body to six hundred members, its size in the Late Republic before Caesar's Dictatorship. (Augustus thought that 300 senators would be enough. This was the traditional size of the Senate throughout the Republic before Sulla.) In 17 B.C. celebration of the Secular Games, which Augustus had perhaps originally projected for 22 B.C., inaugurated and advertised the beginning of a new era in Roman history.

Men and Government

4

The victory of Octavian over Antony, the victory of Augustus over the Republic and the Roman world was the victory not of a single man, but of a faction, of a party, of a whole social class. It is time to turn attention from Augustus himself to analyse the composition of this faction, to examine the working of favour and patronage, to document and illustrate the real nature of a revolution which was as much social as political.

The earliest and closest associates of Octavian in his rise to power, the founder-members, as it were, of his faction can easily be identified. Their names have already been noted in sundry places: Q. Salvidienus Rufus, M. Vipsanius Agrippa, C. Maecenas, diverse in character, ability and achievement, but united by the indecent obscurity of their parentage—or so the Republican nobility would have said. The name Salvidienus was of a type widely distributed in central Italy and not unknown in politics at Rome, but so obvious a parade of alien origin did not please the ambitious Salvidienus. Coins struck in 40 B.C. call him Q. Salvius, Latinizing the too revealing family name. Agrippa, likewise, preferred men to forget that he was called Vipsanius, an ignoble name, never before known at Rome, and to be called simply Marcus Agrippa. The nomenclature of Maecenas presents an odd inconsistency. Tacitus, whom many moderns have followed, called him Cilnius Maecenas. But his family name was Maecenas simply, of unimpeachable Etruscan regularity. Cilnius was the family name of his mother's family. But it possessed what Maecenas did not, the regular termination of a Latin family name. Did Octavian's minister have the vain naivety at some stage of his devious career to attempt unconvincing respectability by adopting the specious form C. Cilnius Maecenas? He was vain enough. Cilnius had another attraction. It was, or was claimed to be, the name of the ancient royal dynasty of the Etruscan town of Arretium (Arezzo). Close attention to apparently pedantic details can sometimes surprisingly illuminate human character and here it confirms what the treachery of Salvidienus abundantly attests: that these new men stood not for any principle of the rights and claims of Italy but, no less than the Roman nobility, for their own power to be sought by any means and in any place. They could easily have been with Antony as many of their kind were, some to the very end.

Salvidienus and Agrippa were, however, with Octavian from the beginning, in the camp at Apollonia. Salvidienus was the older and the more important, earning abuse from Marcus Brutus. He may well have been an officer in Caesar's army. Agrippa was the same age to within a year as Octavian. Where he came from is unknown, as is his family. Even when he had become great and famous, no one could discover who his father was and his character mirrored his peasant origin. Hard and dour, he was better fitted for the harsh realities of a peasant's life than the subtleties of the capital. Even Augustus found it difficult at times to bear with Agrippa's short temper. And he was ambitious, skilled, it was said, in obedience to one man only but lusting to dominate all others. That one man, Augustus, owed him much. In the wars through which he rose to power the strategy, tactics and field command were Agrippa's. A case could be made out that Augustus was Agrippa's creation. Not militarily merely, for Agrippa no less than Augustus was concerned in the constitutional arrangements of the twenties. But one thing Agrippa irretrievably lacked, the charisma which attached to Augustus as Caesar's heir. While Agrippa might succeed Augustus after his death, he could never have supplanted him during his life so as to retain the fullness of power. It is true that once the

25 A bust of Livia Drusilla; *Copenhagen, Glyptotheque ny Carlsberg. Height* 34 cm.

26 A green basalt bust of Livia, which was, until very recently, thought to be of Octavia; *Paris, Musée du Louvre. Height* 32 cm.

27 The head of Cleopatra found at Cherchel, Algeria; *Cherchel Museum. Height* 35.75 cm.

28 The Basilica of Neptune, Rome, built by Agrippa in 25 B.C. to commemorate the victory at Actium.

26

27

31

Augustan Principate was firmly established it discarded its Caesarian origins; but by then Agrippa was dead, an event marked by the nobles' ostentatious refusal to attend his funeral games. They hated Agrippa with vindictive helplessness. He distrusted them, seeing them for what they were, the class which in pursuit of its own glory had destroyed the Republic and would, if it could, destroy the precarious stability and peace established by Augustus. With Augustus' equivocal flirtation with the nobility and his dynastic ambitions Agrippa had little patience. He stood as the visible embodiment of the new order with an ideal of public utility which was remorseless and logical. An ex-consul, he became a commissioner of public works, under the Republic a position reserved for the beginning of a public career, and built aqueducts and repaired sewers; and he advocated the confiscation of art treasures in private possession so that they might be seen and enjoyed by the whole people.

Fig. 10 Coin: Denarius; reverse with the figures of Augustus and Agrippa. *London, British Museum.* (*Actual size*).

Augustus recognized his debt to Agrippa and Agrippa's worth. To honours, ordinary and extra-ordinary, succeeded at length a share in position and public recognition of power. In the settlement of 23 B.C. Agrippa received a grant of proconsular power for five years. The exact nature and extent of his sphere of duty, his *provincia*, is uncertain, but it probably covered all Augustus' provinces in the East and West but not those of the Senate. In the same year Agrippa married Augustus' daughter Julia, widowed by the death of Marcellus. As Maecenas, Agrippa's enemy, put it, Augustus had no choice; he had either to make Agrippa his son-in-law or destroy him. In 23 B.C. Agrippa became publicly deputy leader of Augustus' party and Augustus' partner in the government of the provinces. Five years later he became, it could be said, co-regent. In 18 B.C. his proconsular power was extended, as Augustus' had been in 23 B.C., to cover the senatorial provinces. In addition Agrippa received a share in the tribunician power.

Probity, devotion to duty and a puritanical code of morals were not the only things to come out of Italy. Soon after their arrival in Italy in 44 B.C., Octavian, Salvidienus and Agrippa were joined by C. Maecenas, diplomat, artist and voluptuary. His family was known, his grandfather mentioned in a speech by Cicero, his father recorded on a surviving inscription. They were Etruscan and on his mother's side Maecenas claimed regal descent. Maecenas' contribution to Augustus' power was more subtle, less obvious than that of Agrippa. The triumphs of diplomacy are rarely fit for public commemoration. But we hear of Maecenas on a diplomatic mission to Sextus Pompey in Spain; it was Maecenas who conducted negotiations with Antony's representative in the confrontation at Brundisium; it was he who went to Greece in 38 B.C. to beg Antony's help after Octavian's first disastrous attempt to defeat Sextus Pompey; it was he who exerted himself for Octavian at the conference of Tarentum when the Triumvirate was renewed. While Octavian and Agrippa were in Sicily defeating Pompey, Maecenas was left in charge of Rome as he was again when the armies of Octavian went East to defeat Antony and Cleopatra. Above all, it was Maecenas who organized and directed public opinion and propaganda, not least through his famous circle of poets. The diplomatic arts do not inspire confidence in the sincerity of their practitioners. The grim and puritanical Agrippa hated Maecenas. We can see why. Maecenas, it was said, bathed himself in depravity and luxury worse even than a woman, delighting in precious gems, silks and the charms of the actor Bathyllus. His taste in food was exquisite, extending to the flesh of young donkeys. The style of his verse, like the style of his life, was fantastical and conceited. All this could be borne for none in Augustus' entourage would claim to be above moral suspicion. What was intolerable was Maecenas' vanity, for it was vanity which made him talk too much, as Augustus himself complained. In the end it undid him when in 23 B.C. he betrayed to Terentia the discovery of the conspiracy of Murena.

So when Agrippa died in 12 B.C., Maecenas' influence had already waned and when death came fifteen years later he faced it with self-pity and horror. Salvidienus had gone even earlier. Others could not later repeat these men's experience, no one could know as they knew the innermost secrets of the foundation of Augustus' power. Yet the survival of an old guard beyond the consummation of a revolution can be a mixed blessing; indeed

29 Detail of one of the pillars of the Basilica of Neptune, Rome.

30 Detail of the statue of Augustus from the Via Labicana showing Augustus as Pontifex Maximus; *Rome, Museo delle Terme.*

31 The theatre, Ostia. The theatre, rebuilt at the end of the second century A.D., was originally built with a double colonnaded portico on the initiative of Agrippa.

the relatively early disappearance of Augustus' closest associates from the revolutionary age made its own contribution to the stability of the Principate. As far as was possible T. Statilius Taurus succeeded to the honour and position that would have come to Salvidienus Rufus. To the position of Maecenas succeeded C. Sallustius Crispus, the great-nephew of the historian Sallust. Like Maecenas Sallustius earned a reputation for indolence and vice. Appearances, however, were deceptive. As Tacitus said of him, underneath he possessed a vigorous mind, equal to the greatest affairs and the more incisive because it was cloaked by an appearance of sloth and idleness. Sallustius had once been a partisan of Antony but many of Augustus' closest friends had once been Antonians; Sallustius afterwards served Augustus long and well, acquiring immense wealth and the pleasure gardens on the Pincian hill which passed eventually into legend and the possession of the imperial dynasty. His services did not end on Augustus' death. On the accession of Tiberius, Sallustius accomplished the secret and summary execution of Agrippa Postumus, son of Agrippa and Julia and, therefore, a potential rival to Tiberius and a potential danger to the stability of the state. Sallustius had no son of his own blood but adopted the son of L. Passienus Rufus, consul in 4 B.C. The adopted son, C. Sallustius Passienus Crispus, became a great courtier and the husband of two princesses in succession, of Domitia, the aunt of Nero, and of Nero's mother, Agrippina. Maecenas could be replaced, but no one could succeed the great military men. That was forbidden by the survival of Augustus himself. Indeed, the position and influence of men like Agrippa and Statilius Taurus had been founded precisely on their refusal to use their power and prestige with the soldiers for independent action—unlike Salvidienus. To control the armed proconsuls was the first as it was always the most urgent of Augustus' preoccupations. But from the later Principate two names may be mentioned. M. Lollius was consul in 21 B.C. and annexed the province of Galatia after the death of its king Amyntas. He was successively proconsul of Macedonia in 19 and 18 B.C. and then governor for Augustus of Gallia Comata from 17 to 16 B.C. When in 1 B.C. Gaius Caesar, whom Augustus was promoting as his heir, was sent on a tour of the East, his guide and counsellor was Lollius. But during the tour, in A.D. 2, Lollius, for reasons now obscure and perhaps never publicly divulged, fell suddenly from favour and died, perhaps by suicide. That, at least, was what was given out. To the disgraced Lollius P. Sulpicius Quirinius succeeded as the tutor of Gaius Caesar. He had a long career of faithful service to Augustus. He had campaigned against the Marmaridae, a tribe living in the African desert south of Cyrene, he was consul in 12 B.C. and at some later date governed Galatia and subdued the Homonadenses. Three or four years after the disgrace of Lollius he became legate of Syria. When he died at last, in A.D. 22, Tiberius gave him a state funeral and marked the occasion with a speech in the Senate praising him and abusing Lollius, dead twenty years before.

Agrippa and Statilius Taurus, Maecenas and Sallustius Crispus, Lollius and Sulpicius Quirinius, all of them were new men, Maecenas and Sallustius not even members of the Senate. They were not alone. We know the names of six men who governed Augustus' provinces as legates in the period from 27 to 23 B.C. Only one was an ex-consul, the others were ex-praetors. Five of them certainly had no consular ancestors; if their parents were senators at all, they were obscure and humble in rank. In the first ten years of his constitutional rule Augustus employed not a single noble to command the armies in his provinces and only three men who had reached the consulship. The consulate had been cheapened under the Triumvirs. The great majority of Triumviral consuls had been new men, nineteen in the period 39–33 B.C. as against nine nobles. From 31 to 29 B.C. there were nine consuls, apart from Octavian himself, four new men and five nobles. In 28 B.C. the annual consulate was restored, monopolized at first by Augustus and his closest associates. But of the consuls who held office from 25 to 19 B.C. eight came from new families as against five nobles. The restoration of the Republic, it is evident, did not mean the restoration of the Republican nobility.

The promotion of new families and new men from Italy to power at Rome had been under the Republic a haphazard business, dependent on the interest and ambition of the various factions of the Roman nobility. The civil wars of the end of the Republic had given the new men their chance with the result that there had been an explosive expansion of the governing class at Rome. Augustus' task was to consolidate and institutionalize this social revolution, as was needed by Rome, by Italy and by the empire generally no less than by himself. If Italy was to be stable, the legitimate aspirations of her inhabitants must be fulfilled, and if Rome and her empire were at last to receive proper and efficient government and administration, new men had to be found, promoted and rewarded. If Augustus was to survive, power must be diluted and a counter balance sought to the pretensions of the surviving nobles.

An instrument lay ready to hand in the developing Equestrian Order. To apply this term rigorously to the Republic is to be anachronistic, but for a complex variety of reasons the practice had grown up of applying to what we may very loosely call the Roman middle class the name of *Equites*, knights or cavalry. Not that they now had any connection with horses. Nor was it a term of precise definition, still less of constitutional significance denoting a recognized rank of society, an *ordo*, comparable to the senatorial order. At one extreme the Republican usage covered the non-political members of the upper class, men like Cicero's friend Atticus, whose tastes and style of life were those of the senators and who were superior to most senators in wealth, but who, for whatever reason of personal preference or advantage, had rejected a political career. Below them were the more humble business men, financiers and agents, including the tax collectors, and the leading men of the Roman towns in Italy and the provinces. The lower limit for admission to the *Equites* in this sense was merely that imposed by the natural restraint of each individual's capacity for vanity or flattery. It has been represented that the political history of the last age of the Republic is that of a persistent opposition of the *Equites* to the Senate. The representation is false. The *Equites*, or rather the business men and financiers among them, were concerned with money and their interest was profit. They became politically effective only when their profit was threatened. Increasingly they became a source of political instability. Moreover, in their hands was the collection of the taxes of the empire, farmed out at Rome to companies of speculators. With the connivance of the senatorial governor, the tax collectors could exploit and oppress the inhabitants of a province. If the governor stood out against their demands, political trouble would be expected and even the end of his career—and still the provincials would have to pay. Although Augustus took the collection of the major taxes from the speculators, the whole class still had to be integrated into the body politic.

Drawing on certain partial Republican precedents, the basic qualification for membership of the Equestrian Order was defined as the possession of Roman citizenship and property to the value of 400,000 sesterces. Thus the middle class was given corporate identity not merely in Rome and Italy but throughout the empire. 'I have heard,' wrote the geographer Strabo, 'that at one of the censuses in our time five hundred men of Cadiz were assessed as *Equites*.' Since the qualification for membership of the order was financial, it was to a large extent self-recruiting. Two sources of recruitment were of particular importance. First, common soldiers or their sons gained admittance by military service. Secondly, freedmen, always well represented in financial transactions, had greatly enriched themselves in the wars and proscriptions of the revolutionary period. (One Isidorus, for instance, left on his death 60,000,000 sesterces in ready cash and thousands of slaves and cattle. His funeral must have been magnificent: it cost 1,000,000 sesterces.) In turn, it was the Equestrian Order which supplied recruits for the Senate. The Equestrian Order, in truth, was the cardinal factor in the whole social, military and political structure of the new state of Augustus.

The Equestrian Order not merely supplied recruits for the Senate. It also gradually acquired its own career of public service. In the army this career in the time of Augustus is, unfortunately, a highly obscure subject, but there is evidence to show the beginning of a hierarchy of Equestrian posts with graded honours in which a man might spend most of his active life. In civil life members of the Equestrian Order, drawn from the local aristocracies of the towns of Italy and the provinces, were employed by Augustus as procurators to collect the revenues of his own provinces. A member of the Order might even aspire to govern a province. Some of the provinces acquired by Augustus subsequent to the settlement of 27 B.C., such as Raetia and Noricum, were placed under prefects or procurators of Equestrian standing. The first governor of Judaea after its annexation in A.D. 6 was an *Eques*, Coponius of a respectable family from Tibur. The greatest of all Equestrian posts under Augustus was that of Prefect of Egypt. That land Augustus took as his own possession. Senators were barred from it and it was governed by an Equestrian Prefect in command of three legions. In 2 B.C. another post was created which was eventually to rival the Prefecture of Egypt. In that year two Roman *Equites*, Q. Ostorius Scapula and P. Salvius Aper, were chosen to command the Praetorian Guard. Later still two other peculiarly Equestrian posts were instituted in the city of Rome: that of *Praefectus Vigilum* in A.D. 6 and that of *Praefectus Annonae* soon after. The former commanded a force composed mainly of freed slaves which was responsible for policing the city and guarding it against fire; the latter had charge of the food supply of the capital.

The organization of the Equestrian Order gave recognition and status to the whole class of new men, to the men of wealth and reputation in the towns of Italy and the provinces. It opened to all Roman citizens the possibility of a career of public service, the highest posts of which bestowed power superior to those open to senators, or of entry to the Senate itself. Not that the promotion of men of this class to the Senate was itself a novelty. The new men of the Republic had come from the same background. What was novel was that Augustus provided for the regular and copious recruitment of the Senate from the 'whole flower of the colonies and municipal towns everywhere', as the emperor Claudius was to put it, and that the recruits came not merely from the neighbourhood of Rome and from central Italy but from the most distant corners of the peninsula. Although their names grate on sensibilities attuned to the smooth regularity of the nomenclature of Republican Rome, they were in the main persons of some substance and reputation in their own towns, respectable men who served Augustus and Rome loyally and well. Not that antique virtue attached to all new men, whatever propaganda might claim. Maecenas was no advertisement for moral regeneration; nor was P. Vedius Pollio, son of a freedman grown immensely rich, who fed live slaves to his lampreys. It improved their flavour. Maecenas and Vedius, as it happened, were not senators and many of their class who did attain this dignity were not merely the first but also the last senators in their families. Not that that mattered. A system had been established which replaced them with men of their own kind if not of their own blood.

Among Augustus' new senators can also be discerned names of great moment in later history. From an ancient and honourable family of Ferentinum in Etruria came M. Salvius Otho, who became a senator under Augustus, thanks to the patronage of none other than Livia Drusilla. His son became by the murder of Galba for a brief while the emperor Otho, who was in turn quickly dispatched by L. Vitellius. He was one of the four senatorial sons of P. Vitellius of Nuceria (Nocera dei Pagani) who served with distinction as procurator of Augustus. Vespasius Pollio, from Nursia in the Sabine country, served in the army as an Equestrian officer. His son became a senator. His daughter married the tax collector T. Flavius Sabinus, whose father had been a soldier in the armies of the great Pompey. It was the son of Vespasia and Flavius Sabinus who ended the excesses of the Year of the Four Emperors by putting down Vitellius and founding, as the emperor Vespasian, the Flavian dynasty.

Much has been written about the subservience of the Augustan Senate. Such views misconceive the nature of that august body. The Senate itself, even under the free Republic, had never been the independent originator of policy. That was decided in the private councils of a few leading men, chiefly the senior ex-consuls. The vast majority of senators were content to follow their lead, being known contemptuously as 'foot-men', *pedarii*, since their only contribution to senatorial business was to vote for the proposals of their seniors and betters. Under Augustus the Senate retained its intensely hierarchical habits, only now instead of the many *principes* of the Republic there was only one Princeps and the senior senators were all Augustus' men. The practice of the leading men in the Republican Senate was partially given formal recognition by Augustus' appointment of a committee consisting of the consuls, one member of each of the other colleges of magistrates and fifteen senators chosen by lot and changing every six months. This committee assisted Augustus in the preparation of senatorial business and functioned throughout his reign. It must have been essential in the later years of his life when he rarely entered the Senate House. In A.D. 13 its composition was modified and its powers were so increased as seriously to encroach on those of the Senate itself. Tiberius, when he became emperor, allowed it to lapse. His practice was more Republican, and he took counsel on public business with his old friends and twenty of the leading men of the state. Not that Augustus' committee was the fountain and origin of policy; that began further back, in private and secret consultation with men like Agrippa, Statilius Taurus, Maecenas, Sallustius Crispus, Vedius Pollio and Tiberius and with, we cannot doubt it, the redoubtable Livia Drusilla. Augustus' senators followed his lead from tradition, habit and conviction. They had a keen appreciation of their own interests—and of the interests of Rome. A formidable collection of hard-faced and tough-minded men enriched by civil war and revolution, they had no time for frivolous irresponsibility.

There remained the Republican nobles. They were dangerous, and a century of sedition, revolution and civil war had given ample proof of their destructive proclivities. Moreover, they were the only class which had lost and lost heavily without compensation by the establishment of the Augustan Principate. And what they had lost was what they had most highly prized: independence of political action, freedom of competition for pre-eminent honour and glory, liberty to rule the Roman world according to their own desires and for their own profit. Some nobles had joined Augustus early, a few, perhaps, at the beginning; others, after variegated careers, had made convenient submission in due season, before or after Actium. But Augustus could never trust them, however apparently sincere their acceptance of the new order. If he was ever tempted to, he had only to reflect how many of the Conspirators had earlier received pardon and advancement from Caesar. Yet he could not ignore them. Despite their losses in civil war and proscription, too many survived and the Roman People had always been susceptible to the glamour of a famous name. Augustus needed the nobles for advertisement and utility, now as during his rise to supreme power. They were, after all, the remnants of the ruling caste of the Republic, the heirs to its traditions and experience, the guarantee of the respectability of the new regime. To tame the nobles, to redirect their energies into channels conducive to the welfare of the state and his own survival, that was Augustus' problem. From this point of view the encouragement of the new men, the organization of the Equestrian Order and of a civil service staffed largely by freedmen, the removal from the Senate's control of the most important armed provinces, these were largely negative measures; they reduced the scope and effectiveness of the nobles' capacity for mischief, but positively to bind them to himself Augustus adopted their own favourite political weapon, the marriage alliance. Beginning with his own marriage to Livia Drusilla, Augustus surrounded himself with an increasingly complex network of marriage alliances in which his female kinsfolk in particular were employed to assure the allegiance of important nobles and to satisfy his own dynastic ambitions.

This policy did not however work. Against military usurpation by an armed proconsul Augustus could provide: domestic conspiracy no bond or policy could prevent for such plots were a natural hazard. Immediately after Actium Maecenas, in charge of Rome and Italy, had detected the conspiracy headed by the son of the relegated Triumvir Lepidus. When the younger Lepidus' wife Servilia followed him to death, she extinguished a noble and Patrician family claiming descent from the aristocracy of Rome's parent city, Alba Longa. She had once been betrothed to the young Octavian.

In 23 B.C. came the affair of Varro Murena, involving persons connected with the innermost councils of the government. The conspiracy of Cn. Cornelius Cinna, grandson of Pompey the Great and nephew of Mark Antony, is mysterious. Cinna got off with a caution delivered by Augustus in a speech lasting two hours and gained the consulship for A.D. 5. But the ruin of Augustus' own daughter Julia in 2 B.C. was conducted in a blaze of publicity. Accused of immorality she was summarily banished to an island. Her alleged lovers included five nobles: the ex-consul Iulus Antonius, son of Mark Antony, was executed; T. Quinctius Crispinus, Ti. Sempronius Gracchus, Ap. Claudius Pulcher and a Cornelius Scipio were exiled. The charge may have been moral; the offence must have been political. Julia was a great political lady; the five nobles formed a formidable faction from some of the most powerful houses of the Republican nobility. Ten years later Julia's daughter followed her into exile, having fallen, it was said, into the abandoned habits of her mother. Her lover D. Iunius Silanus was executed and so was her husband L. Aemilius Paullus, on a charge of conspiracy since that of adultery was clearly inappropriate. The survival of Augustus and the homicidal tendencies of the later Julio-Claudian emperors cost the nobility as dearly as the civil wars which ended the Republic. By the time of Trajan and Hadrian descendants of the Republican nobility were portentously rare in public life. When Juvenal mocked the value of pedigrees his examples, the descendants of the nobles, were dead and of no account. After Actium, according to Tacitus, those nobles who escaped death in battle or proscription 'were exalted by wealth and office, as each was ready for slavery, and as they had grown great on revolution, so now they preferred the present dispensation and safety to the old order and danger'. The trouble was that for many of them old habits and attitudes reasserted themselves with peace and safety. In the true conversion of none of them could Augustus trust. Whatever he might do they remained his natural enemies.

Yet superficially and for a long time the nobles were well rewarded. Not only were many of them intimately connected to the imperial family; in the middle years of Augustus' reign they gained far more than their fair share of consulships, the traditional object of aristocratic ambition despite the ravaging of their class in the civil wars and the proscription that had ensured that in the early years of the Augustan Principate there were not many nobles available and eligible for the consulship. These were precarious years of great uncertainty in which both Virgil and Horace testified to the general longing for peace and stability. It is neither surprising nor sinister if the Roman People chose to elect to the consulship those men who seemed to offer the best chance of fulfilling their deepest desire, particularly when those men were supported by a highly efficient propaganda claiming to have saved Rome, Italy and the empire from oriental invasion. When, however, the new order had settled down, when stability seemed assured and, perhaps, some of the glamour had faded, then the ingrained habits of the Roman People reasserted themselves. The Roman People dearly loved a noble name. During the Republic the nobles had successfully controlled the consular elections and a major factor in their control had been the contented acquiescence of the voters. After Augustus' initial popularity had worn off, when he had made it clear that he was not going to be consul himself year after year, and when, perhaps, the government felt secure enough to influence the elections less closely by not always putting up its own members as candidates, then the nobility and the People resumed something of their old electoral relationship. Many of the noble consuls of the middle years of Augustus' reign are men whose fathers through death or defeat in the civil wars had themselves missed the consulate. Many of them, too, feature in the matrimonial and dynastic policy of Augustus. Their consulships will not have been displeasing to him in his aim of taming and using the nobles. But we have no warrant for believing that they were caused by his blatant and open intervention. Such men would have reached the consulate in any age without outside help. But Augustus' attempt to tame the nobles failed. Conspiracy, death and disgrace reduced their numbers and frightened others from public life. At the same time the new governing and administrative class had consolidated and it consisted in part, at least, of men who had grown up wholly within the Augustan system. After A.D. 2 every man who reached the consulship at the minimum age of thirty-three had been born since the battle of Actium and had known nothing but the dispensation of Augustus.

To make revolution permanent, to promote to the Senate and the ruling class the new men from the length and breadth of Italy was one of Augustus' leading objectives. His personal taste was to rule with a coalition of new men and nobles but in this he was frustrated, and by the accession of Tiberius the nobility was irreparably broken. The future lay with the new men. The transformation of the ruling class was not to be contained by geography. Under Caligula two men from Narbonese Gaul reached the consulship, Valerius Asiaticus in A.D. 35, Domitius Afer in 39. Both were of native Gallic stock and Valerius achieved the ultimate distinction of a second consulate in A.D. 46 under Claudius. Caligula was interested in Gaul and the promotion of its inhabitants. So too was Claudius. Under Nero events were controlled and power exercised by Seneca from Corduba in Spain and Burrus from Gallic Vasio. Vespasian, himself a new man from Italy, ruled with an oligarchy composed of municipal Italians and aristocrats from the provinces. Under him men like M. Ulpius Traianus from Spain and Cn. Iulius Agricola from Fréjus not merely reached the Senate but were numbered among the Patricians. The first stage of the process culminated in the elevation to the imperial power of Trajan, a Spaniard married to a woman from Nîmes in Gaul. But it did not stop there: Africa had already produced her first consul in A.D. 80 and ten years later the first consul from Asia is recorded. Between the accession of Hadrian and the death of Commodus men from Africa and the East caught and perhaps overtook those from Italy and the West in numbers of senators if not in numbers of consuls. It was Augustus who had created the essential conditions and had taken the first steps which made this development possible. It was one of his greatest achievements for Rome and for the Western world.

Rome and Italy

5

The city of Rome (cf. map VI, page 117) had grown by the same process of haphazard accretion and with the same lack of conscious thought as the Republican constitution. For many centuries it remained a small town, its inhabitants poor and its population growing but slowly. But the invasion of Italy by Hannibal and the completion of the conquest of the peninsula by Rome attracted a flood of migrants to the capital, which by the early decades of the second century B.C. had reached such proportions that some of Rome's allies in Italy found it difficult to raise the contingents required from them for the Roman army. Twice in ten years these communities had to ask the Roman government to send the migrants back to their native towns. The flood, however, continued unabated until the population of Rome in the last years of the Republic approached one million. Statistical evidence is extremely scanty, but it is clear that the city was seriously overpopulated. The problems were compounded by the fact that even in the time of Augustus the vast majority of the ordinary people of Rome was still crammed within the old city wall. It was not until later in the Imperial Period that the city of Rome was extended significantly beyond this confining boundary. Even in the reign of Constantine three centuries later, the population density in the old city was far higher than that in the suburbs, even though the area of the extra-mural suburbs was twice that within the walls. Since lateral expansion was limited by the city wall, the only way to accommodate the rapidly increasing population was to build upwards. Hence the development in the Late Republic of large apartment blocks, a method of building which brings problems in the best regulated community. At Rome there were no regulations. Such building laws as did exist concerned themselves with sacred property; private building was quite uncontrolled and housing the common people of Rome became a source of profit to speculative builders and speculating landlords.

Slowly and naturally, as in any large city, certain quarters came to be preferred by the aristocratic and wealthy. In the first century B.C. most of the urban plebs were concentrated on the Aventine and Caelian Hills and the Argiletum. In these areas in particular speculators took advantage of the needs of the poor to realize maximum profits by the provision of minimum facilities. Foundations were laid in swampy ground, substandard materials were used, the principles of safe construction were ignored. Roman architects were well aware that a certain height of building demanded a certain thickness of wall. Yet many contractors ignored this ineluctable principle and raised apartment blocks far higher than the walls would support. Such irresponsible parsimony in the service of greed was made worse by the general contracting practice. The contractor quoted a price before building began. Before it was completed the price demanded had often been raised by fifty per cent. Some landlords could not meet this new and exorbitant demand. The uncompleted building was therefore cheaply patched up, often at somebody else's expense, to allow occupation and the collection of rent. Another favourite device to meet and profit by the insatiable demand for housing was to add further storeys to already existing buildings with foundations and walls insufficiently strong to carry the extra load. The inevitable result was the frequent collapse of apartment blocks and houses.

The ancients believed that conflagrations in towns were caused by the height of the buildings. An odd belief, at first sight, but patient of logical explanation. The use of wooden tiles for roofing was one of the very few building practices forbidden by

32 The arch of triumph at Susa, erected by the tribes of the Cottian Alps under M. Iulius Cottius in honour of Augustus, in 8 B.C.

33 Detail of the façade of the Villa Medici, Rome: bas relief showing the temple of Magna Mater as restored in A.D. 3.

34 The Ara Pacis Augustae, Rome: the southern side of the west entrance showing Aeneas sacrificing the white sow to the goddess Juno.

35 The Ara Pacis Augustae: the processional frieze showing the Imperial family.

35

MVNIF.PII.IX.P.M.

SENATVS
POPVLVSQVE ROMANVS
IMP CAESARI DIVI F AVGVSTO
COS VIII DEDIT CLVPEVM
VIRTVTIS CLEMENTIAE
IVSTITIAE PIETATIS ERGA
DEOS PATRIAMQVE

38

39

Republican law. But in order to increase the number of families which could be crammed into existing buildings, the rooms were subdivided by wooden partitions, especially in the upper storeys where the poorest lived. Again, extra storeys added to existing buildings had to be built of wood if they were not to cause the immediate collapse of the whole structure. As this sort of accommodation was taken only by the poorest and showed the least return, there was no incentive for the builder to do even what he did well. Practices in themselves dangerous enough were made doubly so by economizing on materials and by poor and careless methods of construction. To the hazard of collapse, therefore, was added that of fire.

The great surge of migration to Rome coincided with the beginning of a dramatic increase in Rome's wealth from the spoils of the Eastern wars of the first half of the second century B.C. and of the newly acquired empire oversea. Some of this wealth found its way into the Roman treasury; much went to private individuals who were not slow to exploit their new opportunities and to search out new ways to invest their resulting profits to create even more wealth. Behind the irresponsible contractors and avaricious landlords stood ultimately the great magnates and financiers, many of them senators. The activities of Crassus became notorious. Cicero, perhaps more typical of his class, owned apartment blocks which realized a rent of 80,000 sesterces a year. Although he was prepared to let only to tenants who could pay on time, he had difficulty in collecting his rents, and ejection of the defaulting tenants was the result. One of his letters to Atticus is particularly revealing. Two of Cicero's tenements had completely collapsed and the rest were in such imminent danger of doing likewise that not only had the tenants abandoned the place in terror of their lives but even the mice were leaving. Cicero, clearly, had had no repairs done. It was only when the two tenements had fallen down and the other inhabitants had fled, that is, when his income had been cut off, that he instructed the architect Chrysippus to effect the necessary repairs. Chrysippus, however, produced an estimate of costs. Cicero was appalled that he would have to spend good money in this way. He consulted one Vestorius who combined the profession of banker with that of an instructor of building workers. He in some way enabled Cicero to turn his feared loss into an actual profit. The details of this remarkable manoeuvre Cicero, unfortunately, did not disclose.

Life was difficult for the poorer classes in any large city of the ancient world. In Rome of the Late Republic the poor had to endure not merely a normal standard of overcrowded and inadequate housing and exploitation, but also the danger of fire, collapse of their insecurely built and unrepaired dwellings and inundations of the river Tiber. In 60 B.C. a large number of dwellings in Rome collapsed; in 56 B.C. there was an earthquake and two years later came the great flood, when the Tiber overflowed its banks to cover not merely the low lying parts of the city but much of the upper town as well. The flood continued for several days and the bricks of which some houses and apartments were built were so affected by the water that they twisted and disintegrated, causing widespread collapse. The inhabitants who escaped were put in double jeopardy for the houses in which they found lodging themselves collapsed a few years later. The destruction in this period merely intensified the demand for housing and the opportunities of the speculators, and we have no evidence that the government in any way helped to house the homeless. Nor did it intervene when in 50 B.C. the most terrible fire in the history of the Roman Republic totally destroyed no less than fourteen whole wards of the city. This fire was followed in the next year by an earthquake and further fires which consumed the temple of Quirinus as well as many dwellings. The civil wars which preceded Caesar's Dictatorship and which broke out again after his death would hardly have encouraged large scale repair of the damage.

The governmental indifference against which all this happened is worth stressing. It was not merely that it was the ruling class which profited politically and financially by the miseries of the poor. It was also that the city of Rome itself lacked any effective local administration. It is true that the city was divided into wards, *vici*, with officials in

36 The Ara Pacis Augustae: the processional frieze showing the senators, magistrates and priests of Rome.

37 Statue of Augustus from Prima Porta; *Vatican, Museo Chiaramonti and Braccio Nuovo.*

38 Replica of the Clupeus Virtutis of Augustus found at Arles, Provence; *Arles, Musée Lapidaire d'Art Païen. Total diam.* 96.5 cm, *diam. of inscription* 75 cm.

39 Mould for an Arretine ware bowl showing Kalathiskos dancers, signed by Pilemo, a workman in the factory of Perennius; *New York, Metropolitan Museum. Diam.* 19 cm.

charge, but these became increasingly ineffectual in the Late Republic and seem ultimately to have fallen into abeyance. But the simple fact was that the local officials and the city council, for that is what the magistrates of the Roman People and the Senate originally were, were now engaged in the administration of a large empire. The attempt to rule the empire with the governmental and administrative apparatus, largely amateur, of a small city state had many undesirable results, among them this neglect of the physical well-being of the capital and its inhabitants. There was, moreover, no proper police force and no public fire service. There were, it is true, the *Tresviri Nocturni*, but the best they could do was to raise an alarm which no one could answer. All the poor could do was to trust in the good will of some rich citizen who would organize his slaves into a private fire brigade.

The support of the common people was one of the two great pillars on which the power of Augustus rested. Revolutionary politicians, particularly impoverished aristocrats like Catiline and Caesar, had not been slow to turn the grievances of the urban poor to political account. Augustus himself had not neglected to court the poor and when he achieved supreme power the urban plebs became peculiarly his clients. A wholesale programme of slum clearance and rehousing was probably beyond the thinking and the technology of the time, but he did devote large sums of money from the public treasury to rebuilding the dwellings destroyed in the great fire of 50 B.C. He also proposed to introduce building regulations, almost totally neglected by Republican law, and forbade the erection of houses and apartment blocks beyond a maximum height of seventy feet. It is typical of the man that he pressed his point home by reciting to the Senate the speech of the Republican Rutilius 'On the Height of Buildings'. Nero later passed a similar law which was further developed by Vespasian, Trajan and Hadrian. Although, if we may

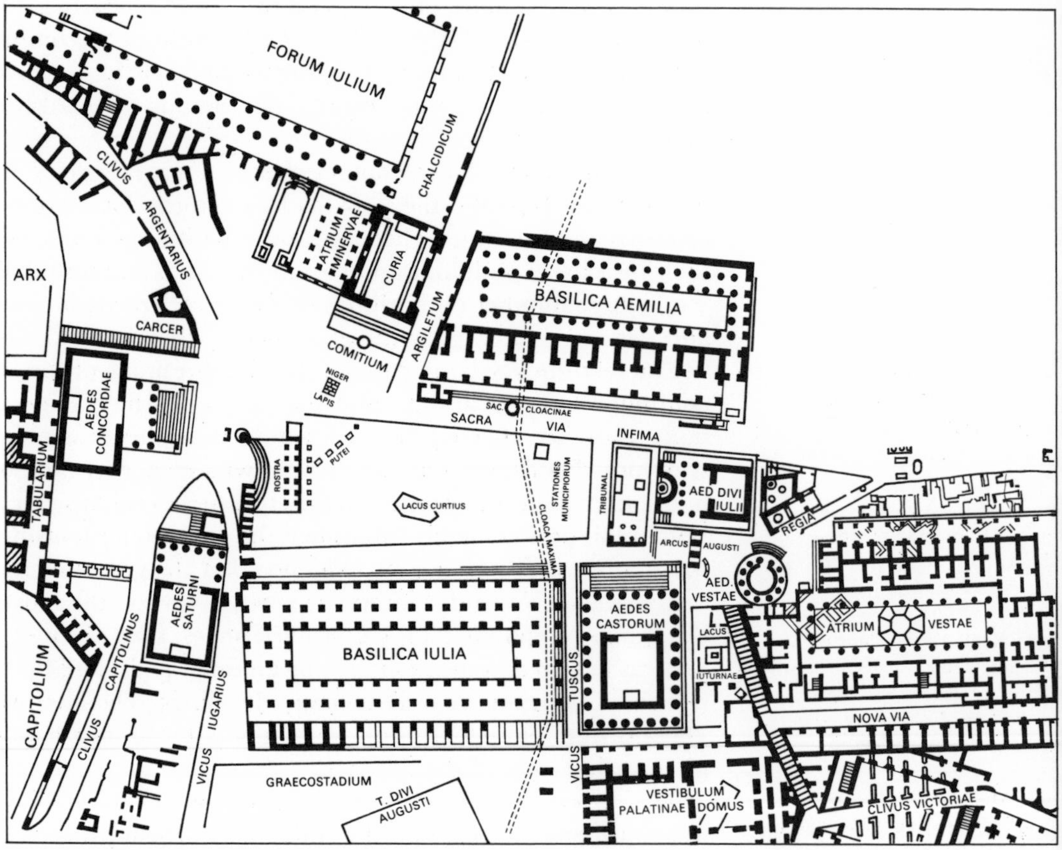

III The Roman Forum.

believe the satirist Juvenal, such laws were frequently evaded, Augustus had taken the first necessary step towards the creation of the building code of the later Imperial Period which controlled the use of building land, laid down standards of construction and encouraged the re-erection of demolished houses. In the later twenties B.C. Egnatius Rufus organized his private slaves into a private fire brigade and brought into sharp focus the Roman populace's fear of fire and the popularity to be won by dealing effectively with it. Egnatius attained the praetorship thereby and even aspired to the consulship. Augustus first in 21 B.C., after a conflagration in 23, put some public slaves under the command of the *aediles* to act as a fire brigade. Further serious fires occurred in 14, 9 and 7 B.C. Finally in A.D. 6 the Watch, *Vigiles,* was established, consisting of seven cohorts of 1,000 freedmen each, under the command of a prefect of Equestrian status. Already in 7 B.C. Augustus had divided the city into fourteen regions and had revived the ward officials, *vicomagistri,* four of whom were elected by each of the 265 wards. Each cohort of the *Vigiles* took charge of two of the Augustan regions. The policing of the city was put in the hands of the three Urban Cohorts, each 1,000 strong, a semi-military body under the ultimate command of the Prefect of the City. In the case of serious disorder assistance could be summoned from the Praetorian Cohorts, Augustus' own guard, comprising nine infantry cohorts and a squadron of cavalry under the command of a pair of prefects of Equestrian rank. Augustus normally kept three of these cohorts in Rome and stationed the other six in various Italian towns.

Fig. 11 Silver folding table from the Hildesheim treasure. *Staatliche Museen, Berlin. Height 70.8 cm.*

Housing conditions and lack of security formed only part of the difficulty of life for the poorer inhabitants of Rome. The supply of food and water was another major problem. Italy in the Late Republic was, on the whole, able to support its own population, but Rome, rapidly expanding and increasingly cosmopolitan, could be fed only with corn imported from abroad. This trade was subject to frequent disruption by warfare, civil and foreign, and to manipulation by speculators. Shortage of food, even actual famine, and consequent rioting were common experiences among the lower classes in Rome of the Late Republic. Famine in 22 B.C. was relieved by Augustus at his own expense, after which he was put in personal charge of the food supply of the capital. This, however, was a temporary charge. More permanent arrangements were made in A.D. 6 when a pair of ex-consuls were entrusted with the care of the corn supply and then a few years later a permanent food commissioner, an Equestrian *Praefectus Annonae,* was appointed. Exact statistics for the Age of Augustus are defective or completely lacking. But in the early Imperial Period nearly 3,600,000 bushels of grain were needed annually for distribution to public servants and the poor in receipt of the corn dole. Further assured supplies were necessary to maintain the market in a stable and reasonable state. Independent merchants still operated in the corn trade from Sardinia, Gaul and some parts of Italy, but it was the tribute in grain from Egypt, Africa and Sicily which conditioned the market. Egypt exported to Rome some 5,000,000 bushels annually, Africa twice as much and Sicily perhaps 2,000,000 bushels. A total import of about 17,000,000 bushels probably left sufficient over, after supplying the free distributions, to meet by sale the normal demand of the Roman market. The organization of this import trade was an immense task for the office of the *Annona.* The grain was carried up the Tiber from the port at Ostia in barges each holding 2,500 bushels and drawn by oxen and at least 6,000 such barge journeys were made annually, an average of twenty-five each working day.

In contrast to the misery of the poor, the wealthy of the last age of the Republic led lives of high sophistication in immense mansions in the fashionable quarters of the city, above all the Palatine, where there lived at various times Sulla, Hortensius, Crassus, Cicero, Mark Antony, Clodius and Milo—and Sulla's freedman Chrysogonus, foreshadowing in the opulence of his domestic arrangements the enormous wealth of the freedmen of the emperors Claudius and Nero. According to Cicero, Chrysogonus' house was crammed with gold and silver vessels from Delos and Corinth, among them an automatic cooker which he bought at an auction at the price of a whole estate, as well as embossed silver, coverlets, pictures, statues and marbles. Chrysogonus had grown rich on

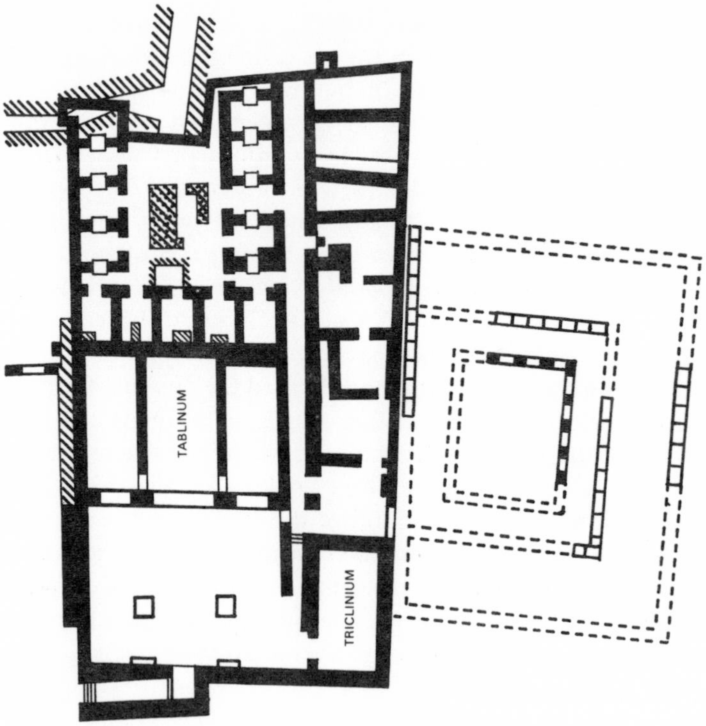

IV Augustus' House

civil war and the Sullan proscriptions. The nobles did not do less well out of the spoils of war and the plunder of the provinces. Their appetite for property was insatiable, and Chrysogonus had been fairly modest in owning only one villa and a number of farms close to Rome in addition to his Palatine palace. Not long afterwards Cicero owned no less than eight country villas and four lodges and was still eager to incur further debt for the acquisition of an additional house. To build in the Late Republic became a verb of political significance. The Republican noble built for ostentation and his own glory and to impress the people of Rome. And he built not merely private palaces and mansions but public monuments. Sulla and Pompey, in particular, devoted a large part of their Eastern booty to the adornment of Rome and the perpetuation of their own names. Sulla rebuilt the great temple of Jupiter Optimus Maximus, destroyed in the civil wars, the Tabularium or Public Record Office, one of the architectural glories of the Rome of his day, and the astonishing temple of Fortuna Primigenia at Praeneste. Pompey erected in the Campus Martius outside the city boundary a complex of buildings which included a garden surrounded by a colonnade, a meeting hall and the earliest and always the most important permanent theatre at Rome with a temple of Venus Victrix at the summit of the auditorium. Occasionally in some crisis the state, that is, the Senate, would order the construction of and vote the funds for a new public building or the repair of an old one. But on the whole the Republican government had neither the funds nor the staff properly to keep up the existing public buildings and amenities, let alone build new ones. For new construction Rome depended on the private munificence and vanity of successful generals, enriched provincial governors and ambitious politicians ready to ruin themselves by debt in the service of self-advertisement. Julius Caesar seems to have had a grandiose plan to improve the city as a whole, to canalize the Tiber and to develop the Campus Martius, but he died before the scheme could be put into effect. Some of his projects were completed by Augustus, others were never carried out. Augustus' attitude in this regard was less radical, more Republican than that of his adoptive father.

Augustus himself lived first in a somewhat plebeian area near the Roman Forum (cf.

map III, page 98), following a well established tradition among Roman demagogues, but later he moved to the Palatine. The nature of his house and his life there is described by Suetonius. The house 'was remarkable neither for its size nor for elegance since it had only short colonnades of Alban stone and rooms without any marble decorations or beautiful floors. For more than forty years he used the same bedroom, in winter and summer alike; although he found the city bad for his health in winter, he always spent the winter there. If he intended to do anything privately and without interruption, he had a private place at the top of the house, which he used to call "Syracuse" and his "little workshop". He took refuge there or in the house of one of his freedmen in the suburbs. When he was ill he took to his bed in Maecenas' house. To get away from the city he went frequently to the coast and islands of Campania or to towns near to Rome such as Lanuvium (Lanuvio), Praeneste or Tibur where he often heard legal cases in the colonnades of the temple of Hercules. Large and opulent palaces displeased him. One, which was built on a very lavish scale by his grand-daughter Julia, he had razed to the ground. His own country villas were modest and decorated not with beautiful statues and pictures, but with terraces, woods and objects remarkable for their age or rarity. For instance, he had at Capreae the colossal bones of huge monsters and wild beasts, which are called the bones of the giants, and the weapons of heroes. The cheapness of his furniture and household goods appears from his beds and tables which still survive, the majority of which scarcely reach the standard of elegance expected of a private citizen. They say that the only bed he slept on was low and modestly covered.' Suetonius went on to record the same modest tastes in food and dress.

Fig. 12 Coin: Denarius; reverse showing the Temple of Jupiter Tonans. *London, British Museum.* (*Actual size*).

This parsimony, which seems to have sprung less from public policy than from personal choice, conditioned perhaps by his Italian upbringing and his perpetual anxiety about his health, contrasted markedly with the opulence of the Republican nobles and some of his own associates such as Maecenas and Vedius Pollio. Augustus' house was not even new, once having belonged to the orator Hortensius. It was destroyed by fire in A.D. 3 and rebuilt, perhaps somewhat more elaborately but still not splendidly, for it was this house which Suetonius saw, preserved after Augustus' death as a national monument. Augustus' successor Tiberius did not live there but began the immense series of imperial palaces which eventually covered almost the whole of the Palatine hill. The so-called Casa di Livia, first excavated in 1869, probably represents the remains of Augustus' house. The three main rooms are decorated with frescoes of mythological and Egyptian scenes.

Augustus himself referred to his own house only incidentally in connection with the various honours and emblems, such as the laurel on his door posts, the oak wreath and the golden shield, he was awarded. Of his public building he left impressive and public record in the *Res Gestae*. 'I built the Senate House and the Chalcidium which adjoins it, the temple of Apollo on the Palatine with its colonnades, the temple of the Deified Julius, the Lupercal, the colonnade near the Circus Flaminius which I permitted to be called the Porticus Octavia after the Octavius who had built an earlier colonnade on the same site, the imperial box in the Circus Maximus, the temples of Jupiter Feretrius and Jupiter Tonans on the Capitol, the temple of Quirinus, the temples of Minerva, Juno Regina and Jupiter Libertatis on the Aventine, the temple of the Lares (cf. plate 55) at the summit of the Sacred Way, the temple of the Penates on the Velia, the temple of Iuventas, the temple of the Great Mother on the Palatine. I repaired the Capitol and the theatre of Pompey, both at great expense, without any inscription of my name. I repaired the water conduits which in very many places were collapsing through age. I doubled the flow of the Marcian aqueduct by connecting it to a new source. I completed the Forum Iulium and the Basilica (cf. plates 67, 82), which was between the temple of Castor (cf. plate 62) and the temple of Saturn, which had been begun and partially built by my father. When the Basilica was destroyed by fire, I began to rebuild it on a larger site under the names of my sons and ordered my heirs to complete it if I did not live to do so. In my sixth consulship (28 B.C.) I repaired on the instigation of the Senate eighty-two temples of the gods within the city and passed over none that needed repairing at that time. In my seventh consulship (27 B.C.) I repaired the Flaminian Way from Rome to Ariminum and all the bridges except the Milvian and the Minucian. On land which I personally owned I built the temple of Mars the Avenger (cf. plate 13) and the Forum of Augustus (cf. plate 2) from the spoils of war. I built the theatre (cf. plates 3, 68) near the temple of Apollo on land mostly purchased from private citizens, which should bear the name of my son-in-law M. Marcellus. I consecrated from the spoils of war gifts on the Capitol, in the temple of the Deified Julius, the temple of Apollo, the temple of Vesta and the temple of Mars the Avenger which cost me about 100,000,000 sesterces.'

Fig. 13 Coin: Aureus; reverse showing the triple arch of Augustus with the inscription CIVIB. ET SIGN. MILIT. A PART. RECUP. The issue commemorates the surrender of Roman captives and military standards by the Parthians and the erection of the triumphal arch. *London, British Museum.* (*Actual size*).

Even this is not the full record of Augustan building in Rome, for it includes only those works for which Augustus himself claimed responsibility. There were also the monuments voted by the Senate, such as the altars of Fortuna Redux and Pax Augusta (cf. plates 34, 35, 36, 51, 52, 53) and the triumphal arches, the triple arch of Augustus (cf. figure 13) on which were displayed the Consular and Triumphal Fasti and the Parthian arch. There were Augustus' own Mausoleum (cf. plate 72), begun in 28 B.C., and the obelisks imported from Egypt. Moreover, Augustus urged his friends and other prominent men to build. Marcius Philippus erected a temple of Hercules and the Muses, L. Cornificus the temple of Diana, C. Asinius Pollio the Atrium Libertatis or Hall of Liberty, L. Munatius Plancus the temple of Saturn, Cornelius Balbus a theatre and T. Statilius Taurus an amphitheatre. Cn. Domitius Calvinus restored the Regia which had been burned down.

Beyond and above all stood Agrippa, second only to Augustus himself in the extent and magnificence of his building operations. His work on the aqueducts and sewers was not merely utilitarian. In addition to the main constructions and repairs he built 700 basins, 500 fountains and 130 distribution points, many of which were finely decorated with, among other things, 300 bronze or marble statues and 400 marble columns. Then there was the Horrea Agrippiana to the south of the Forum, a warehouse with shops for private traders. But Agrippa's most splendid construction was the complex of buildings in the Campus Martius. The geographer Strabo saw it soon after its completion. 'Pompey and the Deified Caesar and Augustus and his sons and friends and wife and sister have surpassed all expense and zeal in beautiful buildings. Most of these are in the Campus Martius which has received, in addition to its natural beauties, deliberate adornment. The size of the Campus is remarkable, affording as it does space not only for chariot racing and all other equestrian pursuits but also for the crowds of people who exercise themselves by playing with balls and hoops and by wrestling. The works of art placed around the Campus, the ground covered by grass throughout the year, the crowns of the hills rising above the river and reaching its bank all present the appearance of a painted stage set and form a spectacle from which it is difficult to tear yourself away. Near this Campus is yet another (Strabo here refers to the Campus of Agrippa) with many colonnades in a circle around it and sacred precincts and three theatres and an amphitheatre and opulent temples, all in close succession to one another so that they seem to declare the rest of the city a mere appendage.'

Agrippa's complex is known to have included the Basilica of Neptune (cf. plates 28,

Fig. 14 Painted frieze from the Sepulchrum Statiliorum, Rome. East wall: left side, scene with Amulius, Numitor and Rhea Silvia. Centre: scene with Mars and Rhea Silvia. Right side: the marriage of Lavinia. *Rome, Museo Nazionale Romano.*

29), which celebrated and commemorated the victory at Actium, the first great set of public baths built in Rome and a Pantheon. The Pantheon seems to have been a temple for the Julian family, containing as it did statues of Mars and Venus, the latter with half of one of Cleopatra's famous pearls in each ear, and of Julius Caesar in the temple proper, while statues of Augustus and Agrippa were placed in the pronaos. This building was destroyed in the great fire under Titus in A.D. 80. Of the reconstruction by Domitian, which was itself destroyed in A.D. 110, we know nothing. The splendid building now standing in Rome is the work of the emperor Hadrian, although Agrippa's inscription from the original building is placed over the entrance (cf. plate 80). Agrippa's Pantheon was circular, but it certainly did not possess the most remarkable feature of Hadrian's building, the dome. The silence of Augustan and later writers, especially the elder Pliny who included in his *Natural History* a list of the architectural marvels of Rome, seems conclusive. It is doubtful whether the Augustan Age possessed either the vision or the technical virtuosity to create a feature of such brilliant originality. Augustan architecture may have been impressive but it was not imaginative.

Augustus' boast that he found Rome a city of brick and left it one of marble is famous. The poets Virgil, Horace and Propertius all bear witness to the impact of the temple of Apollo on the Palatine. It was faced with Carrara marble, used for the first time in Rome, and the doors were of ivory. The brilliant whiteness of the temple itself contrasted with the coloured African marbles used in the colonnades, which contained Greek and Latin libraries established by Augustus where, according to Ovid, all that the learned minds of ancient and modern authors had produced lay open for readers to consult. There was also, beside the books, a statue of Augustus in the guise of Apollo. The last age of the Republic had seen many advances in architectural and constructional technique, especially in the use of concrete and its application to the building of great vaults. The Augustan Age rejected these innovations to produce what may be called a Classical revival, based on Periclean and Hellenistic models, an architecture which was at the same time impressive and extremely dull, the perfect epitome of an official style. The Maison Carrée at Nîmes (cf. plate 41) is a good illustration. The favourite material of the Augustan builders was travertine, the traditional stone of the Republic. It proved ill-advised. Travertine is extremely susceptible to fire. In the great conflagration of Nero's reign not merely the wooden structures burned, but the stone buildings crumbled and collapsed. When the city was rebuilt, concrete faced with brick was used, creating an enormous demand for bricks which the Roman brick yards, accustomed to supply few orders except for roof tiles, found it difficult to meet. The fortunes of the emperor Marcus Aurelius and the Antonine dynasty were ultimately founded in the Neronian fire and the subsequent rebuilding. His ancestors became among the richest men in the empire because they owned brick yards near to Rome and were ready to exploit the new demand and to profit from the shortage.

The vast majority of the Augustan buildings in Rome have almost totally disappeared, the victims of the natural hazards of age, fire and later rebuilding. The few foundation stones of the temple of Apollo which survive hardly suggest that here once stood one of the great glories of Augustan Rome. The Pantheon is not Agrippa's temple and the Senate House which now stands in the Forum, although it contains one of the most magnificent interiors to survive from ancient Rome, represents a rebuilding by Diocletian after Augustus' building was destroyed by fire in A.D. 283. Diocletian, however, rebuilt to the Augustan dimensions. It is not even known what the Chalcidium was. The severe and elegant façade of the theatre of Marcellus survives, although in the later Imperial Period it was robbed of its interior to provide material for the restoration of the Cestian bridge in A.D. 375. Shopkeepers seem to have established themselves in the surviving arches, as they did in more modern times until in 1927–1932 the theatre was freed from the accretions of centuries. In the middle ages it was the fortress of the Pierleoni; in the sixteenth century a palace was built there by the Savelli from whom it passed to the Orsini. The nearby Portico of Octavius, which enclosed the temples of

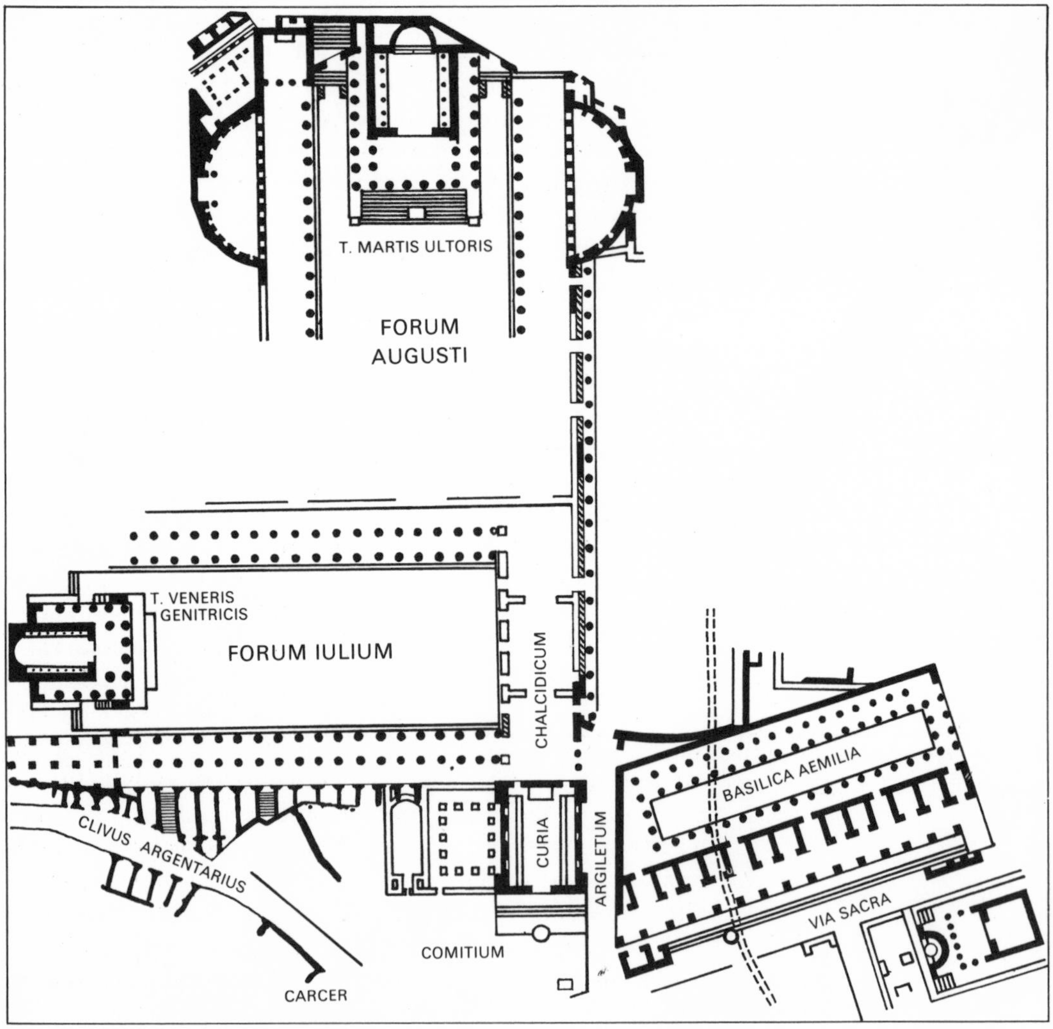

V The Forum of Augustus.

40 Trophy of Augustus from La Turbie, Alpes Maritimes.

41 Maison Carrée, Nîmes. Built originally as a temple, probably in 16 B.C., it is one of the best preserved of all ancient Roman monuments. Painted in the eighteenth century by Hubert Robert, it still looks the same today; *Paris, Musée du Louvre.*

42 Mosaic from Sabratha, Libya, showing the Three Graces; *Sabratha Museum*. 162.5 cm × 108 cm.

43 Mosaic from Sabratha, Libya, showing Diana. Found under a mosaic of Neptune at the Oceanic baths; *Sabratha Museum.* 96.5 cm × 99 cm.

44 The theatre viewed from above, Lepcis Magna. The theatre, completed in A.D. 1–2, was given to the city by a wealthy citizen, Annobal Rufus, who also donated the market.

Jupiter Stator and Juno Regina and was part of a complex of buildings including Greek and Latin libraries, has gone. What remains on the site is from a rebuilding by Septimus Severus. The tale of destruction could be almost endlessly prolonged.

Three Augustan monuments, however, call for detailed comment: the Forum of Augustus (cf. plate 2), the Altar of the Augustan Peace (Ara Pacis Augustae) (cf. plates 34, 35, 36, 51, 52, 53) and Augustus' Mausoleum (cf. plate 72). The Forum was built to the north east of the Roman Forum on land which Augustus owned himself. He could not, however, build as amply as he intended since he was unwilling to expropriate neighbouring owners and the north eastern boundary wall follows an irregular course. It was perhaps this difficulty which caused the long delay between the beginning of the Forum in 37 B.C. and the dedication of the temple of Mars on August 1 thirty-five years later. The massive rear wall, the most impressive feature of the site today, was built not of travertine but of Gabine stone. It sealed the Forum off from the Subura and may have been deliberately planned as a fire break. In the centre of the Forum was the temple of Mars Ultor, the Avenger (cf. plate 13), approached by a flight of steps and surrounded by a colonnade. The cella of the temple ended in an apse which contained statues of Mars and Venus. The boundary walls to the right and left of the temple opened out into two hemicycles or apses. Suetonius says that 'Augustus' reason for building the Forum was the increase in population and the number of law suits which seemed to demand a third Forum since two (i.e. the Roman Forum and the Forum of Caesar) were no longer

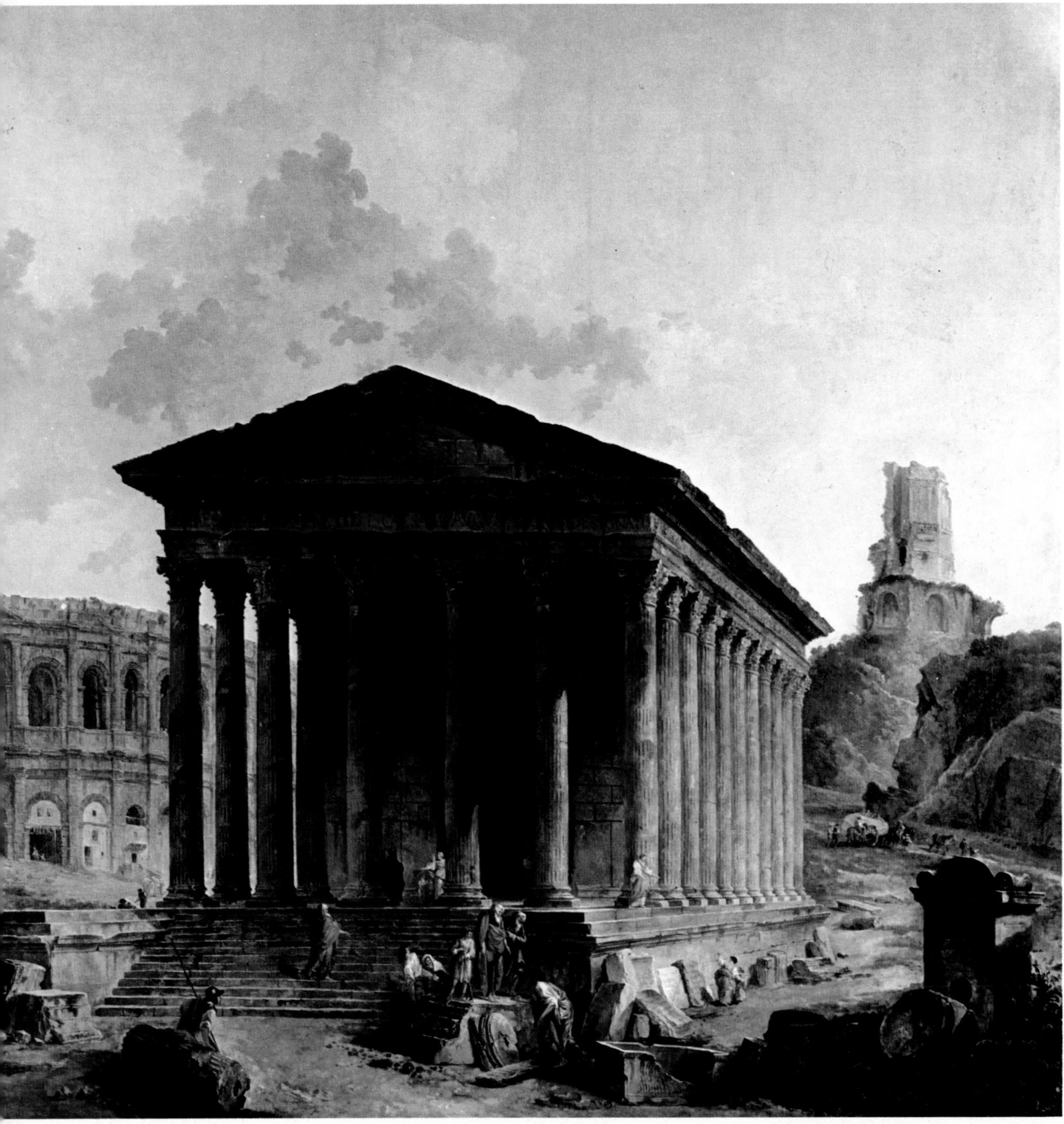

42

43

sufficient. Therefore it was opened to the public in a hurry before the temple of Mars was finished and it was laid down that public prosecutions should be held there away from the rest and the selection of jurors should be by lot. He had vowed to build the temple of Mars during the war of Philippi which he undertook to avenge his father. Therefore he decreed that in it the Senate should deliberate about war and claims for triumphs, that those who were leaving Rome to take up military commands in the provinces should be escorted from it and that those who returned victorious should bring to it the emblems of their triumphs.' Along the colonnades around the Forum stood statues of illustrious generals of the past, each with an inscription recording his great deeds. Niches in the colonnades and hemicycles provided for 108 statues. In the colonnade on the right facing the temple of Mars stood the Julio-Claudians, the family of Caesar and Augustus, beginning with Aeneas; on the other side were the great men of the Republic. Augustus himself may have received special treatment. In the hall on the north west corner of the Forum have been found the marks of the feet and a few fragments of the hand of a colossal statue, which has been supposed to be that of the Princeps. The Forum was Augustus' claim to have restored the Republic given concrete expression; there were gathered the great men of Rome's past like the busts of the ancestors in the atrium of a great Roman house. Not merely were their memories invoked; Augustus proclaimed them as his ancestors by blood or in spirit, thus advertising the continuity between the Republic and the Principate. Exactly the same conception appears in Book VI of Virgil's *Aeneid* in the noble parade of the heroes of the Republic culminating in Caesar Augustus. Augustus himself said on the occasion of the dedication of the statues, 'This I have contrived so that the Roman People may measure me and the Principes of succeeding ages by the standard of the lives of these great men as though by a pattern.'

Fig. 15 Coin: Aureus: reverse showing altar attended by priests with the inscription LUDI SAECUL., commemorating the celebration of the Ludi Saeculares in 17 B.C.

'When I returned to Rome from Spain and Gaul after my successes in those provinces, in the consulship of Ti. Nero and P. Quintilius (13 B.C.) the Senate decreed that an altar of the Augustan Peace should be consecrated in the Campus Martius in honour of my return and ordered the magistrates and the priests and the Vestal Virgins to offer there a sacrifice on every anniversary.' Thus Augustus in the *Res Gestae* recorded the genesis of the Ara Pacis Augustae, the supreme achievement of Augustan art. It stood originally on the west side of the Via Flaminia, the modern Via del Corso, down which Augustus returned to the city. The restoration in the Via di Ripetta has shifted the site a short distance to the south-east and, more important, changed the orientation of the structure. The altar proper was raised by four steps of which the lowest measured about seven by six metres and was surrounded by a precinct wall measuring some 11.6 metres from east to west and 10.5 metres from north to south and 6.3 metres high. The west and east sides had central doorways, that on the west being approached by a flight of steps while that on the east was level with the ground outside. The precinct was open to the sky. The exterior faces of the wall were decorated with relief sculpture, a lower zone of floral scrolls separated from an upper one of figures by a band of 'key pattern' work. On the interior faces there were likewise two zones, vertical fluting surmounted by a series of swags or festoons of fruit and flowers suspended from ox skulls. Above each festoon was a sacrificial dish. The altar itself was also decorated with friezes, the subjects of which included sacrificial animals and the Vestal Virgins. Its two ends were crowned by convoluted pediments, the exterior volutes of which rested on winged lions. The visible parts of the structure were of Carrara marble, the foundation of tufa and travertine. The workmanship throughout is of the highest quality. The great exterior dado of acanthus interwoven with vines and ivy is populated by birds, snakes, insects, frogs and lizards and is in firmly controlled relationship with the figures above. On the north and south walls the pattern comes together in a central calyx from which a thin stalk leads upwards to the central figure of the upper frieze who in each case is walking forward while looking backwards. Thus the whole conception is knit together. The four end panels on either side of the east and west entrances show a similar arrangement.

45 Table of standard volume measures from the market, Lepcis Magna.

46 Pont du Gard built c. A.D. 14, Nîmes, Provence.

47 The market place looking east, Lepcis Magna, built 9–8 B.C.

The most immediately striking feature of the monument is the great processional friezes on the north and south sides. That on the north (cf. plate 36) comprises members of the priestly colleges, magistrates, senators and their families; that on the south (cf. plates 35, 51, 53) depicts Augustus himself, his family and his entourage of priests, officials and magistrates. The head of this procession is at the west, or left side. The first three panels have been seriously damaged, but enough remains to identify the figures on the third as lictors bearing the fasces and a religious attendant with an incense box. On the join with the next panel is the veiled and wreathed figure of Augustus himself. The two wreathed personages on either side of him are probably the consuls of 13 B.C., the older man to the left being P. Quintilius Varus and the younger to the right his colleague the future emperor Tiberius, who was twenty-nine in the year 13. Tiberius is looking back over his shoulder and the man in the background just behind him who looks as if he is whispering in Tiberius' ear with his oddly shaped mouth has tentatively been identified as L. Calpurnius Piso Frugi, an intimate friend of Tiberius.

Following Augustus and the two consuls are the four priests known as *flamines*, easily recognizable from their curious conical caps surmounted by spikes. Then comes a youthful veiled figure with an axe, probably a religious attendant with the ceremonial axe of the pontiffs. He is followed by a grave, impressive figure, about whose identity there has been much controversy. According to the order of precedence he ought to be the Pontifex Maximus. But the Pontifex Maximus in 13 B.C. was the Triumvir Lepidus. It is unlikely that Augustus would have allowed him back to Rome from exile to officiate on this occasion. The figure's face looks nothing like Lepidus' coin portraits. If Augustus leads the procession, then this figure can only represent the great M. Vipsanius Agrippa, the second man in the state. Clinging to Agrippa's toga and clearly experiencing some alarm at the solemn occasion is one of his sons by Julia, presumably the younger, L. Caesar, who was four years old in 13 B.C. He is being comforted by a lady in the background who has stretched forward to touch his head and beside him stands his mother Julia, Augustus' daughter and Agrippa's wife, to whom the child looks up for reassurance (cf. family tree, front endpaper). The young man beside Julia is something of a mystery, but he may be Iulus Antonius, son of Mark Antony and Fulvia, a close friend of Augustus and his sister Octavia before the disgrace of Julia. In 13 B.C. he was Urban Praetor. Next to him in the foreground is his half-sister, the younger Antonia, daughter of Mark Antony by Octavia, Augustus' sister. She is looking at her husband Drusus, the brother of Tiberius, shown in profile, and holding the hand of their two-year-old son Germanicus who wears a miniature toga. Then comes another family group: the elder Antonia, the elder daughter of Octavia, her husband L. Domitius Ahenobarbus and their children Domitia and Cn. Domitius Ahenobarbus who eventually became the father of Nero. The young Cn. Domitius has grabbed hold of his uncle's cloak. The younger Antonia and her husband are obviously chatting to each other, to the great displeasure of the veiled lady behind who has her finger on her lip. She may be that wonderful woman Octavia, Antonia's mother and Augustus' beloved sister, who was still alive in 13 B.C.

The face of the aged man in the background above L. Domitius Ahenobarbus' raised hand looks like a portrait from life. It may be Maecenas. Although only Equestrian in rank, he had served Augustus and the Pax Augusta well enough to be allowed to walk in the procession. On this interpretation of the frieze there is one notable absentee, the empress Livia Drusilla herself. But the west end of the frieze is highly fragmentary and one of the draped figures of which only bits remain was very probably Livia. The surviving heads of lictors some facing forward, some backwards suggest the presence of a personage as prominent as Augustus himself. It is a fascinating composition. As Professor D. R. Dudley has put it, 'This is the high noon of the Principate and Augustus is shown with his family, his friends and his grandchildren. The death of Marcellus is, so far, his only personal loss; death has not touched his friends Agrippa and Maecenas, nor scandal his daughter Julia. The succession seemed amply provided for; who could guess that it would eventually fall on the uncongenial Tiberius?' The two processions balance each other. On one side Augustus and his family embody the Augustan Principate; on the other the senators, magistrates and priests of Rome represent the Roman tradition as they follow the giver of peace. It is another demonstration of continuity with the past and of the Principate as the sole guarantee of peace and stability. The senatorial frieze is as humanly treated as the imperial. Here too we see wives and children, including one importunate little boy who is surely demanding to be carried and a girl with an elaborate coiffure, wearing a necklace and grasping her laurel branch with great solemnity. Where in the world is there a great state monument less pompous and more human?

What are they all doing? The most probable answer is that the friezes represent the procession on the occasion of the foundation of the altar on July 4, 13 B.C., not of the actual dedication after its completion on January 30, 9 B.C. On the foundation day Augustus, the members of his family, the priests, Vestal Virgins and magistrates went in solemn procession to the site chosen for the altar to dedicate it and to offer sacrifice for Augustus' safe return. A temporary altar of wood was no doubt erected for the ceremony, perhaps closely following the form of the later stone altar. The Ara Pacis as we have it possesses a number of features which appear to be direct reminiscences of a wooden structure. What is portrayed is not the final act in the ceremony, but the moment when the procession, having approached the altar from the east from the Via Flaminia and divided to pass it on either side, has paused before reuniting at the main entrance at the west end to begin the dedicatory ceremony. We have here a moment out of history with its participants caught as they were at one particular point of time on July 4, 13 B.C.

Equally important and equally accomplished, although by different sculptors (the two processional friezes show the work of four different hands), are the four end panels with legendary scenes and groups of personifications. On the west wall to the north of the entrance was depicted the suckling of Romulus and Remus by the she-wolf in the presence of the god Mars and the shepherd Faustulus. This panel is now highly fragmentary and the she-wolf has vanished. Its companion on the south side of the west entrance is substantially intact (cf. plate 34). It shows Aeneas sacrificing the white sow to the goddess Juno, at once a sign and a thanksgiving that he has at last arrived at his home in the promised land of Italy. Aeneas stands to the right, grave and veiled for sacrifice. To the left above the head of the attendant offering the dish of fruit is the shrine of the Penates, Aeneas' household gods, proclaiming that he has indeed come home. Behind Aeneas stands the figure of his faithful companion Achates, now almost totally destroyed. The scene is depicted exactly as in Virgil's *Aeneid:* 'Behold a sudden portent, wonderful to see. A white sow with her litter of the same white colour lay stretched among the trees and was seen on the green shore. To you, to you, great Juno, dutiful Aeneas sacrificed her, performing the sacred rites, and placed her with her litter beside the altar'. This was the sign foretold by the god of the river Tiber: 'Here will be your abiding home, here (do not give up) your abiding household'. Thus the two great foundation legends of the city of Rome and of Roman Italy are brought together and the promise of the past, sanctified by divine signs, is now made reality in Augustus' new order.

It is much more than the merely physical homecoming of Augustus from Gaul and Spain which is commemorated. It is the homecoming of the whole race, Rome and Italy at last forged into a unity by Augustus, who is at once the second Romulus and the second Aeneas. The panels on the east side exactly correspond to this conception. On the north side of the entrance was the personification of the city, the goddess Roma herself, answering along the frieze of senators to the foundation legend of Rome; on the south was Italia, connected by the imperial procession with Aeneas' homecoming to Italy and the foundation of the Italian nation (cf. plates 52, 53). The whole structure exhibits the highest level of organization, part answering to part, each bringing out the meaning of the other and all contributing to the tremendous significance of the monument as a whole. Roma has entirely disappeared, but the southern panel survives almost intact. In the centre is Italia, the personification of Italy not only as a political entity but as the motherland of the Italians and of all the inhabitants of the empire. And she is Italy not of the chaotic past, but of the present and the future, of the Pax Augusta. The goddess sits surrounded by the fruits and blessings of peace. She represents the Italy that Virgil praised in the second book of the *Georgics* and the peace that Horace celebrated in his last Ode: 'Your age, Caesar, has given back to the fields rich crops and has restored to Roman Jupiter the standards torn from the arrogant shrines of Parthia; it has closed the temple of Ianus Quirinus, free of wars, restrained licence which wandered disorderly and uncontrolled, removed crime and recalled the ancient ways, through which the Latin name and the strength of Italy have grown and the fame and majesty of empire have spread from the sun's rising to his bed in the west. While Caesar rules affairs, civil madness and violence will not banish peace, nor anger which forges swords and sets at enmity wretched cities. Nor will those who drink the deep Danube break the Julian edicts, nor the Getae, nor the Seres nor the faithless Persians, nor those born by the river Tanais. And we on working days and holy days, amid the gifts of joyful Liber with our children and our wives, will, when we have first solemnly worshipped the gods, sing as our ancestors sang, our song mingled with the Lydian pipes, of Troy and Anchises and the son of bountiful Venus.'

The Forum of Augustus and the Ara Pacis are exactly complementary. The message of both is continuity with the past, that the Augustan Principate was the natural and legitimate successor to the Republic, that the Republic had indeed been restored. The Forum presented this claim straightforwardly in the military sphere. There Augustus was the great general, the servant of Rome's imperial mission, like Aeneas and the other heroes of old, following the duty imposed by heaven to fulfil the decree of Virgil's Jupiter: 'On the Romans I place no limits either of space or of time; I have given them imperial power without end'. The Ara Pacis is an altogether more subtle construction. But the peace and homecoming it proclaimed could not exist apart from the imperial mission of Augustus and Rome. Horace constantly returned to the theme that it was the military power of Rome and Augustus which assured peace and the Sybil in the sixth book of Virgil's *Aeneid* closed the great review of Rome's heroes with the words, 'Do you, Roman, remember to rule the nations with power (these shall be your arts) and to impose the ways of peace, to pardon the humbled and to destroy the arrogant in war.'

The third of what we may term the great foundation monuments of the Augustan Principate is the Mausoleum of Augustus himself (cf. plate 72) in the Campus Martius to the west of the Via Flaminia by the Ara Pacis. The most significant thing about it is its

Fig. 16 Epitaph of Octavia and Marcellus from the Mausoleum of Augustus, Rome.

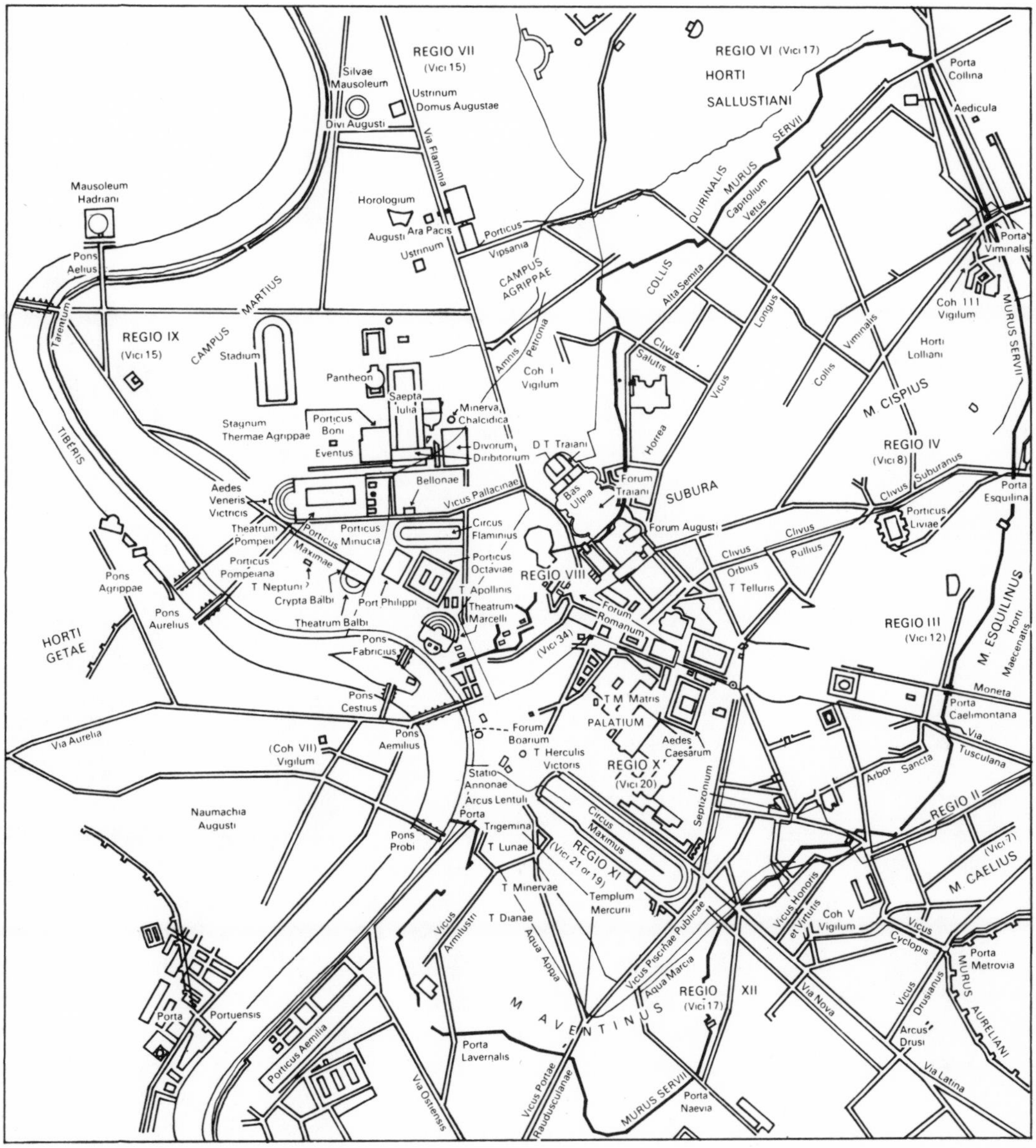

VI Map of Rome.

date: it was begun as early as 28 B.C. Already at the very moment of the restoration of the Republic, Augustus gave visible and public expression to his dynastic and imperial pretensions. Elaborate and bizarre sepulchres were not uncommon in Rome at the time, as witness the pyramid of Cestius (cf. plate 5) and the oven of the baker Eurysaces (cf. plate 48). But the scale of Augustus' tomb was frankly kingly, comparable to the great monuments of Hellenistic and Oriental monarchs. Its central feature was a huge mound some 88.5 metres in diameter and rising to a height of approximately 44 metres, surrounded by an enclosing wall. The burial crypt proper was reached by a long corridor at the outer entrance of which stood two obelisks, now in the Piazza dell' Esquilino and the Piazza del Quirinale. Strabo saw the monument in its original form and left us a description. 'On a high foundation of white marble by the river is a lofty mound, densely covered with evergreen trees to the summit. On the top is a bronze statue of Augustus Caesar; beneath the mound are the tombs of himself and his relations and his intimate friends. Behind is a great sacred enclosure with wonderful colonnades.'

Augustus may have expected to be one of the first to occupy this grandiose tomb. His health was never strong and in 23 B.C. his life was despaired of. In fact, before he died in A.D. 14, the Mausoleum had received the bodies of most of his family and closest

Fig. 17 Porta di S. Ventura, Spello. A gate of the Augustan colony.

associates, the wreck of his dynastic ambitions. Marcellus was the first, dying at the age of nineteen in 23 B.C. In 11 B.C. Octavia was laid to rest beside her son. Their epitaphs survive (cf. figure 16, page 116). The year before Agrippa had been buried there and he was followed by Drusus in 9 B.C. and the young princes Lucius and Gaius Caesar in A.D. 2 and 4. The burial of Augustus himself took place in A.D. 14. His niche is empty, his epitaph lost. His empress Livia survived for another fifteen years and Augustus' daughter and grand-daughter, the two erring Julias, were expressly forbidden by Augustus himself to be buried there. When Germanicus died in Asia, his wife Agrippina brought his ashes home to lie in the Mausoleum. She herself died in exile and it was not until four years later that her son Caligula placed her bones in the tomb. Tiberius was certainly buried there and Caligula and Nerva and, probably, Claudius. By then the Mausoleum may have been full. Trajan was buried at the foot of his column and Hadrian erected a new and even more impressive imperial sepulchre, now the Castel Sant' Angelo.

Augustus and his associates built for many reasons: to repair the depredations of civil war and neglect; to glorify the Princeps, his regime and Rome; for public utility and for another purpose, practical and urgent. The migrant proletariat which flowed to Rome in the second and first centuries B.C. found itself not merely without adequate housing but without employment. In a non-industrial society which made great use of slave labour most of these incomers were not merely unemployed but unemployable. For Rome was a consuming, not a producing city. Its expenditure was balanced by state salaries, products of manufacture and the profits of trade. The importation of food was a major business, but such industry as there was existed only in the small shops of individual artisans. These existed in great numbers, grouped into concentrations of petty manufacturers producing the same articles and organized into trade guilds. But factory production was almost unknown, even of domestic articles for which there must have been a great demand but which were brought in from the manufacturing towns in Italy.

Not even the activities of Agrippa and the imperial Water Board could stimulate the factory production of lead water pipes. Large quantities of standard pipes were needed, the lead came directly to Rome as a fiscal product, the government was concerned with the upkeep of the aqueducts and with the distribution of water to all public places and to all public fountains and distribution points. Yet the pipes were supplied by small shop owners with few slaves, not much capital and not many facilities and they acted not only as manufacturers but as jobbing plumbers. It is as if today each small plumber had to make his own pipes from the raw material not merely for his own use but also to supply the city council workmen when required. There is evidence for the existence of only two large factories in Rome in the early Imperial Period, both of them connected with the processing of state owned materials: one produced red-lead, for which the ore came from the state owned mines in Spain; the other, apparently a private one, reprocessed third grade Egyptian papyrus to make a better paper. Hence the existence of a large, idle and unemployable proletariat, a dangerous source of political instability and an easy tool for revolutionary demagogues. C. Gracchus had in 123 B.C. introduced the corn dole, whereby grain was sold to the poor at a price subsidized by the state. The price was steadily cheapened until it became a free distribution. Such doles were condemned in ancient as in modern times yet it is difficult to see an alternative, unless it is starvation and widespread crime. Augustus considered the abolition of the corn dole, but found himself able only to reduce the number of recipients to 200,000. Transplantation to colonies in Italy and, later, oversea had been one traditional method of reducing the unemployed proletariat of Rome. Public works were another. The Augustan building programme, by creating a demand for unskilled or semi-skilled labour, must have done much to relieve human misery and encourage political stability.

Fig. 18 Coin: Denarius, struck in Spain, 23–22 B.C.; reverse showing the gate of the Augustan colony of Emerita. *London, British Museum.* (*Actual size*).

It was not merely at Rome that the Augustan Principate stimulated building but throughout Italy. The expenses of public construction of town walls, local roads and bridges, water works and sewers, temples, baths, theatres and amphitheatres were borne by the communities concerned. But very frequently part or the whole of the cost of a particular project was contributed by an individual citizen. Civic pride was strong in Italy and some of the wealth acquired by Augustus' new men went to the adornment of their native towns. Augustus himself also gave to the towns of Italy. He contributed, for instance, to the repair of the walls of Tergeste (Trieste), built aqueducts for Venafrum and Brixia (Brescia), paid for the public baths at Bononia (Bologna), the upkeep and running expenses of which were provided by the gift of 400,000 sesterces from a private citizen. Agrippa also spent freely on the theatres at Ostia (cf. plate 31) and at Emerita (Mérida) in Spain, on the baths at Antioch in Syria and many similar projects. One permanent charge on the Roman treasury was the main roads of Italy. In 27 B.C. Augustus repaired the whole of the Via Flaminia from Rome to Ariminum, including all the bridges except the Mulvian and the Minucian. In 20 B.C. a permanent senatorial commission was established to maintain the great highways of Italy, those in the provinces remaining, presumably, the responsibility of their governors. At Rome was set up the Golden Milestone engraved with the distances of the main cities of the empire measured from the gates of the city. The individual towns remained responsible for the upkeep of their local roads, streets and bridges, although for these too benefactions from wealthy individuals were frequent. The towns also had to maintain the imperial post, established by Augustus to speed the passage of official despatches. The post was not available for use by private citizens and by the time of Claudius had become a considerable burden to the towns which had to provide it.

The damage which Italy had suffered in the civil wars was widespread but not permanent. There had been little deliberate devastation. Rather, armies marching and countermarching, proscription and the confiscation of estates had created conditions of insecurity and instability in which agriculture suffered from neglect and the value of land became depressed. What Italy needed for recovery was not direct intervention by the Roman government but a period of peace and security. After Actium, Augustus gave Italy an assurance of the most practical and convincing kind. To settle his demobilized soldiers he did not resort, as many feared, to further proscription and confiscation, but bought the land and recorded in the *Res Gestae* with justifiable pride that he was the first and only general up to his own time to do so. The total cost of land in Italy for the veterans demobilized after Actium and later in the reign he put at some 600,000,000 sesterces. In 29 B.C. alone some 120,000 soldiers received land in Italy and the resettlement of the soldiers of the Triumvirs and of Augustus must have given allotments to about 300,000 men in all. Even when Augustus did confiscate, as in the case of some towns which had supported Antony in the last struggles, he compensated the dispossessed with land elsewhere. The size of the individual plots given to the discharged veterans seems to have been quite traditional, eight to ten *iugera* each (a *iugerum* was equal to about two-thirds of an acre). Thus only about five per cent of Italy's arable land was concerned and the Augustan recolonization avoided, as far as was possible, widespread disruption of the existing agricultural pattern. Later Augusta Praetoria (Aosta) and Augusta Taurinorum (Turin) were founded to check the Alpine Salassi and to guard the Alpine passes and these foundations were followed by much road building in the Alps. Among other routes opened or improved by Augustus were the roads from Aquileia to Nauportus (in Yugoslavia), from Aosta to Lyons and the road over the Brenner Pass. The purpose was military, but the opening of the Alpine routes naturally encouraged the growth of trade between Italy and the north.

Caesar had enacted a law which required Romans to invest a large part of their property in Italian land. The effect was to increase absentee landlordism in Italy, but the law was probably largely ignored during the Triumviral period and Augustus did not revive it. His purchase of land for his veterans and the growth of a general sense of security resulted in a rise in the value of land. Augustus' own estates and those of his family in Italy were modest, consisting in the main merely of old family properties. Estates confiscated by the Triumvirs had not been retained by them, but sold to the great enrichment of certain individuals. Many of Augustus' close associates invested in land outside Italy, Agrippa in Sicily, Egypt and the Thracian Chersonese, Maecenas also in Egypt, Rubellius Blandus in Asia and Africa. L. Tarius Rufus invested his great wealth in estates in Picenum and lost it when he failed as a gentleman farmer.

The main business of Italy was with agriculture of all types. The stability and greatly increased wealth of the Augustan Age resulted in a considerable improvement in horticulture and farming. In particular better fruit stocks were imported and the whole process of wine production developed both in quantity and quality. Rome was supplied with grain largely by the tribute corn of Africa and Egypt, which may have caused a check to cereal production near the capital. Augustus feared that the dependence of a large portion of the population of the city on the corn dole would diminish the production of grain in Italy. But it rapidly became apparent that the problem was a surplus of mouths to feed, not of a saturated market and, despite supplies from oversea, Augustus, Tiberius and Claudius were all exercised by shortage of food at Rome. Outside Rome there appears to have been no shortage. On the contrary, the growth in size of all the cities from Naples to the Alps greatly encouraged cereal production, although it is clear that no farm in Italy approached the productivity of the grain fields of North Africa. Later in the century, however, cereal production in Italy greatly declined, giving place to vineyards and orchards. The best grain lands in the Augustan Age seem to have been the Po Valley, now with the rest of Cisalpine Gaul part of Italy proper, Etruria, despite the prevalence of soil erosion in the sloping fields, and Campania.

In the Late Republic the Roman who wished to impress his guests imported Greek wine. Italian wine was but little thought of and largely unknown outside the peninsula. But the Augustan Age saw a considerable expansion in quantity and a considerable improvement in quality of Italian produced wines. Vine stocks were imported from all over the Mediterranean and farmers from the Po Valley (Augustus himself was particularly fond of the Rhaetic wines from near Comum) to the south became interested in viticulture, to the decline later in the century of the production of grain. Olive oil was

48 The tomb of the baker Vergilius Eurysaces outside the Porta Maggiore, Rome. Built in the form of a baker's oven it has a band of reliefs depicting the work of the bakery. Late Republican or early Augustan.

49 Blue Vase, mid-first century A.D. This is the main surviving example of a complete vase showing the same technique as the Portland Vase; *Naples, Museo Nazionale. Height* 30.4 cm.

50 Silver bucket; *Naples, Museo Nazionale. Height* 30.4 cm.

51 The Ara Pacis Augustae: detail from the frieze of the Imperial family. The tall veiled figure is perhaps Agrippa.

52 The Ara Pacis Augustae: the southern panel of the eastern side showing the goddess Italia sitting surrounded by the fruits and blessings of peace.

VERGILEI EVRYSACIS PISTORIS REDEMPTORIS APPARET

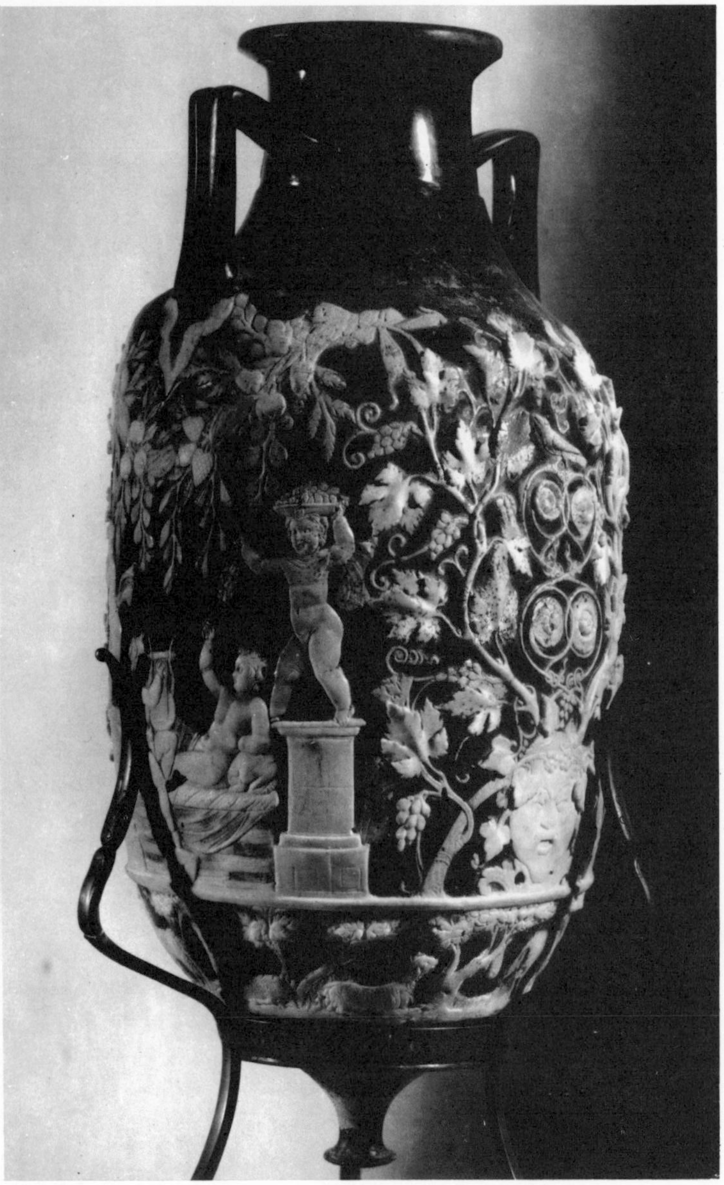

49 50

53

55

56

also produced in vast quantities. Roman Italy, the elder Pliny tells us, did not export this commodity until 52 B.C., although the Greek cities in the south of the peninsula had much earlier built up a flourishing trade in oil. The elder Cato, Varro and Virgil all show their interest in the culture of the olive, which, since it does well on hillsides and requires comparatively little care, was ideally suited to the rather poor and difficult soil of much of Italy. This, no doubt, explains the increase in production, but the quality seems not to have been high and in the second century A.D. oil from Spain began to capture the Roman market. Fruit trees were abundant in this period in the hills of the Po Valley, in Picenum, in Latium and around Capua which was the richest orchard area in Italy. Exactly what kinds of fruit were favoured we do not know, but chief among them was certainly the fig. In the middle of the second century B.C. six cultivated varieties were known; two centuries later the number had risen to twenty-nine. Like the olive the fig was well suited to the condition of much of Italy since it bore well, tolerated poor and dry soil and required no irrigation and little cultivation. Dried figs formed a cheap food for the poor, who lived largely on fruit and vegetables, and Augustus, renowned for the frugality of his meals, greatly enjoyed green figs.

Cattle was raised on farms of all types. Oxen were used as draught animals and for ploughing, and manure was required for the land. But the chief centres of beef and milk production were the large ranches which had grown up in the south of Italy as a result of the devastation during the invasion of Hannibal. The same was true of sheep farming. Most clothing was still made largely of wool and therefore sheep were found on all kinds of property. Throughout Italy there was a great deal of home spinning and home weaving and most farmers met their own and their families' needs from their own wool, but the cities were supplied by the sheep ranches of the south and the north. Strabo mentions the wool of Canusium, Brundisium and Calabria and the sheep of the area around Tarentum are frequently praised from Horace onwards. From the Po Valley Padua in the Augustan Age sent woollen clothing to Rome and was famous for its rugs and coverings, although those from Mutina were considered finer. The soil of the Po Valley was exceedingly rich and progressively turned over to agriculture as the cities of the area grew large enough to create a demand for a steady supply of farm products. Sheep farming therefore became confined to the slopes of the Apennines and the Alps and those lower areas which could not be ploughed. Pigs were raised especially in forests where they could forage for acorns and nuts. According to Strabo there were oak forests in Cisalpine Gaul which yielded such quantities of acorns that Rome was fed mainly on the herds of pigs that came from there. Two centuries earlier Cisalpine Gaul and Etruria had been famous pig country. The Romans were very fond of pork. Poultry farming became at this time a highly specialized and profitable industry with the production, especially near large cities, of choice varieties for the tables of the rich.

While the Italian countryside prospered under Augustus the towns likewise grew in wealth, although of the development of industry it is impossible to speak with certainty. Our information is fragmentary and highly selective. Generally it would appear that the small shop, already noted as typical in Rome, was very common in the Italian towns also and that the making of single articles to individual order prevailed in many industries. Factories developed only in the production of a few commodities and in a few places. Only of a handful of industries have we any certain information. The best iron ore in Italy came from Elba, but the wood necessary for smelting it had apparently run out in the Late Republic. The ore was therefore shipped to Populonia and Puteoli to be smelted and worked. Puteoli in particular had an excellent harbour, plenty of wood and all the rich farmland of Campania as a market for its implements. Every city, including Rome, had its smiths, who, like the plumbers, produced articles from the raw ore, but a rudimentary factory system may have developed at Populonia and Puteoli and perhaps also at the iron mines near Virunum in Noricum, nearly a hundred miles north of Aquileia. Noric iron had a good reputation throughout the Roman world and by it was meant manufactured articles, not the raw ore.

53 The Ara Pacis Augustae: a general view showing both the Imperial procession and the Tellus Italia.

54 The Portland Vase; *London, British Museum. Height* 24.7 cm.

55 The altar of the Augustan Lares: sculptured side showing Aeneas and the miracle of the sow; *Vatican, Museo Chiaramonti and Braccio Nuovo.*

56 The altar of the Gens Augusta from Carthage: sculptured side showing Aeneas fleeing from Troy carrying his father Anchises and leading his son, Iulus Ascanius; *Tunis, Musée du Bardo.*

The Augustan Age saw certain technological innovations in the production of glass (cf. plates 49, 54, 57, 64) which, although their exact nature is unknown, had the effect of making glassware extremely cheap. The result was the growth of factories since the new processes required considerable skill and tractable sand was difficult to find in Italy. Given the problems of bulk transport in the ancient world, glass production concentrated where the sand was suitable. Later in the first century A.D. Pliny mentioned the sand at the mouth of the river Volturnus as being particularly suitable. Glass production in Italy seems fairly soon to have fallen into the hands of oriental experts who, realizing that Rome was by far their best market, migrated and set up factories. The Portland Vase (cf. plate 54) illustrates the technical standard achieved in items made to special order. Another industry which seems to have developed a real factory system, at least at Capua, is the manufacture of bronze and copper ware of all sorts, from ladles and kitchen utensils to busts, *objets d'art,* and elaborate metal furniture. The production of vast numbers of uniform articles in materials which required much more elaborate and specialized techniques than in the iron industry could only have been achieved by heavy capital investment and considerable division of labour.

The clothing and woollen industry presents certain problems. Literature of all kinds is full of references to spinning and weaving by women both slave and free in households throughout Italy and prodigious numbers of spinning whorls have been recovered in excavations. References to spinners and weavers outside the household are very rare and we know nothing of the existence of guilds in these trades. Home produced clothing must have been very generally worn. Even upper class Romans affected such garments to emphasize their gravity and resistance to innovation and frivolity. Augustus kept his family very busy. He made a point of wearing, except on special occasions, clothing spun and woven by his sister, wife, daughter or grand-daughter. Livia's household included no fewer than eighteen slaves concerned with the making and repair of clothing. On the other hand, we hear also of textiles which could hardly have been made thus. Some were imported, especially and predictably the best clothing for women, silk from factories in Asia Minor, fine linen from Egypt. But certain centres in Italy are also known to have produced particularly fine fabrics; Apulia, Padua and Mutina are mentioned for the Augustan Age. Padua sent large quantities of manufactured goods to Rome, yet we have no record of guilds of free spinners and weavers there. The cloth must have been produced in a few large factories run by slave labour.

One of the largest industries in Italy was brickmaking. Building in brick does not seem to have become common at Rome, at least for public buildings, despite Augustus' boast, until the time of Claudius and especially after the Neronian fire. The most important Roman market was for roof tiles. But throughout Italy, particularly in the north, the use of brick was widespread. Conditions were inimical to the development of monopolies or large firms, until the rebuilding of Rome created a concentrated demand and the fortunes of the Antonines. Good clay was abundant in Italy and both the raw material and the final product were too heavy for easy transport. Thus each small area had its own brick works which sent little or nothing of its product beyond its immediate environs, with the exceptions that bricks were sometimes used as ballast in ships, that wealthy Romans were as ready to pay the transport costs of particularly fine or unusual bricks as of any other luxury and that the Tiber afforded the one easy route in Italy for the transport of bulky or heavy articles.

The production of luxury articles in jewels, gold and silver was, as might be expected, organized on the basis of the small shop. There is no evidence that wholesale production played any part in this trade except in the case of silver ware of which large quantities were used at table and which by the middle of the first century A.D. seems to have been made in factories in Campania. The fine cup portraying an elderly bald man from Boscoreale is a splendid example of the standard reached. Quality is also apparent in the Hildesheim treasure (cf. plates 59, 75, 77, 78, back of jacket), perhaps the plate of an Augustan general officer, and the wide range of articles, from utensils and furniture like the silver folding table (cf. figure 11, page 99) to display pieces and Athena (cf. back of jacket) medallion bowls meant to be shown off on specially constructed side boards. One aspect of the gem trade which has almost disappeared today deserves mention. Every Roman with any pretension to dignity had his own seal and took great pride in its being as artistic and distinctive as possible. In the early Imperial Period the aristocratic Roman commanded the services of the very best gem cutters and engravers. Augustus himself summoned Dioscurides, an artist of high ability (cf. figure 19), from the East to make the imperial seal. Dioscurides is an example of a tendency we have already noted with regard to the glass industry: the concentration of wealth at Rome in this age attracted Greek and Oriental artisans to the capital.

Fig. 19 Ringstone, showing Diomedes stealing the Palladium, signed by Dioscurides. *Devonshire Collection, Chatsworth.*

The one field of production in which the Augustan Age was innovatory arose from the same tendency. The best known manufacturer of the red Arretine ware (cf. plates 39, 58), so called from its main centre of production at Arretium, was M. Perennius Tigranus (cf. plate 39), who may have migrated with his slaves to Arretium after the fall of Alexandria in 30 B.C. The restoration of peace and the extension of the military frontiers under Augustus allowed the products of this industry to be sent to the whole Roman world. Arretine ware could be plain or decorated with raised patterns produced in moulds and was not only handsome in appearance but also technically the finest pottery produced in the ancient world. The scale of production varied, but a certain P. Cornelius employed fifty-eight slaves in a single workshop and one of Perennius' mixing vats, of which he had several, had a capacity of some 10,000 gallons. The owning and operation of the furnaces seems to have been a separate enterprise, and a number of potters would take their ware to be fired in one kiln run independently. Although Arretine was probably never the cheapest pottery available, the inhabitants of the Roman empire in the Age of Augustus from Britain to Mesopotamia regarded it as disposable. It was bought, used, broken and discarded. Only very rarely was it mended. But already under Augustus the seeds of the decline of the industry had begun to grow. Settled conditions in Gaul produced an explosive expansion of the Gaulish potteries which began to challenge the brief monopoly of Italian Arretine in Gaul and its neighbours. Under Augustus' successors the whole transalpine market was lost and Gaulish pottery began to invade Italy itself. Much the same happened elsewhere with the result of the progressive loss of markets for the Italian product until by the late first century A.D. Italy was exporting only to North Africa. By the end of the century the Italian industry was dead.

The development of Roman and Italian industry in the Augustan Age presents a haphazard appearance. Monopolistic factory production emerged only under the most exceptional conditions, and not always even then, when the raw material was difficult to obtain and impossible to transport, or when particularly specialized skill was required in the workmen and heavy capital investment by the owner. Generally the small shop, which made and retailed its own products, and custom manufacture were ubiquitous and in no way confined to goods of high quality or infrequent use. The small shop usually co-existed with larger scale production in rudimentary factories in the same industry. Only from the clothing industry does the small shop seem to have been almost entirely absent, although it is found in the finishing and dressmaking trades. Many industries in which conditions seem to us almost to compel the development of a factory system remained obstinately and not entirely explicably wedded to small shop production, the manufacture and supply of lead water pipes in Rome being the most obvious example. Industry received no special encouragement from the Augustan government, not even when the raw material was a state monopoly or the end product was for public use.

Nor was particular encouragement given to trade. Augustus did not take up Caesar's schemes for widespread improvement of canals and harbours. The canal he did construct on the river Po was military in purpose, connected with the stationing of the Adriatic fleet at Ravenna. The clearing of the blocked irrigation channels in Egypt by Roman soldiers was designed not to stimulate trade but to augment the imperial revenues, as was the encouragement of shipping between Egypt and India which would increase the income from Egyptian harbour dues. Even Rome's port at Ostia had to wait until Claudius for proper development. In the Augustan Age it was most unsatisfactory. Strabo refers to the complete lack of any proper harbour there, the silting up of the mouth of the Tiber and the danger incurred by the merchant ships which had to anchor far out at sea, exposed to the south-west winds, while their cargoes were off-loaded into tenders. Many of Rome's imports, in fact, passed through Puteoli, some 120 miles south of the Tiber, where there was a good harbour and merchants had the prospect of return cargoes from Campania. The *Res Gestae* proclaims that Augustus cleared the seas of pirates. But by pirates he meant Sextus Pompey and his troops. Genuine pirates he was not much concerned to prevent and they still, as under the Republic, occasionally infested the coasts of Italy. As on sea, so on land. The roads built by Augustus were primarily for the convenience of the army and the administration. In all of this Augustus followed the traditional policies of the ruling class of the Republic.

Trade, nevertheless, prospered. Italian merchants had been ubiquitous all round the Mediterranean in the later Republic and the Augustan peace brought a great expansion in their activities. Luxury articles from the East began to arrive at Rome in great quantities. From Anatolia and Egypt came linen and fine fabrics. Egypt also supplied Rome with all her paper and the whole western empire with glass from the factories at Alexandria. Alexandria also processed and re-exported to Italy spices and condiments, ointments and perfumes from the Orient. From the East too came jewellery and hand-made furniture. Yet all this illustrates the commercial enterprise of the old trading nations of the East rather than Roman or Italian initiative. The commerce remained largely in the hands of Egyptians, Indians, Syrians, Arabians, Asians who profited by it even more than Italy. Even Gaul, Spain and Africa were stimulated by the new Roman demand for luxuries. In return Italy exported Arretine pottery, glass (cf. plate 49) and bronze (cf. plate 74) and silver ware from Campania (cf. plate 50), which at this period reached very wide markets, although Italy was not to hold them for long. Italian wine and oil also gained wider distribution. But the expansion of Italian industry turned out to be short-lived. In the end it was the landowners and the agriculturalists who held their gains better than the industrialists. Italian and Roman trade was in permanent imbalance. Even at the height of Italian industrial production imports vastly outnumbered and outvalued exports. On the whole, there were no stable markets for Italian products. North Africa and the East were industrially more advanced than Italy and could supply their own markets. Even the western provinces, for a short while the main outlet for Italian manufactures, soon learned to employ their large resources of free labour and raw materials to compete with Italian exports and finally to capture not only their own markets but those of Italy as well. By the middle of the first century A.D. Rome was steadily paying out gold to meet trade deficits. Not that that mattered. Italy's imports were paid for by her income from the whole empire, the tribute of the provinces, imperial salaries and returns from foreign and Italian investments.

Rome and Italy were prosperous as never before. There was no need of direct encouragement or of governmental interference. Augustus had already done all that was necessary, to establish a period of peace and stability in which money was plentiful. The immense wealth of Egypt, both the palace treasures and the cash realized by the sale of a large part of the real estate of the country, was converted into coin and put into circulation, and the supply of money was further increased by the expenditure of the government on land and cash bonuses for the veterans and the vast programme of public works in Rome and Italy. In the early years of his reign Augustus was very concerned to increase the amount of gold and silver coinage in circulation, even melting down the many silver statues set up in his honour in Rome and in the provinces. He seems to have followed with some success a rudimentary quantitative theory of money. His successor Tiberius followed the opposite policy of extreme public parsimony which resulted in shortage of money, a rapid rise in interest rates and a serious financial crisis.

Prosperity was not Augustus' only or greatest gift to Italy. We who speak easily and naturally of Italy are not always aware how slowly the realization developed that the multiplicity of nations and tribes which inhabited the Italian peninsula had a community of interest which united them against the rest of the world. The country had been populated over a long period of time by migrants from the hinterland of Europe displaced by population pressures or merely wandering. They came in small waves and the geography of the country, with the long spine of the Apennines, few large plains and an abundance of small valleys, encouraged the establishment of separate settlements; from the East came the Etruscans and the Greeks who had planted their colonies in southern Italy and Sicily. The whole country was thus fragmented into a large number of independent states or tribes of different ethnic sub-groups, with their own political organizations, customs and dialects. Political pressure from the Etruscans in central Italy and the civilizing influence from the Greeks in the south facilitated the coalescence of the tribes and peoples into larger units, but the expansion of Roman power was as much divisive as cohesive. For the Roman conquest of Italy proceeded on the classic principle of divide and control. When Rome emerged as mistress of Italy, the land she ruled was a patchwork of areas of Roman territory, colonies of Roman citizens, towns with various forms of half-citizenship and a large number of technically independent allies whose relations with Rome were in each case defined by treaty—and all were inextricably mingled together. Rome was concerned with the stability, not the strength of Italy. Although such events as the invasion of the Greek condottiere Pyrrhus and the ever present threat of the Gauls gave birth to the first glimmerings of the idea of Italian unity, it was not until the last quarter of the second century B.C. that the Italians found a cause which really united them, the demand for Roman citizenship. When they realized that the Roman nobility was interested in their claims only as they affected politics at Rome and that they were used merely to serve the ambitions of politicians in the power struggles of the capital, the Italians laid the foundations of national unity. In the revolt of the Italian allies which broke out in 91 B.C. *Italia* was the name of the rebel confederacy. When, less than sixty years later, Octavian before Actium invoked the *consensus Italiae*, he appealed not to an existing reality, but to a deep-felt aspiration. The unity of Italy and the further unity of Italy with Rome is prominent in Horace's poetry and forms one of the great themes of Virgil's *Aeneid.* That poem describes the foundation struggle not of a single city, but of a unified nation. 'So great a task it was to found the Roman race': the last word in the line is as important as its beginning. Rome was to exist not merely as a city built with hands but as a natural entity arising from a union with Italy in which Italy would give strength to Rome. The separate and divided Italy which Turnus defends against Aeneas in the last books of the poem was an anachronism. What Jupiter decreed at the beginning of the *Aeneid* Juno acknowledged at its end: 'Let there be Latium, let there be kings at Alba through the ages, let there be the Roman race powerful with the strength of Italy.' On the shield of Aeneas Virgil placed Augustus himself, the visible symbol of national unity, 'leading into battle the Italians with the senators and the people of Rome and the gods of the home and state.' It was not the least of the achievements of Augustus that under him the unity of Italy moved from an imperfectly formulated aspiration or a propaganda fraud to solid and enduring reality.

The Empire and the Army

6

By conquest, bequest and default the Roman Republic acquired an overseas empire, but resolutely refused to provide proper civil administration for the provinces. The most that was done was to establish a military presence (the main function of a Republican provincial governor was military, to command the legions stationed in his province) and to arrange for the collection of taxes. This meant that the provincials, if they caused no trouble, enjoyed a quite remarkable amount of freedom. It also meant that, especially in the East, they suffered greatly from the lack of proper government when Rome, in assuming control of a country, destroyed the existing central authority without replacing it by her own. The Senate, indeed, was extremely reluctant to assume direct responsibility for territory oversea, which not infrequently embroiled Rome in quite unnecessary warfare as in Greece in the first half of the second century B.C. When annexation became unavoidable, the Senate's preference was to reduce Rome's commitment to the minimum. Thus, for instance, Italy's northern frontier was exposed to continual raids from the Gauls in Europe. Moreover, the vital road from Italy to the Roman provinces in Spain required protection. Yet as late as 125 to 120 B.C. a major war fought in Transalpine Gaul did not lead to annexation. It was years later, when the danger from the north had become quite inescapable, that a colony was established at Narbo Martius (Narbonne) and even this foundation was opposed by the majority of the Senate. It was not until the Germans had come down on Gaul and northern Italy, before Marius' final victory, and successive Roman armies had suffered shattering defeat, that the Senate accepted that to leave this vital area to the protection of two or three isolated Roman garrisons, helped only by Massilia, was highly dangerous and the province of Transalpine Gaul was established.

Again, Cyrene, a wealthy and well organized country, was left to Rome by its last king, Ptolemy Apion, when he died in 96 B.C. The Senate made no attempt to annex, still less to govern and administer this unfortunate kingdom which was allowed for the next two decades to drift into anarchy. All that the Senate did was to arrange for some of Cyrene's income to be diverted to Rome and even this was not systematically done. No regular system of tax collection was instituted. Cyrene was not organized until 75–74 B.C. when a desperate shortage of grain and money at Rome resulted in popular unrest and compelled action. Egypt also was bequeathed to Rome in 88 B.C. by Ptolemy Alexander I, a bequest staggering in its wealth. Yet once more the Senate did nothing. Egypt became the playground of rival and dubious claimants to the throne. Agitation at Rome in the sixties for annexation came to nothing and in 59 B.C. Ptolemy Auletes bought through Julius Caesar recognition by Rome as king of Egypt for 144,000,000 sesterces, borrowed from Roman business men. The Romans, however, were more easily satisfied than Ptolemy's subjects who a few years later again expelled him. This time it cost him the fantastic sum of 240,000,000 sesterces, more than the total of all Rome's revenues from the whole empire before Pompey's conquest of the East, to regain his throne. Even the province Asia, which was, according to Cicero in 66 B.C., by far the most profitable of lands (the other Roman provinces produced merely enough to pay for themselves) was probably treated much the same as Cyrene when it was first accepted by Rome as a bequest from Attalus III. It was not until a decade later, in 123 B.C., that C. Gracchus arranged for the efficient collection of its revenues. It was Pompey who carried this attitude to its final conclusion. He claimed to have found Asia a frontier province and left it the centre of the empire. His claim was founded on the buffer of client states on the eastern boundaries of the Roman provinces. They represent his great contribution to Roman imperial theory, for he made them pay tribute to Rome. It was the perfect solution: taxation with no responsibility for government and administration.

Since public channels were inefficient or non-existent, the provincial who sought redress or protection had to betake himself to private sources. The Roman patron, on the whole, faithfully protected the interests of his provincial client, whether it was an individual, a city or a whole kingdom. But the Roman noble was also concerned to use his provincial clients for his own profit, financial and political. The lack of any real system of provincial administration encouraged the growth of a network of personal ties dangerous to Rome and disastrous to the provinces. For if he protected his provincial client, the Roman noble also exploited him; the provincial was caught between the Roman governor and his staff, the Roman tax collector and any Roman noble who had an interest in his country. Behind the business man and the tax collector, who bulk large in modern accounts of the misgovernment of the empire, lay the vast wealth of the leading members of the Senate, the ultimate recipients of the profits of the provinces whether they were extorted by the tax collectors or exacted by the governors. As Professor Ernst Badian has written, not over harshly, no administration in history has ever devoted itself so wholeheartedly to fleecing its subjects for the private benefit of its ruling class as Rome of the last age of the Republic. And in return Rome gave her subjects neither adequate government nor tolerable peace. Triumph hunting, no less than the pursuit of wealth, was a favourite occupation of the Roman nobility. From the second century B.C. onward we hear again and again of wars unnecessarily begun and unnecessarily prolonged to serve the insatiable appetite of the Roman noble for prestige and military glory. In Caesar, as usual, the characteristics of his class reached their consummation. He deliberately began a major foreign war in Gaul, prosecuted it with unsurpassed brutality and treachery, followed it by a march on Rome and civil war—all for his own personal glory and profit.

Fig. 20 Coin: Sestertius; obverse with an oak wreath between two laurel branches and the inscription OB CIVIS SERVATOS, commemorating the honours and emblems bestowed on Augustus by the Senate in 27 B.C. *London, British Museum.* (*Actual size*).

After the victory at Actium the whole Roman world was Augustus' personal possession, all its inhabitants his own personal clients. But this power, private and personal, lying beyond the constitution, had to be made regular and legitimate. Systems of administration had to be evolved to mediate it and make it effective. The settlement of 27 B.C. had been largely concerned with the provinces. Augustus took a large *provincia*: Spain, Gaul and Syria. The Senate continued to administer the rest: Africa, Illyricum, Macedonia with Achaea, Asia, Bithynia-Pontus, Crete and Cyrene, Sardinia and Corsica, Sicily (cf. map I, page 9). It was not that Augustus took all the armed provinces. The senatorial proconsuls of Illyricum, Macedonia and Africa, provinces close to Italy and, as the civil wars had demonstrated, dangerous to Rome, all had armies under their command. But their legions totalled only some five or six. Augustus commanded a large army, twenty legions or more. His portion was almost exactly that held by Pompey, Caesar and Crassus from 55 B.C., a clear demonstration of its political and military importance. Moreover, Spain, Gaul and Syria were precisely those areas in which serious and continued warfare was intended or apprehended. Not that the arrangements of 27 B.C. were immutable or the division absolute. Africa retained its one legion to the end of Augustus' reign, but in 12 B.C. Augustus took over Illyricum and some time later the army of Macedonia was withdrawn and assigned to the governor of the new province of Moesia. All such acquisitions and creations were retained by Augustus: Galatia, Raetia, Noricum and Judaea. He also took and kept Sardinia in A.D. 6. The Senate received in turn various pacified territories, Cyprus and southern Gaul, Gallia Narbonensis, in 22 B.C., southern Spain, Baetica, at some unknown date. The number of senatorial provinces was thus increased: there were ten in A.D. 14 as against eight in 27 B.C. Useful for conferring position and honour on senators, these additions conferred no additional power. The senatorial provinces continued to be governed, as before, by proconsuls, who might be ex-consuls or ex-praetors, holding office for one year only. Gradually, but not as the result of any specific enactment, a distinction arose between consular and praetorian provinces. Africa and Asia emerged as the senior governorships in the Senate's gift and were governed by ex-consuls; the rest had ex-praetors at their heads.

Augustus divided his vast *provincia* into regions to be administered by legates drawing their power and authority from him. The division varied according to the needs of each particular territory and the necessities of a particular time. It was a very flexible arrangement, well suited to the large, imperfectly conquered and inadequately organized areas which constituted much of his portion. It also enhanced his own safety. For Augustus began the process which eventually, to ensure that no provincial governor could challenge the emperor's power, fragmented the Roman empire into almost a hundred provinces, each too small for adequate administration and serious defence. Spain, for instance, which in the Late Republic had been under a single governor of consular rank, was now governed by two or three legates, inferior in standing and power and subject to Augustus himself. As in the senatorial provinces, so in Augustus' portion the distinction between consular and praetorian governorships emerged slowly and gradually as, equally slowly and gradually, his arrangements for his *provincia* crystallized into a number of distinct commands or separate provinces. Some of Augustus' governors were not senators at all, but drawn from the Equestrian Order. To give provincial governorships to non-senators, to divorce, in effect, the governing of the provinces from the magistracies of the Roman People, was one of Augustus' most radical innovations.

Yet the distinction of senatorial and imperial provinces was one of convenience merely. It does not disclose opposing centres of power and authority. It is easy but erroneous to suppose that, since the name remained the same, the Augustan Senate retained all the habits and attitudes of the Senate of the Late Republic. It was, on the contrary, a very different body in composition and function. The emperor Tiberius' troubled relations with the Senate arose largely from his refusal to realize this. To expect a body of experienced and able administrators to return to the Republican practice of initiating policy was unrealistic folly and a failure to accept what was properly the emperor's responsibility. Augustus had a keen appreciation of the Senate's function and an ideal of the standards to be expected in public life. His preference for the reduction of the membership of the Senate to its traditional Republican and pre-revolutionary number of 300 is revealing. In his revisions or purges of the Senate it is natural to look for a crude political motive, the removal of opposition. But membership of the Senate was for life and a man entered it with the quaestorship held at the age of twenty-five. The passage of years would reveal the incapacity for public service or the unworthiness for public dignity of many individuals. Periodical reviews were necessary for the good of Rome and the dignity of the Senate. It was not Augustus, in origin a new man from Italy, who treated the Senate with contempt but the Patrician noble Julius Caesar and, after Augustus, Tiberius and the arrogant line of the Claudian dynasty. Augustus did not establish a partnership or dyarchy with the Senate, nor was the Senate a body in opposition to him. It became a valuable and trusted organ of Augustus' government. This and much else becomes evident from the arrangements for the eastern provinces.

The Greek East presented Augustus with problems of peculiar difficulty. Two centuries of Roman involvement in the area had led to the establishment of large *clientelae* by many Roman noble houses. Pompey, who had conquered and organized the East, had stood in the Late Republic as its supreme patron. Whole kingdoms, tetrarchies and provinces owed personal allegiance to him. Although Pompey's following was shattered in civil war, Brutus and Cassius inherited and used what they could of his clients. Antony succeeded Brutus and Cassius as lord of the East. For well over a decade before Actium the East had been in the power of Augustus' enemies, who had not neglected to secure the loyalty of its inhabitants while exploiting them after the Republican fashion. At Rome Augustus had a large body of men with hereditary ties with Eastern lands and considerable experience gained there under his enemies. It is no wonder that he regarded the East as a matter of particular personal concern and a subject for personal supervision. In 23 B.C.

57 Prismatic bottles of glass of the first century A.D.; *Turin, Museo di Antichità. Heights* (from l. to r.), 26 cm, 19 cm, 26 cm.

58 Arretine ware bowl from Capua with reliefs of the Seasons from the Factory of Cn. Ateius; *London, British Museum. Height* 19 cm.

59 Medallion bowl with Hercules strangling two snakes in high relief from the Hildesheim hoard; *Berlin, Staatliche Museen. Diam.* 21.4 cm.

60 Clasp of gold necklace found at Pompeii; *Naples, Museo Nazionale.*

61 The Aqua Julia built in Rome by Agrippa in 33 B.C. above the Aqua Marcia (144–140 B.C.) and the Aqua Tepula (125 B.C.). The channels of all three aqueducts ran together within the city from the Porta Maggiore. The inscriptions refer to the restoration of the conduits by Augustus in 5 B.C., Titus in A.D. 79 and Caracalla in A.D. 212–213.

57

58

IMP CAESAR

64

and again from 18 to 13 B.C. Agrippa toured and inspected the East and between Agrippa's two visits Augustus himself was there, from 22 to 19 B.C. In 6 B.C. Tiberius went to Rhodes, perhaps originally as superintendent of the East. His sojourn there turned, however, into morose and self-imposed exile and in 2 B.C. his powers ran out and were not renewed by Augustus. But immediately a new member of the imperial family appeared in the East, the young Gaius Caesar, consul designate and already possessing proconsular power.

An Antonian past was no disqualification from service in the East under Augustus nor was membership of a Republican house with hereditary eastern clients. But something more than mere experience and influence with the communities was demanded. Many men amply qualified in these ways were not employed by Augustus although they, and many others, lived on at Rome with honour and, sometimes, the friendship of the Princeps. But he never trusted them with a province. Experience and provincial connections were desirable, but above all loyalty to the new regime which made past allegiance irrelevant.

It is remarkable how many Eastern governors served in both senatorial and imperial provinces. Nor will documentary evidence support the notion of distinct systems of administration. Augustus issued edicts to the whole empire, senatorial and imperial provinces alike. From Cyme in Asia, for instance, comes an inscription ordering the restitution of public and sacred property in every province of the empire by virtue of a general pronouncement of Augustus and Agrippa in 27 B.C. The stone also has a consequent letter to the city of Cyme by L. Vinicius, proconsul of Asia, who regarded himself as bound by Augustus' orders. Again, in 12 B.C. Augustus by edict protected the traditional right of Jews to send money to Jerusalem. The initiative had come from the Jewish communities of two senatorial provinces, Asia and Cyrene. The classic case of Augustus concerning himself with particular senatorial provinces is Cyrene, from which four edicts of Augustus are preserved on a famous inscription. The long series of embassies from the senatorial provinces to Augustus is particularly illuminating since they began before the division of the provinces in 27 B.C. and were clearly unaffected by it. The subjects of the envoys' requests were diverse: remission of tribute, aid after a natural disaster, punishment of a murderer, funds for public buildings. In some cases we know that Augustus in response gave orders to the appropriate senatorial governor.

Both Augustus and the Senate made regulations affecting all the provinces. Not infrequently they acted together. But if the Senate decreed a law, for instance, this law was valid throughout the empire. Changes in private and public law made by the Senate affected all provinces, imperial and senatorial alike. The text exists, in fact, of a decree of the Senate issued in 4 B.C. on the procedure to be followed in cases of maladministration by provincial governors. It refers to all provinces. The division of the empire between Augustus and the Senate had therefore only one practical consequence: there were now two types of provincial governorship, differing in method of appointment and length of tenure, in other words a mere administrative convenience.

The ultimate guarantee of the well-being of the provincials was Augustus himself. It was not merely that for the provincials as for the Italians his presence and power stood against the return of civil war and the disintegration of the empire. Wealthy beyond any man and supreme in honour and prestige he had no incentive to rob and exploit the provinces. His immense power, lying beyond the governors, the Senate and the courts, was always there to be stimulated by initiative or pressure from below. And he provided as far as was possible (against human greed or folly it is impossible to provide) sound and just administration. Above all, he broke the unholy alliance of the senatorial nobility and the companies of tax collectors which had bled the provinces under the Republic. To secure fair and just taxation Augustus undertook surveys of the resources of the various provinces. Gaul, for instance, was subject to such censuses in 27 and 12 B.C. and in A.D. 14, just after Augustus' death. The disgusting Vedius Pollio perhaps superintended a similar assessment of Asia shortly after Actium and the census of Sulpicius Quirinius of Judaea in A.D. 6 is famous. On the basis of such returns taxes were collected. The chief

62 The Temple of Castor, Rome, consecrated in 484 B.C., restored in 117 B.C. and rebuilt by Tiberius who in A.D. 6 dedicated it in the names of his brother, Drusus, and himself.

63 One of the obelisks imported from Egypt in 10 B.C. now in the Piazza del Popolo, Rome. It was erected by Augustus on the Spina of the Circus Maximus.

64 First-century glass bottle; *Turin, Museo di Antichità. Height* 32 cm.

direct taxes levied on provincials were a land tax and a property tax, which in backward areas became a poll tax (i.e. a per capita tax). The land tax was paid not merely by natives but also by Roman citizens resident in the provinces. A very few communities were granted the exemption enjoyed by the whole of Italy. Other towns were exempted from the property tax. Augustus could and did grant such exemptions to individuals and communities for honour and reward. The indirect taxes were harbour and customs dues of up to five per cent, a tax on the manumission and sale of slaves, which was also levied in Italy, and a requisition of grain for the governor and his staff. Death duties were paid only by Roman citizens in the provinces.

In the imperial provinces the direct taxes were collected by a procurator of Equestrian rank whose appointment was quite separate from that of the governor and his staff. The indirect taxes were still farmed to independent contractors, *publicani*, but they were now closely supervised. In the senatorial provinces all financial affairs were in the hands of the quaestor, who could employ *publicani* if necessary. In any senatorial province in which Augustus personally owned property there was a procurator, who would, no doubt, let his eye range beyond the boundaries of his immediate and official assignment. Legislation and administrative arrangements, however efficient, do not produce virtue and abuses continued to occur. But now the opportunities were less and retribution more swift and sure. The ultimate deterrent was Augustus' own displeasure and the abrupt end of career or life. Unrest in the provinces struck at Augustus himself. It was from him that all honour and office now flowed. The owner of the Roman world could dispose as he pleased.

The proper administration of the provinces was essential to Rome. She existed on the provincial revenues. Moreover, maladministration producing refusal of the provincials to co-operate would provoke either the necessity for armed intervention or the collapse of Roman control. For as in the Republic so under Augustus Roman provincial administration relied on the co-operation of the provincials themselves. The Romans made no attempt to dictate or arrange the forms of local government. The administrative system which was imposed was for the province as a whole. It accepted the existing communities whether cities or, in the more primitive areas, tribes as the units through which it worked. The Roman empire has been described, rightly, as a vast experiment in local self-government. If there was no attempt to impose particular forms of local government, still less is there any sign of the deliberate propagation of Roman civilization and culture among the provincials. The attitude of Augustus to the spread of Roman citizenship is indicative. It is, unfortunately, often impossible to distinguish Augustus' work in this sphere from that of Julius Caesar, but the fundamental principle is clear enough. Although the age of Caesar and Augustus saw the first large scale extension of the Roman citizenship in the provinces, it was limited to those areas in which there already existed a considerable body of Italian immigrants. These might be legionary veterans settled in a colony after discharge from the army or, much more rarely, Roman civilians similarly established in formal settlements. There was also much casual emigration from Italy of farmers, merchants and business men. Roman business men domiciled in provincial towns grouped themselves together for the administration of their own affairs. Such groups, too, formed a nucleus which could lead to an eventual grant of citizenship to the whole town. The grant of Roman citizenship or of the lesser status known as the Latin Right came only at the end of a long process of self-Romanization by the provincial communities. It was a passive recognition of a state of affairs which had arisen naturally, not an active instrument of government policy. The grant of any form of Roman civic rights to the purely native communities in the provinces is almost unknown.

The view that Augustus retreated sharply from the lavish liberality with which Caesar extended Roman citizenship in the provinces is difficult to support. The differences between the practices of the two men are to be explained not by any deliberate divergence of policy but by the different situations in which they found themselves and the different conditions with which they had to deal. Caesar was a pioneer. Before him only one Roman colony had been founded outside Italy, that at Narbo. For him colonial foundation was an instrument of power, to bind to himself in a revolutionary age the legionary soldiers and the civilian poor. Similarly generous grants of rights and privileges assured him the support of communities in the provinces, whose decisive importance for the game of power politics at Rome had been demonstrated in the first century B.C. Caesar's attitude was essentially that of the other monarchic faction leaders of the Late Republic, notably Pompey. The provinces were there to be used to influence the balance of power at Rome: any method which would ensure their support was to be employed. Augustus after Actium was concerned not with revolution but with stability and order, for the good of Rome and his own power. Thus Antony to secure the island's allegiance had given full Roman citizenship to the whole of Sicily, which still remained in part Greek rather than Roman in population and culture. Augustus rescinded the wholesale grant and replaced it by a gradual extension of citizenship to individual communities, assisting the process by the foundation of colonies.

Fig. 21 Coin: Denarius; reverse showing Celtiberian trophy, struck in Spain to commemorate the Spanish Wars of Augustus. *London, British Museum.* (*Actual size*).

Colonies of legionary veterans were founded by Augustus all over the Roman empire in very large numbers. The purpose of these foundations was simple, straightforward and traditional: to provide a livelihood for discharged soldiers and to form centres of Roman power for the control of occupied territory. It had been the practice in the Republic to settle in a conquered country a proportion, at least, of the army which had conquered it. This had been the way in which Rome had controlled Italy and its export to the empire overseas, when this was acquired, was a natural development. If a colony induced the surrounding natives to adopt Roman customs or to learn Latin, this was to Rome's benefit. But it was not the primary purpose of the colony, merely an accidental by-product. The purpose of all such colonies, with the exception of a few purely civilian foundations, was military. Augustus followed closely traditional practice. What makes his colonial foundations particularly important is the largeness of scale. The influence of these colonies on the neighbouring natives differed sharply in the West from that which they exerted in the East. It is only in the western provinces that we can speak properly of Romanization. When Roman power expanded into Europe it met comparatively primitive culture and comparatively backward, mostly tribal, social structure. It was, on the whole, the Roman veteran colonies which determined the pattern of urbanization for western Europe and to this the Augustan foundations made a large contribution. In this part of the empire the spread of Roman customs and the Latin language was rapid, for they were filling, as it were, a vacuum.

For the Augustan Age we have the evidence of Strabo for this process in Spain and Gaul. Of Hispania Ulterior, roughly modern Andalusia, he wrote, 'With the general prosperity of the country gentleness and urbanity have come to the Turdetani and to the Celts also, through their being their neighbours or their kinsfolk. But less to the Celts than to the Turdetani, since the former live for the most part in country villages. The Turdetani, however, and especially those who live around the river Baetis, have completely changed to the Roman way of life and do not remember even their native language any more. Most of them have received Latin rights and accepted Romans as colonists so that they are not far short of being all Romans. The cities which have been recently settled, Pax Augusta among the Celts, Augusta Emerita among the Turduli, Caesar Augusta near the Celtiberi and some other foundations, show clearly the change to the urban way of life I have mentioned. Indeed, all the Spaniards of this type are called toga-wearers and among them are the Celtiberi, who were once regarded as the most brutish and bestial of all'. It was at Cadiz in this part of Spain that Strabo says there were 500 men who possessed the Equestrian census, a greater number than in any Italian city except Patavium (Padua). Some of its sons were fantastically wealthy. Cornelius Balbus built under Augustus a whole new city, Puerto Real, on the mainland of Spain opposite the island of Cadiz. Similarly of the Volcae Arecomisci of Narbonese Gaul, the modern Provence, Strabo wrote, 'They are no longer barbarians but have been changed for the most part to the Roman way of life both in speech and in habits and some even in their civic customs. The metropolis of the Arecomisci is Nemausus (Nîmes), which, although it is inferior to Narbo in number of foreigners and merchants, surpasses it in number of citizens. For Nemausus has under its authority twenty-four villages whose inhabitants are of the same race as its own people and which are exceptionally well populated and contribute to its expenses. It has also what are called Latin rights so that those thought worthy of the offices of aedile and quaestor at Nemausus become Roman citizens. For this reason the tribe is not subject to the orders of praetors sent out from Rome.' Of the prosperity and urban culture of Nîmes and its area in the Augustan Age the remains of the amphitheatre and the magnificent aqueduct of the Pont du Gard (cf. plate 46) and of the theatre at Orange (cf. plate 22), as well as the insipid official architecture of the Maison Carrée (cf. plate 41) provide clear evidence.

In the East matters were very different. Caesar had used his colonies both for the resettlement of veterans and Italians dispossessed by colonial foundations in Italy and also to drain off the surplus population of Rome. Buthrotum, for instance, was colonized with emigrants from Rome and the colonists at Corinth were mainly freedmen from the capital. The majority of these would be Greeks, hardly the best vehicles of the Romanization of their native land. Augustus was concerned only with veterans and displaced Italians. The latter formed the populations of the colonies at Dyrrachium and Cnossos. But such civilian colonies served only to provide homes for the dispossessed. They had no military value, which is why Augustus founded only two. The remainder of the Italian dispossessed were dispersed among the veteran colonies. It was in the veteran colony that strength lay. Communications along the North African coast were protected by a chain of colonies along the coast of Mauretania. The Pisidian colonies controlled the brigandage of the Homonadenses; Heliopolis and Berytus (Beirut) in Syria watched the Ituraeans, equally addicted to banditry. Berytus was a strong post: Quinctilius Varus collected 1,500 soldiers there. It was also a focus for Near Eastern commerce. Similarly Alexandria in the Troad occupied a valuable site for trade with Thrace, Bithynia and Asia; Patrae was as important economically as Corinth. But these were incidental benefits. Augustus realized that a colony could perform several functions at once, but his chief pre-occupation was to pay off his veterans and to garrison his empire. If trade was also encouraged, so much the better, but it was not his main purpose.

Still less was it his purpose to make the Greeks speak Latin. There were simply not enough colonies founded in the East to infect the natives with Roman ways. The East already possessed its own civilization and urban culture, developed to a high pitch over many centuries. It was Greece, after all, which had given to Rome the whole concept of town planning and most of her educational system. For the inhabitants of Greece and Asia Roman culture and the Latin language had no attraction. Their own they considered immeasurably superior. The Greeks went on being as Greek as they had ever been and when eventually, some centuries later, they did call themselves Romaioi, all they meant was that they were citizens of the Roman empire and possessed the resultant rights. Culturally and linguistically they remained Greek. It was not the natives who were Romanized by the Roman and Italian colonists, but the colonists who were Hellenized by the natives. Many of Augustus' colonies exhibit a progressive decline in the use of Latin even for official purposes.

Nowhere was the tenacity of Hellenistic civilization more dramatically shown than in Italy itself, in the cities of Tarentum, Rhegium and Neapolis, which according to Strabo still in his day retained their Greek character. Neapolis clung to its Greek heritage so strongly that it accepted Roman citizenship after the Italian rebellion only with the greatest reluctance. The Greek language continued in public and private use well into the Imperial Period. In the early second century A.D. Tacitus could still call it a Greek city and as late as the reign of Hadrian the chief local magistrate had a Greek title. Strabo says that many traces of Greek culture were preserved at Naples and Greek names were used even though the people were Roman citizens. In part this astonishing survival was due to the Roman passion for the superficialities of Greek life. From the moment the two races came into contact Greek culture exercised a potent fascination on the Romans. By the second century B.C. it had mounted to a regular mania among the Roman upper class for the advertisement of status through the possession of Greek tutors, Greek works of art, proficiency in the obscurer dialects of the Greek language. Too much should not be made of this Greek capture of Rome. Rooted in the Roman sense of cultural inferiority, the progressive Hellenization of Rome was restricted to the superficial and its influence hardly salutary. Roman art is at its worst when most Greek. Nor was the Roman sense of inferiority justified. It was Virgil who met the challenge: 'Others will forge statues of bronze that breathe more softly, others will draw living faces from the marble, others plead cases better and measure the wanderings of the heavens and name the stars as they rise: do you, Roman, remember to rule the nations with imperial power (these will be your arts) and impose the habit of peace, to pardon the humbled and to destroy the arrogant in war.' It was not mere chauvinism. Virgil was right. A people born neither to enjoy peace themselves nor to allow it to others, the Greeks had failed in the one essential art, that of establishing security and stability in human society. This was Rome's great contribution and Augustus was a large part of it.

Nevertheless the people of Neapolis made great profit from Roman Hellenomania. Strabo described the place in the Age of Augustus: 'Neapolis has springs of hot water and elaborate bathing places in no way inferior to those at Baiae, although it has far fewer people than Baiae. Because at Baiae palace has been built on palace, a new city has arisen there not inferior to Dicaearchia. The Greeks who come from Rome to retire at Neapolis, those who have worked in education or because of old age or illness wish to live in relaxation, intensify the Greek way of life there. Some of the Romans, too, delight in this way of life and seeing the great number of men of the same culture who live there gladly fall in love with the place and make their abodes there.' In A.D. 2 Neapolis instituted sacred games to be celebrated every five years in honour of Augustus. These games, grandiloquently called the Italica Romaea Sebasta Isolympica, were the first to be established in Italy and it was not for over a century that they received a rival when the Eusebeia were established at Puteoli in A.D. 138. The contests in the Neapolitan games were gymnastic, musical and literary. According to Strabo, they rivalled the most famous games of Greece and inscriptions preserve their advertisement by the town council of Neapolis at Olympia itself. Augustus attended the Isolympica at Neapolis shortly before his death and provided himself with a private Greek retreat on the island of Capri which he took from Neapolis. Capri was as Hellenic in character as Neapolis and Augustus made no attempt to Romanize it. In A.D. 14 he still regularly observed the exercises of Greek youths training in the Greek fashion on Capri and it was there in the same year that he gave Greek clothing to Romans and Roman clothing to Greeks, stipulating that each should wear the other's dress and speak the other's language. Yet despite his taste for Greek ways and his proficiency in Greek literature, he never learned to speak or write Greek fluently.

Augustus' philhellenism partly merely reflected a craving common among the Roman upper class. But to some extent it was an act of policy. Half his empire was Greek and that the wealthier half. In the East he appeared, as other Romans before him, as the patron of the Greek way of life in both senatorial and imperial provinces, thus maintaining indirectly his own personal pre-eminence. He built up cities and organized leagues so that the Greeks would be able, as far as was possible, to administer themselves, thus easing the strain on Rome. Once he had assured himself that the administrative units were viable and that the right men were in control, he interfered only to keep the provincial machinery running smoothly or to relieve hardship, as when in 12 B.C. the province Asia suffered widespread earthquake and he paid from his own treasure the province's tribute for the whole year. Thus in the East as in the West peace and stability were established and with them prosperity returned to this troubled area. At Patrae, famous for the large number and the charm of its women, the textile industry flourished. Corinth prospered on trade and banking. Athens gained a new forum, a temple of Augustus and Rome and a vast concert hall in honour of Agrippa. Altogether unusual was the re-erection in Athens of a fifth-century temple of Ares systematically dismantled from some unknown site. Ares was the Greek counterpart of the Roman Mars, for whom Augustus had a special regard. Ephesus, favourably sited for commerce with Asia, grew, according to Strabo, more prosperous every day. So did Apamea, which received exports from Italy and Greece. Strabo also testifies to the thriving condition of Laodicea, which produced excellent wool, of the unusually fertile country around Sardis, of Cyzicus, Tyre and Syrian Antioch.

New cities arose also with names like Caesarea, Sebaste or Sebastopolis, Sebastos being the Greek for Augustus, and old ones changed their names to honour the emperor. Under Augustus began the building of the great road system of Asia Minor. But there was no large admission of Greeks to any grade of the Roman citizenship, wherein Augustus' practice differed from that of Caesar. Augustus' policy was slow, orderly and deliberate. The traditionally necessary Romanization, present in the western provinces, was absent from the East. Augustus, too, was concerned with the integration of Rome and Italy. The wider question of the enfranchisement of the Greek East and the admission of Greeks to office at Rome was postponed. Not that non-Italians were deliberately excluded from high office. Cornelius Balbus from Spanish Cadiz and Cornelius Gallus of native Gallic stock both found important employment under Augustus. Greeks, too, were used at court and in the eastern provinces. On some of them Augustus conferred the citizenship. Q. Pompeius Macer, son of Augustus' procurator of Asia and grandson of the Greek freedman Theophanes of Mytilene, was prophetic. He became a senator and was praetor in the year after Augustus' death.

It was Rome's heaven given duty, Virgil claimed, in imposing peace to destroy the arrogant in war. The Ara Pacis was balanced by the Forum of Augustus with its proud parade of Rome's great captains. The Augustan Age saw not only peace and prosperity within the provinces, but on the frontiers of the empire a planned programme of aggression without parallel in Roman history. It began early, with the ten years' war in Spain from 28 to 19 B.C. Spain had been in Roman occupation for two centuries, but the conquest of that difficult land and intractable people was still far from complete. In particular, the Cantabrians and Asturians, whose territory stretched from the western Pyrenees to northern Portugal, remained independent and wild. They had seized the opportunities afforded by the confusion of the civil wars to extend their raids and domination southwards into the Roman sphere of influence. Velleius Paterculus alleged that Augustus in person in 26 and 25 B.C. so completed the conquest of Spain that thereafter it was free even from robbers and bandits. In fact, the process was long, arduous and bloody, commencing already in the Triumviral Period, when C. Domitius Calvinus, who governed Spain from 39 to 36 B.C., and the five proconsuls who followed him all celebrated triumphs. Augustus' campaigns in 26 and 25 B.C. undermined his health and although his propaganda claimed the complete subjugation of the whole peninsula, in fact the reduction of Asturia was left to his legates C. Antistius Vetus and P. Carisius. The war dragged on until 19 B.C. when Agrippa with remorseless patience imposed a settlement by massacre and enslavement. The rebellious and conquered hill tribes were moved down into the valleys; new towns were founded, veteran colonies established. The old province of Hispania Ulterior was divided into Baetica, the most highly Romanized area, which was placed under senatorial administration, and Lusitania, retained under the control of Augustus.

Gaul, after Caesar's brutal conquest, also needed organization, although sporadic uprisings continued as late as 12 B.C. Here too the most Romanized and urbanized area, Narbonese Gaul, was transferred to administration by the Senate. The rest was divided into three parts, Aquitania, Belgica and Lugdunensis. Each was in charge of a legate who was subordinate to Augustus' governor of Gaul as a whole. The really serious military problem in the West was the northern frontier. That Roman occupation stopped at the Alps is the severest indictment of the military policy of the Republican nobility. While army after army was sent to gain glory and loot in the East, northern Italy lay open to the invader. As late as the end of the second century B.C. the Cimbri and Teutones had overcome five consular armies north of the Alps and were halted by Marius only in the Po valley. Traffic across the high passes between Italy, Gaul and the Rhine was prevented and there was no land communication between the western and eastern halves of the empire, between Italy and Illyricum. Augustus' plans for establishing a proper northern frontier earn him and his generals a high place in the annals of military history. The aim was to move the frontier from the Alps to the line of the Rhine and the Danube and then to eliminate the dangerous re-entrant angle at the sources of the two rivers in the Black Forest region by advancing to the Elbe. The grand strategy was worked out in the three years that Augustus spent at Lugdunum (Lyons) from 16 to 13 B.C.

But before then valuable preliminary work had been done. In 25 B.C. Varro Murena had opened the route to the Great St Bernard by the virtual annihilation of the Salassi, 44,000 of whom were sold into slavery. At the same time M. Vinicius may have been operating on the same line, but from the north, in the Valais. In 17 or 16 B.C. P. Silius Nerva, proconsul in Illyricum, reduced the peoples of the Alpine valleys from Como eastward, and a raid by Pannonians and others from Noricum on Istria gave Rome a pretext for annexing the kingdom of Noricum. In 15 B.C. the great campaign opened, conducted by Augustus' stepsons Tiberius and Drusus, to conquer the Alps. The important consideration was to prevent the Alpine tribes from escaping northwards across the mountains. Therefore, while Drusus advanced northwards from Italy, Tiberius marched eastwards from the upper Rhine to meet in the heart of enemy country, Raetia, that is, eastern Switzerland, the northern Tyrol and southern Bavaria. The plan was overwhelmingly successful. Together Tiberius and Drusus overran all the territory as far as the Danube and with Noricum also in Roman hands the northern frontier was dramatically transformed and the armies of the Rhine and of Illyricum could now be linked by a route north of the Alps. The Alps troubled Rome no more. High above Monaco Augustus set a monument recording the achievements of his stepsons. The inscription recorded that under Augustus' leadership and auspices all the Alpine tribes from the Adriatic to the Mediterranean had been brought under the control of the Roman People. Then followed the names of forty-five tribes, to which must be added the fifteen states of the Cottiani in the extreme west, which M. Julius Cottius, son of the native chieftain Donnus, ruled with the rank of a Roman prefect. The remains of the trophy survive at La Turbie (cf. plate 40).

This was merely the first stage. Central to Augustus' policy was Illyricum. It was not lust for conquest, certainly not lust for wealth which led Augustus to commit so much of his resources to this hard and difficult country, but the necessity of forging the link between the two halves of the Roman empire by securing the land route from Italy to the East. The route was that of the modern railway between Italy and Turkey: from Aquileia in north-eastern Italy across the Julian Alps to Ljubljana (ancient Emona) and down the valley of the Save to Sremska Mitrovica (Sirmium), Belgrade (Singidunum), Niš (Naissus), Sofia (Serdica) and Istanbul (Byzantium). When Augustus left Lugdunum in 13 B.C. the strategy had been agreed: while Drusus remained in Gaul to commence the push over the Rhine, Agrippa and M. Vinicius were to conquer Illyricum, for which the foundation had already been laid in the campaigns of Octavian from 35 to 33 B.C. But the first year's campaigning and the harsh winter of central Europe broke Agrippa's health. He returned to Italy and died early in 12 B.C. Thus it was that Tiberius came to Illyricum and, apart from the period of his self-imposed exile in Rhodes from 6 B.C. to A.D. 4, dominated Augustus' European strategy until he himself succeeded to the imperial power. Augustus never faltered in the belief in Tiberius' loyalty, that he could be entrusted with the safety of the empire in the greatest emergency; no other Roman of the age spent so long commanding so many armies on active service. The fighting in Illyricum was long and difficult, with many reverses and revolts. At last, in 9 B.C., the Pannonians and Dalmatians were finally subdued and Augustus could claim 'the peoples of Pannonia, which before my Principate no army of the Roman People had ever approached, I brought under the rule of the Roman People after they had been conquered by Ti. Nero, who was then my stepson and legate, and I extended the boundaries of Illyricum to the banks of the river Danube'. Meanwhile Drusus from Gaul advanced in great sweeps from the Rhine to the Elbe. When he died towards the end of the summer of 10 B.C. following a fall from his horse, Tiberius, fresh from the conquest of Illyricum, continued and completed his work. In 7 B.C. Tiberius was recalled to Rome, celebrated a triumph and, in the following year, departed for the East and exile.

With the death of Drusus and the departure of Tiberius our sources lose interest in the northern frontier until the great revolt of Pannonia in A.D. 6. But brief hints reveal a staggering design. Beyond the Danube in Transylvania lived the Dacians, a people which in the first century B.C. had grown in strength and national cohesion and which was able from its native stronghold to menace the western end of the Black Sea, Macedonia, Thrace and the Aegean, the Hungarian plain and the middle Danube. Caesar had already noted their menace. At his death he was planning an expedition against them. Now Augustus proposed nothing less than the conquest and annexation of Dacia. Had he succeeded the Roman frontier would have stood not on the Rhine and the Danube but on the Elbe and the Dniester. In A.D. 4 Tiberius had returned to the command of the European armies, this time in Germany. Two years later he was ready to launch the final attack on Dacia in a converging movement with twelve legions, involving that hallmark of Augustan strategy, the co-ordinated action of different armies over a wide area. But in A.D. 6 the whole of Dalmatia and Pannonia rose in revolt. Roman residents were massacred and Italy was once more in peril. Tiberius hurried to the area. The great weakness of Augustus' military policy was exposed. For his own safety he had banished the armies to the frontiers; there was no central reserve of troops on which to draw; the legions of Illyricum were reduced by high casualties and mutinous; new recruits were unobtainable; Tiberius could only fight his way to Siscia and wait for the arrival of reinforcements from the East. Yet by slow and brutal warfare Illyricum was recovered. The Pannonians surrendered in A.D. 8. The valleys of southern Illyricum and Dalmatia were secured in the following year by wholesale massacre. Pannonia became a separate province, governed by an imperial legate; Illyricum was soon renamed Dalmatia; the conquest of Dacia was abandoned.

Hardly had the Roman position in Illyricum been recovered than the northern section of Augustus' grand frontier design collapsed in ruins. In A.D. 9 P. Quinctilius Varus was ambushed in the Teutoburgowald beyond the Rhine by the German Arminius and perished with the loss of three legions. Augustus was shattered. For several months he would neither shave nor cut his hair and frequently banged his head on the door shouting 'Quinctilius Varus, give me back my legions'. The anniversary of the disaster he observed as a day of sorrow and mourning. Indeed, although Tiberius held the Rhine, all the gains of the past years to the Elbe were lost and would never be regained. But this was not the only nor the most important loss. Augustus' anguish was not mere senility. To replace Varus' army he had to find three new permanent legions and this, on top of the losses in Illyricum, proved impossible. The number of volunteers for the army sufficed only and barely to maintain the existing legions. The legions of Varus were never replaced. From A.D. 9 the military establishment of the Roman empire was permanently reduced until Augustus' death from twenty-eight to twenty-five legions. Even the larger number, as recent events had demonstrated, was hardly sufficient for the defence of the frontiers. Yet before Actium the Roman world had supported nearly three times as many legions in the East and in the West. Augustus was caught between converging trends ultimately of his own contriving. For his own safety and the security of his regime the army had to be kept as small as possible. Disaffection in the legions, on which the ambition of a usurper might feed, precluded conscription and force. Nor could

65 Soldier's arm piece; *Naples, Museo Nazionale.* 19 cm × 33 cm.

66 Armour: breast plate; *Naples, Museo Nazionale.* 28 cm × 45 cm.

67 Basilica Julia viewed from one of its arches, Rome.

68 Detail of the arcades of the theatre of Marcellus, Rome.

69 The Rostra of Augustus in Rome, showing dowel holes for attaching the ships' beaks which decorated it.

65 66

70

71

72

73

74

the cities of the empire now be compelled to pay for pressed legions. That way lay unrest and revolt. At the same time with the return of prosperity and security to the empire, military service lost much of its attractiveness; civilian life was now more congenial and rewarding. Italians, Gauls, Spaniards and Asians were no longer ready to lose their wealth or their lives fighting in barren lands for little loot. Augustus' distress becomes intelligible. All thought of further conquest, even if it would have afforded a better frontier and greater security, had to be abandoned. That was bad enough; but what was worse was the realization that even the restricted frontier of the Rhine and the Danube might not be held if further disaster came. It is no wonder that Augustus left to his successor the advice, written in his own hand, that the empire must be restricted to its present boundaries.

Another great land frontier lay in the East (cf. map page 9). Here the problems and solutions were different. The principles of Rome's defence of the Eastern frontier had long been laid down: the provinces were to be protected from the power of Parthia by a buffer of client kingdoms. In the sixties of the first century B.C. Pompey had reduced the chaotic result of Republican irresponsibility to some sort of order. After him Antony before the final confrontation with Octavian had subjected the East to a thorough reorganization. Augustus' method was simple: he accepted and confirmed Antony's arrangements almost in their entirety and advertised the reconquest of the East for Rome. Augustus' treatment of the many petty tyrants who infested the area is particularly revealing: three were put down permanently, on the island of Cos, at Amisus and at Heraclea Pontica on the south coast of the Black Sea (the tyrant of Heraclea at least should not have been surprised; shortly before Actium he slaughtered all the Roman inhabitants of his city), but elsewhere a curious pattern emerged: Augustus would depose an Antonian ruler only to reinstate him or his family at a later date. At Hieropolis-Castabala in Cilicia, for instance, Tarcondimotus had been so devoted to Antony as to take the name Philantonius. He fell at Actium and was succeeded by his son whom Octavian deposed in 30 B.C. Ten years later, however, the son was restored to all his father's possessions, with the exception of certain coastal districts given to the king of Cappadocia. Similarly in the kingdom of Emesa in Syria Octavian deposed the Antonian ruler and incorporated the kingdom in the Roman province of Syria. But again, ten years later, in the same year as the restoration of the son of Tarcondimotus, the Antonian dynasty was re-established and the king given Roman citizenship. At Tarsus, Comana in Pontus and Olbia in Cilicia Aspera much the same happened.

As his experience of Eastern affairs deepened Augustus realized that his first victorious reactions were not conducive to good order. In fact his second thoughts bear remarkable testimony to the excellence of Antony's dispositions. Elsewhere Antony's arrangements were not even temporarily disturbed. The bandit Cleon continued to rule in Gordioucome in Mysia with his territory enlarged. In gratitude he renamed his capital Juliopolis. The tyrants of Caranitis and Amaseia were likewise left in power, although when they died their kingdoms were annexed. Carana, the capital of Caranitis, was renamed Sebastopolis; Amaseia became part of the Roman province of Pontus. Of the great Eastern kings only two were deposed and one of those had been unreliable even to Antony. Of the kings maintained in their possessions by Augustus no less than five had been active partisans of Antony. Asandar, ruler of the Bosporan kingdom on the northern shore of the Black Sea, remained uncommitted in the Roman civil wars. His kingdom supplied food for Asia Minor and protected it from devastating invasion by the northern barbarians. Neither Antony nor Augustus disturbed him and he reigned for at least twenty-nine years.

The kings of Pontus, Paphlagonia, Galatia and Cappadocia were Antony's creations. In Pontus Augustus confirmed the rule of Polemo, depriving him of Antony's gift of Lesser Armenia only to bestow it on another Antonian, the former king of Media, who was temporarily without a kingdom. When the Median died in 20 B.C., Lesser Armenia was given by Augustus to Archelaus of Cappadocia. Deiotarus in Paphlagonia, Amyntas in Galatia, to which Antony had added all or part of Pamphylia and Cilicia Aspera,

70 Marble bust of Cicero; *London, Wellington Museum. Height* 63.3 cm.

71 Medallion bowl from the Boscoreale hoard showing portrait head of an elderly man in high relief. *Paris, Musée du Louvre.*

72 Mausoleum of Augustus in Rome showing the entrance.

73 Marble table pedestal; *Naples, Museo Nazionale. Height of sphinx* 89 cm.

74 Bronze ewer; *Naples, Museo Nazionale. Height* 23 cm.

Archelaus in Cappadocia – all passed without difficulty into Augustus' empire. When Amyntas was killed in 25 B.C. by the Homonadenses, Galatia was organized as a Roman province, thus irretrievably fixing Roman control in central Asia Minor. Cilicia Aspera, an ungovernable territory, was not included in the new province: Archelaus of Cappadocia was saddled with its administration. When Deiotarus of Paphlagonia died in 6 B.C. his country was added to the province of Cilicia. In Judaea Herod had naturally chosen Antony and, equally naturally, had transferred his allegiance to Octavian at the right time. His lands were enlarged to the east of the Jordan and by Abelene in the north. But the ambitions of Herod and the intrigues of his family made him not entirely satisfactory. When he died in 4 B.C. Augustus partitioned his realm between the rival claimants, Archelaus and Antipas. Archelaus soon had to be removed, to Vienne in Narbonese Gaul. In A.D. 6 Judaea became a province under an imperial procurator.

The two kings deposed by Octavian were Malchus, king of the Nabataean Arabs, and Mithridates of Commagene. Malchus was tiresomely disloyal to Antony and an enemy of Herod of Judaea. Obodas II of an old Arabian royal family took his place. In Commagene Octavian replaced Mithridates with Antiochus, only rapidly to learn the unwisdom of tampering with Antony's arrangements. Antiochus had to be executed in 29 B.C. His successor fared not much better. He murdered a rival and Augustus had to deprive him of his throne. He was succeeded by the son of his murdered rival. Thus the provinces, Syria, on which the military defence of the East rested, Galatia, Cilicia, Bithynia-Pontus and Asia, were protected by a ring of client states large and small. Diplomacy was the preferred method of Augustus' defence of the Eastern frontier; the aim was to safeguard the provinces without direct Roman involvement and responsibility. Beyond lay Parthia and between Parthia and the Roman East was Armenia, facing both east and west, towards Asia Minor and towards the Iranian plateau. Augustus had an unsettled debt with Parthia, the defeats of Crassus and Antony. But true to his policy in the East, in dramatic contrast to that on the northern frontier, he rejected the *casus belli.* The good behaviour of Artaxes of Armenia was assured by holding his brothers as hostages at Rome and by establishing his enemy Artavasdes on the throne of Lesser Armenia. Since these actions could hardly be construed as friendly to Armenia, Phraates of Parthia opened diplomatic relations with Rome. He was involved with an Armenian pretender Tiridates, who eventually kidnapped one of Phraates' sons and fled to Rome. Phraates demanded his return. At the same time the Armenians requested that Artaxes should be replaced by his younger brother Tigranes who had spent ten years in Rome. Augustus recognized both the gravity of the situation and the opportunities it offered. He himself went to the East and ordered Tiberius to advance with an army from Macedonia through Armenia. The show of force was enough. Phraates restored the Roman standards captured from Crassus and Antony and Tigranes was crowned king of Armenia, after Artaxes had been conveniently murdered, by no less a personage than Tiberius himself. All of which was hailed and advertised at Rome as a famous victory. A triumphal arch was erected. Coins celebrated the handing over of the standards and the submission of Armenia. The surrender of the standards formed the centre piece of the breastplate on the famous statue of Augustus from Prima Porta (cf. plate 37). The standards were finally laid up in the temple of Mars Ultor, dedicated in 2 B.C. Phraates gave earnest of his pacific intentions by sending all four of his sons to live in Rome. But the vital kingdom of Armenia remained a problem. Tigranes died about 6 B.C. and shortly afterwards Augustus sent out his grandson, the young Gaius Caesar. He met Phraataces, the new king of Parthia, in A.D. 1 and renewed agreement with his kingdom. Armenia remained weak, beset by dynastic intrigue and the unwillingness of the natives to endure a client king. But the alternatives of complete abandonment or complete annexation of Armenia were alike unthinkable. The former would unduly have encouraged, the latter unduly provoked Parthia. Augustus' diplomacy was hardly spectacular, but it passed the essential test: it worked. In the forty-five years that Augustus was in sole charge of the Roman world the eastern frontier saw no major war. Above all, a war with Parthia, for which there was pressure at Rome in the years after Actium but which there was no certainty that Rome would win, was avoided.

For a government so militaristic and aggressive as that of the Roman Republic, the military system remained curiously haphazard and amateur. At formation level, in the legion and below, organization and performance were alike good. But just as there was no general conception of the principles of the constitution or of provincial administration so military policy remained a series of particular reactions to particular situations. The basic concept was that of a citizen army, recruited annually by conscription for a single short campaign, in which service was a positive right not a burdensome duty and which could be commanded by whoever filled the chief elective offices of state for that year. The acquisition of an oversea empire destroyed the validity of this approach. It became necessary for armies to be stationed permanently in the provinces. These frontier armies became standing forces and in the Late Republic a permanent military establishment was stationed exactly in those areas in which Augustus afterwards concentrated his troops, Spain, Gaul, Macedonia and Syria. But these armies remained small, scarcely adequate for defence under normal conditions and quite incapable of withstanding a determined invasion. Nor were they integrated into a general strategy of frontier defence. That simply did not exist, as the northern frontier of Italy amply demonstrates. Emergencies of defence or campaigns of conquest or retaliation were still met by a development of the citizen army of early Rome. A force, often a very large one, was raised for the specific crisis and demobilized when the crisis had passed. It was these emergency armies which had destroyed the Republic. For the ruling oligarchy, instead of establishing proper control over them and making proper provision for their demobilization, preferred to use them as instruments of their own political ambitions. They became client armies and their patrons sought to use them exactly as they had used their civilian clients. But the capacity of a civilian client for mischief through rioting or the ballot box was necessarily limited. When the clients were soldiers to deploy one's own or to attempt to erode one's opponent's *clientela* led straight to civil war.

Fig. 22 *Above* Coin: Denarius; reverse showing kneeling Armenian with inscription CAESAR DIVI F ARME CAPT, commemorating the conquest of Armenia in 20 B.C. *London, British Museum.* (*Actual size*).

Fig. 23 *Below* Coin: Aureus; reverse showing the Temple of Mars Ultor. *London, British Museum.* (*Actual size*).

Augustus rose to power through civil war and proscription by the relentless manipulation of the client army. After Actium the first and most urgent of his pre-occupations was to control the armies, to prevent himself suffering the fate of the Marian party against Sulla, of Pompey against Caesar, of Brutus and Cassius against Antony, of Antony against himself. It was not a subject patient of legislation. To march beyond the boundaries of your province with your army and without express authorization by the Senate and the Roman People had long been illegal under the Republic. It was no defence against a man determined or desperate enough and backed by an army of faithful clients. Augustus' solution was simple in conception, complex in execution and, typically, hardly innovatory: the client armies would remain, but they would all be clients of a single patron, himself. If he retained the allegiance of the soldiers, then the ambitious and armed proconsuls would be powerless. Not that this solution emerged from conscious debate and careful weighing of alternatives. It was simply that Augustus' position after Actium was maintained and enhanced. He had become after the defeat of Antony the owner of the whole Roman world. That the vast majority of its inhabitants, civil and military, were his own personal and private clients was the essential basis of his power and position. His treatment of the army, like his restoration of the Republic and his provincial arrangements, was but to institutionalize and make permanent and public this fundamental fact. But it limited or modified his ultimate power no more than his acceptance of certain formal powers in the settlements of 27 and 23 B.C. or his alleged division of the provinces with the Senate.

The civil wars of the Late Republic had revealed the essential truth about the client armies: that their allegiance, like that of civilian clients, went where they saw or could be persuaded that the greatest benefits lay. If their demands were not met or if they received a better offer, transference of allegiance was easy and rapid. This characteristic Augustus knew well: he had exploited it against Antony. The principal material benefits were two: pay during service and the provision of a gratuity in land or money after discharge.

Augustus' vast personal wealth (his private income alone was greater than all the public revenues of the Roman state and he recorded in the *Res Gestae* that he four times bailed out the treasury from his own pocket) enabled him to keep both benefits firmly in his own hands. The mere fact that no individual, not even the Roman treasury could in any way approach Augustus' own fortune made the soldiers less likely to look elsewhere for benefits. The great demobilization after Actium and the way the discharged troops were settled formed a proclamation to the armies no less than to the civilian populations of Italy and the provinces. For it demonstrated to the soldiers not only to whom they must look for their benefits but also that Augustus had the resources to provide them. Succeeding years made it clear that the resettlement of his veterans was to be Augustus' permanent care and the lesson was reinforced by extraordinary donations to the troops and the veteran colonists.

Augustus made only one major innovation, but that affected the nature of the whole army. He abolished the emergency army which had fought most of the wars of the Late Republic and which had afforded large opportunities for ambitious generals. Instead the frontier force was enlarged to a permanent wartime establishment. The size of the army retained after the demobilization after Actium, twenty-eight legions, was the product of a complex set of calculations. The safety of Augustus himself demanded that the army should be no larger than absolute military necessity dictated. At the same time the safety of Rome and the empire had to be provided for. Economic resources entered the calculation; so did the available supply of volunteers and the foreseeable amount of work for the army, for an idle army is a dangerous one. Augustus succeeded in preventing armed usurpation. But twenty-eight legions dispersed on the frontiers placed a heavy burden on Rome's economic resources and, as the aftermath of the Varian disaster showed, on the sources of recruitment. Much better would have been a smaller frontier force backed by a central mobile reserve in Italy. But that the safety of Augustus would not allow.

As it happened, Augustus' system just worked, although even he was slow to learn the limitations it imposed. Pay, bonuses and gratuities after service were the essentials in securing the loyalty of the legions. The dispersal of the armies to the frontiers was a valuable precaution. We must not forget also the simple passage of time. In many respects the most important thing that Augustus did was a sheer accident of nature: he lived until A.D. 14. Thus a whole generation had grown up which knew only his dispensation. Use and the passage of time assured the stability of the system; it changed the nature of the Senate and of the whole administration, and it changed too the nature of the army. The purpose of the grand demobilization after Actium was not merely to reduce in size an army too big for Rome's needs and resources and the safety of Augustus; it also removed from service those soldiers who had learned their concept of loyalty in the treacheries of civil war. In the Augustan army as established thereafter the annual rate of retirement was, on average, about 9,000 men and the normal length of service sixteen years. Thus by 15 B.C. the whole army consisted of men recruited by Augustus as Princeps. They had known no other terms and conditions of service. In 13 B.C., in addition to the formal fixing of the term of service at sixteen years, the resettlement of veterans on land, Italian and provincial, which Augustus bought with his own funds, was given up and instead a cash bounty was paid. In A.D. 6 the provision of this bounty became at last a function of the state instead of the personal gift of Augustus as a private patron. In that year he established the military treasury, the *aerarium militare*, with an initial gift of 170,000,000 sesterces from his own fortune and provided for its future by the institution of two new taxes, a sales tax and death duties.

The first veterans to receive the cash bounty under the arrangements of 13 B.C. would be those who had formed the first intake into the army after the great demobilization of the years 30 and 29 B.C. The first veterans to be provided for from the *aerarium militare* would be the first army intake born since Actium. Double coincidence is possible, but it seems likely that these two developments mark two deliberate stages in Augustus' growing confidence in the loyalty of his soldiers. To secure this loyalty he had had to make himself personally responsible for all aspects of military service. No longer, as under the Republic, were individual generals to decide when their soldiers should be discharged or what provision should be made for them after discharge. Everything was to come from Augustus and to be seen to come from him and to be in the gift of no one else. There was to be one patron and one only. In A.D. 6 this patronage was made institutional. The junior officers, centurions and military tribunes, were probably easier to deal with than the common soldiers or the army commanders, for if any vestige of higher loyalty survived it remained with them. Serjeants-major and subalterns are in any army the staunchest defenders of tradition. When Sulla marched on Rome all his military tribunes save one deserted him. To the centurions especially Augustus had opened whole new fields of opportunity by his organization of the Equestrian career both civil and military, but for the senior officers and commanders no general rules could apply, and careful selection was the only method. Many anomalies in the careers of prominent men, especially in the earlier years of Augustus' Principate, are doubtless to be explained by the operation of the loyalty test. The major military operations were conducted either by men like Agrippa whose allegiance had been tried in the years of civil war or by members of Augustus' own family, especially by Drusus and Tiberius.

Augustus succeeded in his chief purpose. Domestic conspiracy, not the armed proconsul, was his major danger. He handed on to his successor an army whose loyalties lay firmly with the emperor. So long as the emperor could claim to be even by the most tenuous links of adoption the heir of Caesar, the army knew whom to obey, were he a Caligula, a Claudius or a Nero, and obeyed readily. It was only when the dynastic link was broken, as it was with the suicide of Nero, that the Roman world exploded once more into civil war. The army, without a focus for its loyalty, was an easy prey for the ambitions of unscrupulous men. At the same time the soldiers realized the ultimate right and power of a client—to appoint his own patron. The Year of the Four Emperors revealed not the failure of the Augustan approach, but its essential soundness. Subsequent events confirmed it: the history of the first four centuries of the Roman imperial system, as dynasty succeeded dynasty, demonstrates clearly, despite the military anarchy of the third century A.D., the adherence of the army to the hereditary principle, the strength of the bond between the emperor and his military clients and the importance of that bond for the stability and peace of the Roman empire.

The Imperial Cult

7

It is difficult for anyone brought up in even the vestiges of the Christian tradition, or, indeed, that of any mystery religion which emphasizes personal responsibility and individual salvation, fully to comprehend the Roman state religion. Devoted almost exclusively to the formal performance of empty ritual it appears so devoid of spiritual content that we may easily suppose that no Roman took it seriously. Yet Augustus spent considerable time and a great deal of money on the construction or repair of temples and the encouragement of the state religion. To condemn his actions as the cynical manipulation of religion for political purposes and personal glory misses the important point: there is no profit in manipulating, cynically or otherwise, something in which few people believe. A system of religious observance which lasted a thousand years and which was abolished only with unrest and disquiet is not lightly to be dismissed.

Many Romans, especially among the upper classes, appear to have taken it very seriously indeed. The official religion of the Romans belonged to a concept of an ordered society in which the basic unit was not the individual but a group, above all, the family. The fundamental purpose of religion was to secure not the salvation of an individual soul but the continued existence and well being of the group by assuring the favour of the gods. Just as the cults in individual families secured this at one level, so the state cults acted at the highest level to ensure the favour of the gods for the group in which all other groups were subsumed, the *respublica*. Modern notions of personal faith and individual responsibility are irrelevant and misleading. Of course no Roman believed in his gods in the same way as a Christian believes in the redemptive power of Christ, and belief of that type was not demanded. The Roman state religion was political in that it was concerned with maintaining the existence and promoting the welfare of the commonwealth in its relations with the gods just as the civil administration did in its relations with citizens, allies and friends and the military with enemies. The breakdown of the traditional concept of Roman society as based on the family, not on the individual, was marked by the importation and growing popularity of the individualistic and romantic mystery religions from the East.

But by definition none of these cults could supplant the state religion until one of them, Christianity, adopted the essentials of the Roman attitude. Conversely, individual belief, provided that it did not lead to public disturbance, was no concern of the official religion. There was no notion of sin, morality being regarded as the private concern of the individual and only recognized by the civil authorities in so far as immorality endangered the stability and welfare of the state. The concept was of religious crime, acts of sacrilege which disrupted Rome's relations with the gods. Thus, when Augustus repaired temples, restored cults and encouraged the state religion, this formed an essential and inescapable part of his re-establishment of a stable and ordered society. As with all other aspects of the restoration of the *respublica*, he, a Roman whose mind moved in Roman categories, never considered the possibility of not doing so. The detailed arrangements were no doubt conducive to his convenience, but the basic action was as natural and inevitable for him as speaking Latin.

In one direction Roman religion received under Augustus a great and important extension, the cult of the emperor and of his family. Here, as elsewhere, the division of the empire, rooted in nature, into East and West made its effect. In the East the worship of the ruler as a god had long been established and widely diffused. The Greeks had developed their own practice, altogether more subtle and sensible than the crude deification of the living rulers of their oriental neighbours. Among the Greeks divine honours were the ultimate accolade that could be conferred on a mortal man, implying not that his nature had in any way been changed nor that he was suddenly endowed with supernatural powers and attributes, but simply that his services to his fellow men had been such as to merit extraordinary recognition. A man so honoured did not become a god in life nor did anyone suppose for a moment that he did. Alexander the Great may under the influence of Persian and oriental belief have gone beyond the sane moderation of the Greeks and when his general Ptolemy grabbed for himself the kingdom of Egypt after Alexander's death he inherited and accepted the worship the Egyptians had traditionally paid to their native Pharaohs. Gradually the Greeks in Egypt became infected with native practices and attitudes and developed their own form of ruler worship. When Augustus after Actium and the death of Cleopatra succeeded to the realm of the Ptolemies, he too assumed the position and cults of the Pharaoh. It was the economical solution. The alternative was the destruction of a complex system of government and administration which had endured and developed for many thousand years and the labour and danger of imposing a new one.

Fig. 24 Emerald cameo of Augustus wearing a laurel wreath. *London, British Museum.* (*Actual size*).

The Egyptians worshipped Augustus as they had worshipped the Ptolemies before him and the Pharaohs before them. From Philae and elsewhere come monumental representations of Augustus as the Pharaoh and inscriptions name him as the king of Egypt with the titles of Horus, Re and other divinities which the Ptolemies had inherited from the Pharaohs. His statue was probably erected in all the temples and the priests no doubt hailed him, as they had done Alexander, as the son of all the gods and goddesses of Egypt. The Egyptian Greeks too hailed Augustus as a god and accorded him the special forms of worship which they had developed under the Ptolemies. His particular cult title among the Egyptian Greeks was Zeus the Liberator, Zeus Eleutherios, and the temple to Antony which Cleopatra had begun in Alexandria was completed as a temple to Augustus. Various other cities followed the example of Alexandria and erected temples to the new god-king of Egypt. Augustus' acceptance of this worship was prompted not by insane megalomania but by considered policy, to assure effective government and the loyalty of his subjects. Egypt, in fact, provides only the most extreme example of Augustus' general policy throughout the East, to take over wherever possible existing local conditions and to develop them for his own purposes.

The Greek practice of according divine honours and titles to prominent individuals was, above all, a method of assuring a superior power of a community's loyalty and proper attitudes or of attracting that power's interest and benevolence. When Rome began to establish control over Greek lands, her representatives naturally and inevitably became the objects of such attentions. When in 212 B.C. Claudius Marcellus captured Syracuse, its inhabitants promptly hailed him as saviour and established in his honour a great festival which was celebrated annually until its abolition in the first century B.C. by the infamous C. Verres to enhance his own glory. Verres, for all his oppression of the Sicilians, was nevertheless named by the Syracusans as patron and saviour of all Sicily. After his defeat of Philip of Macedon Titus Flamininus had been showered with such honours. Throughout Greece he was proclaimed saviour. The Chalcidians linked him with Heracles in the dedication of a gymnasium and with Apollo in that of a Delphinium. More, they instituted a cult of Flamininus with a regular priesthood and a hymn celebrating Flamininus, Zeus, Rome and the Roman Faith. Flamininus was not displeased. He responded with a votive offering after the Greek custom at Delphi. The inscription described him as godlike and he claimed descent from the gods by calling himself the son of Aeneas. Honour to a mortal might conveniently and without disrespect be combined with the worship of a god. The Chalcidians linked Flamininus variously with Heracles, Apollo, Zeus and Roma. The last deity was unknown to the religion of the Romans. She was a Greek creation, a personification of the city of Rome. In 195 B.C. Smyrna erected a temple to the goddess Roma, a diplomatic action designed to attract the benevolence not of any one Roman general but of the whole government of Rome. Other cities hastened to imitate Smyrna's example by establishing temples and festivals in honour of Roma. Spontaneous expression of gratitude hardened into political calculation. Divine honours to Roman generals in the East became regular and Roman governors came to regard them as no more than their due. Sulla in 86 B.C. sacked Athens and prevailed on the pro-Roman aristocracy which he established in power to create a cult of him. Cicero, although from political calculation he refused a temple which the people of Asia wished to erect to him and his brother when the latter was proconsul of Asia, was very angry when a certain Pelops of Byzantium neglected to obtain an honorary decree for him. Cicero in turn incurred the wrath of his predecessor in the governorship of Cilicia, Ap. Claudius Pulcher, who considered him tardy in securing the completion of a temple in his honour. After Pompey's defeat of the pirates and Mithridates and his organization of the East, Asia was full of temples dedicated to him as god and saviour. When Julius Caesar emerged as victor in civil war, the same cities compliantly accorded him the same honours and titles. After Caesar's death Antony was a god in the East: in Egypt he capered as Osiris and at Athens he was the new Dionysus. At Athens, too, the name of the Panathenaic festival was changed to the Antonaia.

Some of these cults were very persistent. Flamininus was still worshipped three centuries after his death. Others were evanescent. The cult which Sulla extorted from the Athenians lasted only a few years. More and more the cults of Romans in the East became expressions of diplomacy. The case of Mithridates is decisive. In the first century B.C. he interrupted Roman dominance in the East and overran Asia. The cities acclaimed him in the same terms as they had done the Roman governors who had gone before him. He became a god, the father and saviour of Asia. When Roman rule was re-established, Romans again received the same enthusiastic deification, and when Octavian defeated Antony he naturally and inevitably fell heir to the whole tradition. There was no need of considered policy or of deliberate encouragement. The cities and communities of the East hailed him as benefactor, saviour and patron simply because he now represented the superior power and they wished to establish with him the diplomatic links which had served them under the Republic.

Dedications to Augustus are known in great numbers from all over Greece and the East. In addition to the common and widespread acclamations as saviour, benefactor, patron and the like he was in many places worshipped as a god with his own priesthood. To all of this Augustus must have consented, but in one respect he intervened to direct the proliferation of cults. He laid it down that his worship must be joined with that of Roma. While excessive adulation might arouse suspicion at Rome, Augustus' acceptance of divine honours was an act of policy to bind the peoples of the East more closely to him, not now as a revolutionary faction leader, but as the head and embodiment of the Roman state. Roma was by now a well established goddess in the Greek East and the sharing of her worship presented no difficulty; thus the joint cult became widely diffused. Although a private individual might make a simple dedication, the cults themselves were in the hands of the cities or of leagues or associations of cities. These leagues or associations were in origin purely secular. They existed already under the Republic and Augustus had no need to create them or entrust the new cult to them. It was natural that an existing association of the cities of any particular province, formed for quite other purposes, should take responsibility for cult observance at provincial level. It was a development not displeasing to Augustus. In the cities the cults of Augustus alone, which continued to flourish unsuppressed, and of Augustus and Roma, gave to the wealthy and influential friends of Rome opportunities to acquire prestige and distinction by holding the priesthoods. The advance of the worship from city to provincial level increased the distinction and widened the influence of the men who became provincial high priests. These were the same as those on whom Augustus relied in the secular government of the East.

As such cults became established a further development appeared. From the worship of the individual Augustus emerged the worship of the Augustan dynasty. Hereditary king-

75 Kantharos with handles in the form of twisted branches from the Hildesheim hoard; *Berlin, Staatliche Museen. Diam.* 10.5 cm, *height* (*with handles*) 11.1 cm.

76 Garden fresco from the Villa of Livia at Prima Porta; *Rome, Museo delle Terme.*

75

77

78

ship had been the common form of government in the Hellenistic East and dynastic cults had grown up beside those of individual benefactors. Earlier cults of Roman magistrates had been, naturally, of particular individuals not of families or dynasties. But now Augustus' family became the object of worship similar to that accorded to the families of Hellenistic kings. Nor was it merely those members with especial contacts with the East who were so honoured. Cults of Agrippa, Drusus, Gaius and Lucius Caesar might be regarded as the normal working of Eastern diplomatic practice. The dynastic nature of the cults is put beyond doubt by the inclusion of the imperial women, especially Livia and Julia. This development was advantageous to both sides. For Augustus it multiplied the ties which bound the peoples of the East to him; for the Greeks it opened new avenues to the patronage and benevolence of the Princeps himself. But further extension Augustus could not allow. The practice of establishing cults to individual Roman magistrates had survived from the Republic and their continued proliferation might end by stifling that of the imperial dynasty. Nor could Augustus permit other Romans thus to establish their *clientela* and advertise their glory in the East or anywhere else in the Roman world. That would infringe his own prerogative and erode the basis of his own power.

The last example of the establishment of a cult of a Roman governor in his own province is that for C. Marcius Censorinus, consul in 8 B.C. In A.D. 11 Augustus prohibited the paying of all honours, religious or secular, to governors by provincials both during their term of office and for a period of sixty days afterwards. The reason given was the necessity to control the corruption occasioned by demands for dedications, testimonies and eulogies. That was certainly true, but equally the measure was aimed at reducing the bestowal of excessive honours on Romans outside the imperial dynasty. Honorific inscriptions to Roman magistrates became more modest in tone under Augustus. The title 'benefactor', often literally true, was allowed, but the more extreme epithets such as 'saviour' or 'founder' (of a city) were restricted to Augustus and his family. But, significantly, the more extravagant honours continued to be bestowed unabated by Greeks on prominent fellow citizens. At Gytheum the Spartan C. Julius Eurycles received a cult in the latter part of Augustus' Principate. Even more remarkably, at Thyatira the high priest of the cult of Augustus, C. Julius Xenon, himself became the object of a cult. These were civilians and non-Romans who posed no challenge to the power of Augustus or to the imperial cult. When, after Augustus, Greeks from the East began to reach high office at Rome they too were debarred from receiving worship.

In Rome and the West matters stood very differently. The Roman state religion had no concept of divine honours paid to a man during life nor of deification after death. Romulus, the founder of the city, had been received among the gods, but no other mortal, dead or alive, had followed that path. The Roman general celebrating his triumph was, in a sense, a god for a day, but that position was by definition ephemeral; no cult accrued, no religious honours. The illustrious dead were accorded homage and honour, but in historical times the distinction was observed between mortality, however heroic, and divinity. When apparently religious honours were bestowed on the dead, they remained the concern of individuals and families. In no case was the cult of a pre-eminent man administered by public priests. The wholly excessive religious honours paid to Caesar reveal not an attempt to found a divine monarchy, but his insatiable appetite for distinction in the assertion of the prestige which was the ruling passion of his life and which finally undid him. Cicero might rail at the statue of Caesar with the inscription 'To the unconquered God' set up in the temple of Quirinus, the deified Romulus, but it was the secular honours which aroused the fury of Caesar's opponents. Nevertheless the enshrinement of Caesar in the state cult with his own priest, Antony, marked a radical departure from the normal course of Roman religion. Octavian after Caesar's death was quick to take advantage of it. In 44 B.C. and for long years afterwards Caesar's name and inheritance was Octavian's principal asset. The formal deification of the dead Caesar was, with the ratification of his adoption of Octavian and the implementation of the provisions of his will, the chief means by which Octavian asserted at the beginning the reality of his claim to be Caesar's heir. And for this reason

77 Simpulum with cast handle in the form of branches and leaf decoration from the Hildesheim hoard; *Berlin, Staatliche Museen. Diam.* 8.2 cm, *height* (with handle) 11.1 cm.

78 Silver dish with slightly raised flange decorated with acanthus scroll ornament in relief and edged with an ovolo, from the Hildesheim hoard; *Berlin, Staatliche Museen. Diam.* 31 cm.

Antony, who as priest of the cult had been most intimately concerned in the divine honours paid to Caesar during his life, opposed deification after his death as resolutely as he opposed recognition of Octavian's adoption. He capitulated only when it was brought home to him that not thus easily could Octavian be defeated. One of the first acts of the Triumvirate was indeed the deification of Julius Caesar.

It is clear why Octavian persisted. Below the official state religion there existed a wide range of belief and observance, some of it of great antiquity surviving from the old native Latin religion which had existed before the development of the Graeco-Etruscan state cult, some of it of much more recent origin deriving from the multifarious mystery religions of the East, none of it contained within the limits and distinctions of official religion. Whatever may have been the sacerdotal theory, the lower orders of society at Rome were prepared to pay divine honours to mortal men, dead and living. The common people of Rome, freedmen and slaves, were passionately devoted to Caesar and it was to their informal and popular religious attitudes that he appealed in his lifetime and Octavian after his death. Caesar's riotous funeral put the possibilities beyond doubt. The Roman mob seized Caesar's body, carried it to the Capitol and attempted to inter it in the great temple of Jupiter. His death, wrote Suetonius, translated him among the gods not merely on the lips of men passing decrees, but also in the firm conviction of the common people. The Roman masses had made up their minds on the question before Octavian had even started for Rome. He was not the man to neglect to profit by it.

Fig. 25 Coin: Denarius; reverse showing the comet which appeared during Octavian's celebration of the games in honour of Caesar's victory at Thapsus in 44 B.C., with the inscription DIVUS IULIUS. *London, British Museum.* (*Actual size*).

Useful as Caesar and Caesar's cult were to the revolutionary Octavian, he was a most embarrassing parent for Augustus, the restorer of legitimate and ordered government. In the years after Actium the Caesarian claims gradually receded. The historian Livy doubted whether Caesar's birth had been a blessing or a curse. Virgil in the *Aeneid* made the Sibyl exhort Caesar to lay down his arms before Pompey. From the Odes of Horace all mention of Caesar the man is absent; only the Julian Star, the comet, is there, the purified soul of Caesar. Nor would it do for Augustus to recall Caesar's religious extravagances even had they been to his liking. The Augustan cult which eventually developed at Rome was in sharp and striking contrast to the practice of Caesar. Although the Roman state cult did not admit the divinity of mortal men, there existed in private and family devotion the worship of the Genius and the Lares: the Genius represented, as it were, the guardian spirit of the master of the house, especially the generative power that secured the continuity of the family; the Lar was the spirit of the deified ancestor, the original founder of the family. In 30 B.C. the Senate, among many examples of adulation after Actium, decreed that at all banquets both public and private a libation should be poured to the Genius of Augustus. The custom became general. In every household Augustus' Genius received worship with the family's own private gods, the Lares. But there is no evidence that Augustus deliberately directed or encouraged the cult. Rather it took natural root as an expression of that Roman gratitude for peace and stability established and guaranteed by the person and power of Augustus to which Virgil and Horace bear eloquent testimony. Just as the Genius of a single family assured the continued existence of that family, so the Genius of Augustus assured the continuity of the sum of families which made up the Roman state.

When in 13 B.C. the Triumvir Lepidus died, the office of Pontifex Maximus became vacant and on March 6, 12 B.C. Augustus was elected to fill the vacancy by a multitude greater than Rome had ever seen before which flocked to the city from all Italy. The day was entered in the calendar as one of the most important dates in the Roman sacred year. As Pontifex Maximus Augustus should have lived in the official residence in the Forum. He, however, was unwilling to move and instead made part of his own house public domain. The effect was to make his private household cults part of the official state religion. From this time not only the Genius of Augustus but the Lares of his house, which hitherto seem to have been objects only of private devotion within his family, received public worship Shrines of the Lares were found not only in every Roman house but also at the crossroads of the city, where they represented the spirits of the dead in general.

Augustus restored these crossroad sanctuaries. In them were placed new statues of the Lares of Augustus, no longer vague spirits of the dead but the ancestors of his own house. And between the statues of the Lares he set another to his own Genius. Significantly the cult belonged especially to the lower classes, to slaves and freedmen. Each ward elected annually four freedmen 'masters' and four slave 'ministers' to manage the worship, which included the sacrifice of a pig to the Lares and of a bull, a potent symbol, to the Genius.

The cult of the Lares of his house and of his own Genius reveals most clearly and most accurately Augustus' view of his own position in the state and in religion. An Italian from a sacerdotal family, he appealed to a level of religious observance more ancient than that which appeared in the state religion of Rome. The devotion concerned the basic unit of society, the family, emphasizing the personal basis of his power and position. His Genius and his ancestors were worshipped as those of the master of the Roman world considered in this case as a single family. Poets in gratitude and flattery might hail Augustus in divine terms. But divinity was precisely what he studied to avoid. He could have had it for the asking from the lips of pliant senators and in the hearts of many men and his rejection of the opportunity was perhaps due as much to sincere belief as to crafty calculation. Not thus did he, the least prone of all men to self-delusion, conceive his role, but as the father of his family, the patron of his clients.

Fig. 26 *Above* Coin: Denarius, struck 29–27 B.C.; reverse showing Octavian as pontifex with oxen. This may refer to Octavian as a founder of cities, perhaps specifically as the (second) founder of Rome. The obverse has the head of Octavian's patron deity, Apollo. *London, British Museum. (Actual size).*

Fig. 27 *Below* Coin: Aureus, struck in Gaul; reverse showing the altar of Augustus at Lugdunum with the inscription ROM ET AVG. *London, British Museum. (Actual size).*

The worship of the Augustan Lares and Genius spread rapidly throughout Italy, where it acquired special characteristics. At Rome the centres of the official cult were in Augustus' own house on the Palatine, in the temple of Mars Ultor and on the Capitol. The sacrifices in these places were conducted by the pontiffs, with Augustus himself as Pontifex Maximus, the high priest of his own Genius. In Italy in addition to the crossroad shrines to the Lares and the Genius there arose special temples for the Genius, called Augustea, which had their own priests. The cult, in other words, became spontaneously a municipal concern, in which all members of a community, not merely its lower classes, participated. The importance of the municipal cult was increased by the creation of new offices, half-priestly and half-administrative, called Augustales. These were a more important group of freedmen than those who became 'masters' of the cult at the crossroads in all the towns. Once again we see Augustus' concern in the pursuit of stable social conditions to establish a proper dignity and status for all classes or, from another point of view, to multiply the ties which bound the members of all orders of society to him.

It is in the western provinces that the deliberate use of religion to secure loyalty to the Augustan regime is most noticeable. In the West, unlike the East, religious belief and observance were local and tribal; there was little development of religious diplomacy nor could spontaneous growth of the imperial cult be expected except in the highly Romanized areas. Elsewhere, since there existed few institutions which he could turn to his own use, Augustus himself established the cult observance at particularly important centres. In 12 B.C. at Lugdunum, which had become the commercial and political capital of the three Gallic provinces, there was erected a great altar to Rome and Augustus. Coins from the imperial mint at Lugdunum show its form (cf. figure 27). The central marble altar, decorated with imperial emblems, was flanked by two granite columns surmounted by statues of Victory and surrounded by statues representing the sixty-four Gallic tribes who had built the altar and who assembled every year to worship there. This is the only example under Augustus of anything like the eastern leagues becoming established in the West. The cult at Lugdunum was in charge of a high priest chosen each year from the most distinguished citizens of the province.

Gaul was now peaceful and settled and the Narbonese province in particular was highly Romanized and it is precisely from this province that most of the evidence for the Augustan cult in the Gauls comes. At Narbo itself the municipality dedicated in A.D. 11 an altar to the Numen (that is, the divine power, probably equivalent to the Genius) of Augustus. Annual sacrifice was offered on Augustus' birthday, a two days' festival, by three Roman *Equites* and three freedmen. Other celebrations took place on the anniversary of Augustus' first investment with power and on the date when he settled a dispute between the people of Narbo and the town council. Narbo also had an altar to the Pax Augusta, typical of many monuments erected by communities in Italy and the West which were suggested by and sometimes modelled on those put up at Rome by Augustus, his family and his closest associates. At Nîmes the inscription recording the gift of the Maison Carrée to the people by Agrippa was replaced by a dedication to Gaius and Lucius Caesar. Bacterrae had a special priest of Augustus and Vienne an altar to him erected by the inhabitants of a particular ward. The great altar at Lugdunum provided a focal point for the loyalty of the three pacified provinces.

Fig. 28 Coin: Aureus, struck c. 39 B.C.; reverse showing Aeneas carrying Anchises. The obverse shows the head of Octavian and the coin commemorates the descent of the Julian gens from Venus. Similar coins of the same date record the origin of Mark Antony's family from Anteon, a son of Hercules, and that of Lepidus from the Vestal Virgin Aemilia. *London, British Museum.* (*Actual size*).

The principle was extended when in about 9 B.C. a similar altar to Rome and Augustus was established at the tribal capital of the Ubii, the modern Cologne, whom Agrippa had earlier settled at their own request on the west bank of the Rhine. This altar formed a similar focus for the two Germanies. When in 2 B.C. L. Domitius Ahenobarbus advanced to the Elbe, he built an altar to Augustus on the banks of the river. This, however, had to be abandoned in the great retreat which followed Varus' disaster, but again the intention is clear. No such central monuments are known from Spain, unless the altar of Rome and Augustus at Tarraco was a provincial rather than a municipal one, nor did the Spanish provinces yet have leagues such as that which worshipped at the altar at Lugdunum. In all the western provinces the veteran colonists provided particular centres of devotion to the Genius of Augustus, which they would worship not so much as part of the general cult but specifically as the attendant spirit of their founder and patron. In Africa the cult was not organized until the reign of Vespasian, under whom provincial leagues or councils for cult purposes appear also in Narbonese Gaul and Baetica in Spain. Surviving Augustan dedications from Africa, in fact, present a curiously disorganized picture which suggests the exuberant enthusiasm of undirected devotion. At Carthage was established a colony of veterans. It possessed a temple and altar to the Gens Augusta (cf. plate 56), described as the first with this dedication. The altar shows the goddess Roma, the god Apollo and Aeneas escaping from Troy with his father Anchises and his son Ascanius. It was perhaps here that the colonists worshipped the Genius of Augustus as the founder and patron of the colony. At Lepcis Magna (cf. plates 44, 45, 47) there was a priesthood of Augustus held by natives and a chalcidium, colonnade, gate and road were dedicated to the Numen of Augustus.

The significant aspect of Augustus' religious policy is the extent to which it did not exist. There was no attempt to force the inhabitants of the Roman empire to conform to a system of belief and observance dictated from Rome. Still less did a megalomaniac emperor insanely extort from his subjects recognition of his own divinity. Native religions were, on the whole, left undisturbed. Towards them Augustus observed the traditional policy of the Roman Republic with regard to the cults of the provinces overseas and to foreign religions imported into Rome. Such rites were tolerated if they did not endanger public safety by fostering immorality, encouraging disorder or impeding the public cults of the state religion which ensured the peace with the gods. In the establishment of the imperial cult the initiative came almost everywhere from the provincials. In the East Augustus benefited from long established Hellenistic practices and intervened only when the cult was operating to regulate and direct it. In Rome and Italy the worship of the emperor's Genius, following easily and naturally from the traditional cult of the Genius of the head of the family, grew from an adulatory decree of the Senate. It was only after some eighteen years had passed and the cult was seen to be firmly established in private worship that Augustus made it part of public religion. It was only in the western provinces that the imperial cult was to any extent imposed from Rome and there, significantly enough, it failed to take firm root. Everywhere the purpose was political and diplomatic. The person of Augustus was the focus of the empire's loyalty and the imperial cult in one or other of its forms allowed the expression of this loyalty.

The Imperial Dynasty

8

If Augustus was serious about the stability of his new regime, then it was necessary to provide a peaceful and orderly transference of power on his death. The problem was sharp and immediate, for it was not mere fanciful flattery or the adulation of poets that his person alone stood against the chaos of civil war. His official position and titles he could not formally bequeath: they were in the gift of the Senate and the Roman People. But it was not here that his difficulty resided. In one sense there could be no successor to Augustus: his experience, the benefits he had conferred on Rome and the empire, the prestige and influence which flowed therefrom were unique. What Augustus could transmit to his successor were his own personal possessions. In the sense that the whole Roman world was his by right of conquest his successor, although he could not repeat the conquest, could receive the result in the form of the clientship of the whole empire. Hereditary patronage was an established feature of Roman political life. The allegiance of the clients of the great houses of the Republican nobility had descended regularly from father to son. Now there was one patron in place of many, one Princeps instead of a multitude of *principes*. The principle stood. Augustus could hand on precisely that network of extra-constitutional relationships which formed the bedrock of his power. To his clients, the urban proletariat, the provincials and, above all, the army, he could indicate to whom they must transfer their allegiance on his death. The struggle to establish himself as Caesar's heir had taught him much. His successor must be not only clearly and unequivocally designated, but also in position to take up his inheritance at once and without opposition. Adoption to supply an heir to political power had a long history in Republican Rome. The young Octavian had experienced its disadvantages. To put the issue beyond doubt his successor should be of his own family and his own blood so that Augustus' dynastic aspirations were dictated as much by public necessity as by private ambition. Nor was it a remote and distant contingency for which he had to provide. The precarious state of his health and the danger of conspiracy made it imperative that from the moment he emerged as master of the Roman world there should always be an heir apparent and that his identity should be known to Augustus' clients, civil and military. But there was much more to Augustus' dynastic policy than the discovery and designation of an heir. The remnants of the Republican nobility were his chief and natural enemies. No law or constitutional settlement could prevent their ambition. Augustus endeavoured to moderate their selfishness and to canalize their destructive vitality by binding them to himself, by so enmeshing them in matrimonial and dynastic alliances that their interests became identical with his own.

The central problem which faced Augustus was simple and insurmountable: he had no son. All his efforts turned, therefore, to finding a substitute son by adoption and matrimonial alliance. If his successor could not be of his own blood, the welfare of the state and his own ambition demanded that at least he must be of his own family. His nearest male relative was M. Claudius Marcellus, born in 42 B.C. to his sister Octavia by her first marriage to C. Claudius Marcellus, consul in 50 B.C. It was on Marcellus that Augustus set his first hopes. In 25 B.C. he was married to Augustus' only child, his daughter Julia. Marcellus' career was advanced by extraordinary dispensations so that he would become consul ten years before the minimum age allowed by law. It was not to the liking of the hard men who had fought with Octavian from Philippi to Actium and Agrippa in particular disapproved the advancement of the young Marcellus and his exorbitant honours. Rumour at Rome spoke of a breach between Augustus and his greatest marshal, so that when Agrippa left for the East his motives were variously conjectured as disgust and resentment or rejection and relegation by Augustus. Neither was true. In the East Agrippa continued to command provinces and armies. He was not, therefore, politically suspect. But the danger was plain enough. If Augustus persisted in pressing the claims of Marcellus and his own dynastic ambitions against the wishes of the leading men of his own faction, to whom he owed more than, perhaps, he cared to acknowledge, he would end by wrecking not merely his own party but the fabric of the state he was striving to establish. Marcellus' name had already been coupled with that of Augustus in the trial of M. Primus. An hereditary despotism masquerading behind the façade of the restored Republic, that was what Varro Murena and Primus attempted to suggest. Augustus retreated. When early in 23 B.C. he lay close to death, he handed over the state papers to his colleague in the consulship, L. Calpurnius Piso, and his signet ring to Agrippa, but there was no word of Marcellus. When he recovered he offered to read his will to the Senate to allay suspicions of monarchical designs, an offer that the Senate refused as it was not necessary for them to accept it. Whatever Augustus' intentions he was not free to indulge them without restraint while Agrippa, Statilius Taurus and the other great marshals survived; that would come later, as part of the process of the consolidation of the Principate.

Fig. 29 *Above* Coin: Denarius; reverse showing the heads of Augustus' daughter Julia and her sons Gaius and Lucius Caesar. *London, British Museum.* (*Actual size*).

Fig. 30 *Below* Glass cameo of Tiberius. *London, British Museum.* (*Actual size*).

Meanwhile Agrippa received a share in Augustus' power. Marcellus might eventually succeed but Agrippa had saved the restored Republic. His view was, as usual, hard, practical and correct. Peace and stability demanded a strong man at the centre of power and Augustus might die at any moment leaving Marcellus who was young, untried and, as yet, weak. His over-rapid promotion placed in jeopardy the safety of Rome and the empire. In the fullness of time and experience Augustus' ambitions for Marcellus might be realized, but now Agrippa was there as Augustus' acknowledged vice-gerent to guard against sudden catastrophe. As it happened Marcellus died prematurely, in 22 B.C., and Agrippa advanced in outward recognition of his power and position. From vice-gerent he became almost co-regent and with the increase in his constitutional powers and position went matrimonial advancement. His first wife was the heiress Caecilia Attica, daughter of Cicero's friend the magnate Atticus; his second was Marcella, daughter of Augustus' sister Octavia and sister to Marcellus; his third was Augustus' own daughter, Julia, whom he married in 21 B.C. after the death of her husband Marcellus. In 20 B.C. a son was born, named Gaius. Another, Lucius, followed in 17 B.C. In addition there were three other children, the younger Julia, Agrippina and Agrippa Postumus, brutal and vicious, born after his father's death in 12 B.C.

Augustus' dynastic plans had been thwarted by Agrippa and the death of Marcellus, but not annihilated. Agrippa had been right in 23 B.C., but ultimately Augustus was correct in his belief that full dynastic succession was necessary to ensure the greatest possibility of the orderly transference of power on his death. He, therefore, turned to the sons of Agrippa and Julia and in 17 B.C. adopted Gaius and Lucius as his own sons. But complications again arose. By his marriage to Livia Drusilla Augustus had penetrated the inner circle of the Republican nobility. She brought him no son of his own, no daughter either, but two boys by her previous marriage, Tiberius Claudius Nero and Nero Claudius Drusus. When Agrippa died in 12 B.C. Tiberius was forced to divorce Agrippa's daughter, whom he passionately loved, and marry Agrippa's widow (Augustus' daughter), to succeed to Agrippa's position in the ambitions and government of Augustus. In 12 B.C. Augustus was faced by a similar situation to that of eleven years before. The succession had to be assured, but the nearest heir was too young to succeed if death came to the Princeps soon. Therefore a trustworthy person connected with the imperial family must be marked out as a surrogate successor until the true heir was able to assume his position.

Like Agrippa Tiberius received the tribunician power in 6 B.C. for five years. Like Agrippa Tiberius became Augustus' great marshal, conquering Illyricum and in Germany extending the conquests of his brother Drusus. But Tiberius was not Agrippa. He was at all times and consciously a Roman aristocrat, ambitious, demanding recognition, sensitive in his pride and dignity, fundamentally out of sympathy with what Augustus was doing. To fight wars for another man's glory, to hold position as the temporary substitute for another man's children, never to know glory or position in his own right—this was the negation of aristocratic ambition. More, since 12 B.C. Tiberius had hardly been seen in Rome and in 6 B.C. there was no urgent reason for him to go to the East. Augustus did not fear Tiberius as a rival any more than he had feared Agrippa. He would not have put him in command of great armies if he had. But it seemed almost as if Augustus deliberately prevented Tiberius from acquiring personal popularity in the capital and without that Tiberius could never hope to succeed. At the same time Tiberius saw the young Gaius and Lucius Caesar honoured and advanced and from his mission to the East he withdrew against Augustus' threats and the pleading of Livia into exile on Rhodes, where he nourished himself, so it was said, on anger, pretence and secret lusts.

Fig. 31 Coin: Aureus; obverse showing the head of Gaius Caesar. The coin commemorates Augustus' adoption of Gaius in 17 B.C. *London, British Museum. (Actual size).*

Tiberius' withdrawal, however, revealed the full measure of Augustus' plans for Gaius and Lucius. In 6 B.C. although agitation arose that Gaius should be made consul, Augustus expressed public disapproval, but the following year the Senate voted that Gaius should become consul in five years' time, in A.D. 1, when he would be but twenty, thirteen years below the minimum legal age. The Equestrian Order hailed Gaius as their leader under the title Princeps Iuventutis. The two orders, Senatorial and Equestrian, which together formed the governing and administrative class of Rome, united in recognition of the adopted son of Augustus as their designated prince. Three years later the Senate voted that Lucius, Gaius' junior by three years, should have the consulate of A.D. 4. In 2 B.C. also a centurion set up at the colony of Acerrae in Campania an altar to the two princes with a verse inscription: 'When the time laid down by the gods demands you, Caesar, and you seek in heaven the throne from which you rule the world, let these two be here to govern this land in your place and rule us with their prayers favoured by the gods.' On his birthday in A.D. 1 Augustus wrote to Gaius and Lucius in a private letter, 'As you see, I have come through my sixty-third year, the common climacteric of all older men. I pray the gods that we all may be allowed to pass in safety whatever time remains for me with the republic in the most favoured state and with you performing heroically and succeeding to my position.'

Divorce, marriage and adoption Augustus manipulated as ruthlessly as any Republican noble. Males were rare in the line of Caesar and Augustus, but he had at his disposal a large number of female relations whom he distributed strategically among the members of his faction and the Republican nobility. The family tree (cf. front endpaper) makes Augustus' purpose patent. The imperial dynasty was to form an integrated whole and artfully locked into it were the leading families of the nobility. From them, again, reached out further matrimonial tentacles to embrace other men prominent in the government. Augustus in his search for stability put himself at the head of a faction of a type characteristic of the politics of the Roman Republic. It did not work. In 2 B.C. the scheme was shattered by the scandal which ruined Julia and five nobles and showed that the Republican nobility had not yet learned that its ambitions and intrigues were outdated. When Julia was banished Augustus did not consult her husband, the exiled Tiberius, but merely sent his daughter a divorce decree in Tiberius' name. Tiberius' pleas for a reconciliation with Julia found her father unrelenting as also did Tiberius' request for permission to visit his own relatives. He had abandoned them eagerly enough, replied Augustus; he must learn to do without them. Tiberius was in a perilous situation. In an attempt to escape attention he lived away from the sea, hoping thus to evade those who put in at Rhodes, but the exile had become an object of curiosity. No general or magistrate who was travelling anywhere in the East failed to call on him. This was sensible, for dynastic politics are subject to imponderable reverses and Tiberius' mother was the empress Livia.

Honoured and advanced at Rome, it remained to exhibit the heir apparent to the armies and the provinces. In 1 B.C. Gaius Caesar, consul designate and invested with proconsular power, visited the Danube and the Balkans and passed from there to the East, to settle under the care and guidance of M. Lollius the problem of Armenia. At Samos Tiberius came to pay his respects, but he received a cold reception, thanks, it was said, to the all-powerful Lollius who was Augustus' man. He had no reason to love the exile of Rhodes who had supplanted him in the Gallic command and had caused his labours to be depreciated, a trifling defeat magnified into irreparable disaster. It was Tiberius who was now a step away from disaster. Augustus suspected him of treasonable correspondence and the citizens of Nemausus threw down his statues and busts. At a private banquet in the presence of Gaius Caesar and Lollius a man offered to sail to Rhodes and return with the head of the exile. Tiberius' proud spirit was broken and he begged to be allowed to return to Rome. His mother supported him and Augustus agreed – if Gaius Caesar gave his consent and Tiberius lived as a private citizen. Gaius, now at odds with Lollius, consented and in the eighth year of his exile Tiberius came back to the capital. Meanwhile disagreement with Gaius Caesar was fatal for Lollius who fell suddenly from favour and died. The published reason was trivial, bribes accepted from foreign kings, but the real cause lies buried in the intrigues that surrounded the exile Tiberius. Lollius' successor as guide and counsellor of Gaius Caesar, P. Sulpicius Quirinius, managed to combine advancement by Augustus with assiduous cultivation of Tiberius for which in due course he had his reward. In A.D. 3 he, a new man from the small town of Lanuvium, got the Patrician Aemilia Lepida for his wife, perhaps through the machinations of Livia, and from Tiberius as emperor came the legateship of Syria and a state funeral with a public laudation in the Senate by Tiberius himself.

Tiberius lived at Rome, his life precarious. If Augustus spared him, Gaius, when he acceded to the imperial power, assuredly would not, but on February 21, A.D. 4, Gaius Caesar died as a result of wounds received on campaign in Armenia. Two years earlier his younger brother Lucius had succumbed to disease at Massilia. Augustus' hopes and ambitions lay in ruins. He was sixty-seven years old and would never see the succession established for one of his own blood. He turned to Tiberius in bitterness and frustration which endured for the rest of his life and which found memorable expression in the preamble to his will: 'Since cruel fortune has torn away from me my sons Gaius and Lucius, let Tiberius Caesar be heir to two-thirds of my estate.' Augustus adopted Tiberius from necessity, not choice. The safety of the state demanded that the succession be assured and there was no time to train another young heir. But the dynasty could still remain Augustan, not Claudian; Tiberius was compelled to adopt his brother's son Germanicus even though he had a son, Drusus Caesar, whose mother was Agrippa's daughter Vipsania. For Germanicus perpetuated the line of the Octavii as his grandmother was Octavia and he married Agrippina, daughter of Julia and Agrippa; he therefore transmitted the blood not merely of the municipal Octavii and Vipsanii but of the noble Antonii and Claudii to his son, the emperor Caligula. Thus Augustus reached out from beyond the grave to secure the imperial succession for one of his own blood, but not in the way he had intended; Germanicus himself died early in Tiberius' reign at the age of thirty-four, poisoned, it was believed, by Tiberius who also did away with two of Germanicus' sons. Augustus remained true to his ruthless self. Tiberius was to have what could not be avoided, the succession for himself, but of founding his own dynasty he was to be cheated. To rub the point home Augustus himself adopted the last surviving son of his daughter Julia and Agrippa, the brutish Agrippa Postumus.

It was not merely Augustus who needed Tiberius, but the Roman empire and not on some occasion in the future, but presently. Equipped once more with tribunician power and a special command, Tiberius was sent to the northern frontier. After two campaigns in Germany he passed to Illyricum to complete the conquest of Dacia. Instead he found himself faced with the most serious foreign war since those with Carthage, for thus the revolt of Illyricum was called. For three years he was occupied with the remorseless subjugation of that difficult country. Scarcely was that task completed when Varus and his three legions perished and Germany was lost. Tiberius did not return to Rome until A.D. 12 and these disasters sharpened the problem of the succession. What if Augustus died when Tiberius was far away on the frontiers fighting not for empty glory but for the security of the empire and of Italy? The succession must be quite clear without possibility

79 Fresco from Pompeii depicting Theseus and the Minotaur; *Naples, Museo Nazionale.* 88 cm × 96 cm.

80 The Pantheon in Rome showing the inscription of Agrippa, from an engraving by Giovanni Battista Piranesi; *London, British Museum. Height* (excluding the inscription) 48.1 cm, *width* 70.8 cm.

81 The Gemma Augustea; onyx cameo showing in the upper half the apotheosis of Augustus, who in the guise of Jupiter shares a throne with Roma while he is crowned by Oikoumene; *Vienna, Kunsthistorisches Museum. Height* 19 cm, *width* 23 cm.

M·AGRIPPA·L·F·COS·TERTIV
Portico AB, Acroterio CD, e Frontespizio E contemporanei per ciò che dimostra la interna
loro costruttura, ed aggiunti posteriormente da Agrippa alla parte rotonda del Pantheon, come si
ravvisa alle lett. DF, BG, H dalla medesima costruttura sciolta da quella del tempio. I Parte dell'acroterio interotta col frontespizio K sotto il Pontificato d'Urbano VIII per ridurre le parti CE, L, in forma di
torri ad uso di Campanile. M N circonferenza della finestra, per cui scende il lume nel tempio. O Colon-
ne solide di marmo Sienite di palmi 6 di diametro, e di 59 d'altezza 2, e 3 Canali e forami ne' quali
Piranesi F.
Veduta del P
oggi Chiesa di S.

...n d'Agrippa
...' Martyres
...rovansi bassirilievi di bronzo

erano incastrate le lettere di metallo della iscrizione d'Agrippa. P Iscrizione degl'Imperadori L. Settimio Severo, e Caracalla restauratori del Pantheon. Q Una delle pietre con forami a' quali anticamente raccomandavansi le corde della tenda che si spiegava per le solennità. RS Angolo del portico rifabbricato sotto il Pontificato d'Alessandro VII. T Gradi moderni. V Avanzi degli ornamenti di stucco de' quali era rivestita la circonferenza del Pantheon. XY Cornici ove si ravvisano alcune porzioni degli stucchi che coprivano e adornavano l'odierna rozzezza delle medesime...

83

84

Fig. 32 Sardonyx cameo signed by Epityndianos of the profile of Germanicus. *London, British Museum.* 2.1 × 1.8 cm.

of ambiguity or alternative focus of loyalty. Two personages survived who might provide such a focus: the younger Julia and Agrippa Postumus, the grandchildren of Augustus. In A.D. 7 Agrippa, whom Augustus had adopted only three years before, was banished to an island. The next year Julia followed her brother into exile on another conveniently barren island. Like her mother she was accused of immorality, but not only was her alleged lover put to death but her husband also. Conspiracy, warned by the fate of Agrippa Postumus, might be suspected and a convenient pretext for Augustus' ruthlessness.

Through disappointment and frustration, through death and conspiracy Augustus pursued his own ambition and the welfare of the Roman world. If the two could be combined, well and good; if they conflicted, Augustus was remorseless in the sacrifice of ambition and his own family. Suetonius recorded his prayer, 'May I be permitted to establish the commonwealth safely and securely on its foundation and to reap the fruit of that achievement, which is what I desire, so that I shall be called the author of the best possible government and that as I am dying I shall take with me the hope that the foundations of the commonwealth which I have laid will remain in their place unshaken.' Augustus' regulation of the succession shows how seriously he meant it and what it cost him.

The stage was thus cleared for the final act. In A.D. 13 Tiberius, receiving powers equal to those of Augustus in the provinces and over the armies, became almost co-regent—almost, but not quite, for Augustus still reserved to himself supreme authority in Rome and Italy. Together Tiberius and Augustus conducted a census but when their term of office ended in the middle of the year A.D. 14, Tiberius was to leave for Illyricum. Augustus' health, however, was finally failing. Men saw the signs and omens to confirm them. Despite dire predictions Augustus proposed to escort Tiberius in his journey to Illyricum as far as Beneventum. They reached Astura, where Augustus so far forgot his usual caution as to go on board ship at night, and he developed diarrhoea, from which further illness followed. Nevertheless he sailed round the coast of Campania to his villa at Capri, where he spent four days in rest and diversion. Then he crossed to Naples and there, although still suffering, watched the quinquennial games established in his honour. With Tiberius he travelled on to Beneventum and on his way back his illness grew worse. At Nola he took to his bed and called Tiberius back; after a long conversation with his heir he died there on August 19, A.D. 14, just thirty-five days before his seventy-sixth birthday. His body was escorted to Rome, where the senators vied with each other in proposing extravagant honours. Two eulogies were delivered, one by Tiberius before the temple of the Deified Julius, the other from the old rostra by Tiberius' son Drusus. The corpse was carried by senators to the Campus Martius and cremated, and a convenient ex-praetor swore that he had seen the soul of the Princeps ascending to heaven. Augustus' ashes, collected by the leading men of the Equestrian Order, were placed in his great Mausoleum.

Augustus had provided well. At Rome the consuls, the prefect of the praetorian cohorts and the prefect of the corn supply, the other magistrates, the Senate, soldiers and populace swore a personal oath of allegiance to Tiberius. This was the essence of the Principate. Tiberius had succeeded to Augustus' position as patron of Rome and the empire and all else was formality, the regularization of this personal and private power. Tiberius summoned the Senate, careful to define the right by which he did so as possessor of tribunician power. Augustus' will, made on April 3, A.D. 13, was read; Tiberius received two-thirds of his estate, Livia one-third, and both were instructed to assume his name, to be called Augustus and Augusta. It was the Roman custom to appoint besides the principal heirs secondary and tertiary heirs, who could inherit if those named above them died or refused to accept the legacy, a practice dictated originally by caution, which became a method of paying a posthumous compliment. Augustus' heirs in the second degree were Drusus, Tiberius' son, Germanicus and the latter's three sons. In the third degree he named many relatives and friends.

To the Roman People he left 40,000,000 sesterces; to his own two tribes 3,500,000; to the soldiers of the praetorian guard 1,000 each; to those of the urban cohorts 500 each; to the legionaries 300 each. These sums he ordered to be paid at once. He had kept the money

82 The Basilica Julia, Rome.

83 Detail of the *Monumentum Ancyranum*: part of the Latin text of the Res Gestae from the temple of Augustus and Roma, Ankara.

84 Detail showing the first lines of the Latin text of the Res Gestae from the temple of Augustus and Roma, Ankara.

by him in cash and ready, mindful of his own difficulties over the implementation of Caesar's will and that the rapid accession of wealth is a powerful suasion of loyalty. Payment of other legacies to individuals, some of which amounted to 20,000 sesterces, he directed to be delayed for a year on the ground that his estate was too small. He claimed that, although he had received 1,400,000,000 sesterces in the previous twenty years under the wills of his friends, he had spent nearly all of it, as well as what he had inherited from his natural and adoptive fathers, for the good of the commonwealth so that not more than 150,000,000 sesterces remained for his own heirs.

Augustus could still distinguish part of his vast wealth as his own personal and private possession. But rapidly under his successors, since the same officials handled the emperor's public and private finances and since the emperor ceased to render accounts for his receipt and expenditure of public funds, the distinction between his personal and his public wealth disappeared. All public revenues and property passed into the free disposal of the emperor and the emperor's private income and property became assimilated to the public funds he administered. Because the imperial revenues had become essential to the financial solvency of the state, all imperial property and income became attached to the imperial position. A man who became emperor automatically fell heir to the patrimony of all his predecessors and, in turn, lost all testamentary rights over his own private property, which was absorbed into the imperial estate.

In addition to his will Augustus left three other documents: the directions for his funeral; the text of the *Res Gestae* (cf. plates 83, 84); and a statement of account for the whole empire. This last was immensely detailed. It included the numbers of soldiers in service in all parts of the empire, the amount of money in the state treasury at Rome and the various provincial treasuries, details of arrears of taxation and the names of slaves and freedmen from whom even more detailed accounts could be obtained. The publication of such a balance sheet had been a regular practice of Augustus, but Tiberius in his later years gave up the custom and, after a short-lived revival under Caligula, they ceased permanently to be issued. It thus became impossible for anyone outside the imperial bureaucracy to check the emperor's income and expenditure.

Augustus was serious in his intention that the system he had established should survive the dangerous dislocation of his own death. Eighteen months before that event at last occurred he had given secret instructions to his secretary of state, Sallustius Crispus, that Agrippa Postumus should not survive him. The execution was performed speedily and summarily, but no report of the deed was made to the Senate and Tiberius is said to have delayed publication of the news of Augustus' death until he knew that Agrippa was dead.

Thus the imperial power passed. Not that Augustus' dynastic legacy was entirely happy; Augustus had known the essential truth about Tiberius, that fundamentally he was out of sympathy with the whole idea of the Augustan Principate. Tiberius' reluctance to assume the fullness of the imperial position and power, his failure fully to comprehend the true nature of the Augustan system, stemmed ultimately from his character as a Republican noble and issued finally in typically Republican irresponsibility. His successors were incompetent, bloodthirsty, corrupt, mad. It was not until Vespasian, another Italian new man, seized the imperial power that Rome and the empire received a ruler who in any way approached Augustus. Yet the variously unsatisfactory nature of the Julio-Claudians demonstrates conclusively the success and strength of the Augustan system. For all that a Caligula, a Claudius, a Nero could do by design or neglect, Rome, Italy and the empire continued to be governed, stability and security continued to be assured. If the history of the Julio-Claudian dynasty demonstrates the ultimate irrelevance of the personality of the individual emperor, the civil war which followed Nero's death reveals the necessity for the existence of the imperial position. Only thus could the great mass of empire stand in balance and chaos be prevented. The Year of the Four Emperors taught that for stability a strong monarchy, providing a central, visible focus of loyalty, was essential. Augustus had learned the lesson a century before.

Epilogue: The Personality of Augustus

Augustus, born the son of a small town Italian banker, passed by adoption into the Patrician clan of the Iulii, by marriage into the heart of the Roman nobility. Returning to Rome at the age of eighteen in the middle of one of the most murderous epochs of European history, he spent the next thirteen years in the remorseless pursuit of his own ambition through cajolery and bribery, fraud and treachery, murder and civil war until he emerged at the age of thirty-two as sole master of the Roman world. The last forty-five years of his life were consumed in the consolidation of his personal power through the establishment of peace and a stable social order, thus laying down the essentials of the form of government which was to rule Rome and her empire for the next three centuries. The achievements stand on record, a cause of wonder and surmise. The motives of the man and his personality remain elusive.

Various statues and portrait busts disclose how Augustus wished to appear. Most impressive is the great martial figure from Prima Porta (cf. plate 37). It represents Augustus as a general addressing his troops, but not as a dashing world conqueror. He is in his middle years, the face grave and firm, dedicated to duty. It is the note which recurs in other portraits, Augustus as the father of his country in peace and war, like Virgil's Aeneas. In the centre of the breastplate of the Prima Porta statue stands a scene depicting the return of the standards captured from Crassus and Antony by the Parthians. Above, under a figure representing the sky, is the sun in his chariot preceded by the dawn with the moon giving place to them. Below is Mother Earth with a cornucopia and two children, representing the prosperity which comes with peace. On either side are Augustus' two particular divine patrons, Apollo with his lyre and Diana on a stag.

The statue does not, however, represent Augustus as he really was. He was not in life so impressive a figure. Suetonius has left us a description: 'He was very handsome and most graceful at all stages of his life, although he cared nothing for any sort of finery. He was so uninterested in how his hair was dressed that he would set several barbers to work at once in a hurry and he would have his beard clipped at one time and shaved at another and while the barbers were working he would read or even write something. His expression both when he was talking and in silence was so calm and mild that a certain Gallic noble confessed to his own countrymen that it had softened him and prevented him from his plan of hurling Augustus over a precipice when, during a crossing of the Alps, he had been allowed to approach him under the pretext of talking with him. Augustus' eyes were clear and bright and he liked men to think that there was a sort of divine power in them. He was very pleased if anyone at whom he looked keenly lowered his face as if before the light of the sun. In old age he did not see very well with his left eye. His teeth were widely separated, small and dirty. His hair was slightly curly and yellowish. His ears were small. His nose protruded somewhat at the top and bent rather inwards at the bottom. His complexion was between dark and fair. He was short (although his freedman Julius Marathus, who kept his records, informs us that he was over five feet six inches in height), but this was disguised by the good proportions of his figure and only apparent if someone taller stood beside him. His body is said to have been spotty, with birthmarks scattered all over his chest and belly in the shape, arrangement and number of the stars of the constellation of the Great Bear and with rough places like ringworm caused by the itching of his body and the constant vigorous use of the strigil. His left hip, thigh and leg were not very strong and he often limped, but he tried to strengthen them by treating them with a poultice of sand and reeds. He also sometimes found the forefinger of his right hand so weak when it was numb and contracted with cold that he could scarcely write even when it was supported by a horn finger stall. He complained of his bladder, too, and was relieved of pain only after he had passed stones in his urine.'

As to Augustus' personal habits we have a deal of miscellaneous information. If we may believe everything we are told, which we assuredly may not, his sexual tastes and experience were wide and varied. He is accused variously of homosexuality (Julius Caesar and A. Hirtius are named as his lovers and it is alleged that he singed his legs with hot nutshells to make the hair grow more softly), the defloration of young virgins, who were brought to him from all over the empire even by his own wife, fornication with grown girls, whom his friends stripped and inspected before passing them on to him, adultery with respectable matrons, including the wife of an ex-consul taken from her husband's table under his very eyes and returned with her hair dishevelled and her ears blushing. When marriage and divorce are matters of high politics, affection naturally finds its expression in adultery. Sexual freedom in this respect was a prerogative of the Roman noble, female as well as male. As for the rest, the authorities for Augustus' scandalous practices, where they are named, turn out to be his enemies.

Physically, it is clear, the man was a coward. Wars and battles terrified him into illness. At Philippi he skulked in a marsh. His fear of thunder and lightning was such that he took with him everywhere a seal skin, reputed among the ancients to share with the laurel the distinction of never being struck by lightning, and at the first sign of a violent storm he would hide in an underground room, since it was believed that lightning did not penetrate more than five feet into the ground. Like most Romans of the upper class he was an hypochondriac. In winter he would wear an under vest, a woollen chest protector, four tunics, a thick toga and wrap his legs in wool. The sun he avoided in winter as in summer and never went out, even at home, without a broad brimmed hat. At all times he took the greatest care of his health. Roman hypochondria sprang not so much from idle self-indulgence as from a keen appreciation of the limitations of medical science. When pneumonia was almost invariably fatal, excessive precautions would be taken to avoid catching cold. Augustus had good reason to be solicitous for his health. His constitution was always weak and, throughout his earlier life at least, further debilitated by repeated illness. His disorders were, we may suspect, to some extent psychosomatic, the product of a nervous and timid temperament exposed to quite extraordinary strain.

Augustus was not an attractive person. He lacked glamour and panache, still more the vigorous masculinity of a Mark Antony. Puny, sickly, cowardly—the type is recognizable, as is the ruthlessness which often co-exists with physical cowardice. What commands admiration is high moral courage and a firm grasp of reality. It was no weakling who survived the Triumviral Period to achieve supreme power and to set in order the government of Rome and the empire. The politicians of the last age of the Republic had to an almost incredible extent lost contact with reality. To them nothing mattered but their power and prestige in the narrow arena of politics at Rome. To serve the fantasies of a handful of power-mad men the city, Italy and the provinces were alternately neglected and exploited. Augustus originated from Italy. Intent as any Republican noble on self-aggrandisement, he was free from the preconceptions of the Roman nobility as to the nature of power and the way to win it. He retained to the end the marks of his origin, epitomized in the frugality of his life, and it allowed him to establish his power on real foundations and in response to real aspirations. Augustus knew what men wanted and manipulated it to secure and maintain his power on a sure basis. What men wanted after a century of civil war and the rumour of war was peace, order and security, like the husband who wrote in the eulogy of his dead wife (the so-called *Laudatio Turiae*), 'The world was at peace, the republic was restored and at last we enjoyed tranquil and prosperous times. We hoped for children, which for some time fortune had withheld'. This above all Augustus knew, that the whole Roman world yearned for that peace in which children would be longed-for blessings not causes of worry and sorrow.

Here lay the surest guarantee of his own power. From this all else flowed, even his greatest achievements, the unity of Italy, the incorporation of its inhabitants into the Roman government, the creation, for the first time, of the Roman empire as an entity in place of the discrete provinces which had previously existed, and of the ever present danger of a split between East and West with the atrophy of the West, nourished by the revenues of the East, as the inevitable result. Rome once more became outward looking. The myopic Rome-centrism of the Late Republic gave place to a system in which Rome, Italy and the provinces interacted to the benefit of all. Not that all abuses vanished. Ambition and greed are immutable in human nature. But now retribution and redress were surer and swifter. Augustus had no cause to condone oppression and misgovernment by his agents. On the contrary, they and the unrest they caused struck at the basis of his power. Augustus was the patron of the whole empire, an informal and unofficial position which was personal to him, institutionalized under his successors. Under the Roman Republic there had been a multiplicity of patrons as there had been a multiplicity of *principes*. Now there was one Princeps and one patron, whose interests were identified not with the petty power struggle at Rome, but with the needs of the whole empire, for on those needs he had founded his power. It was a relation of mutual benefit and mutual obligation. To the provincials it opened informal channels of communication which they could now use with greater assurance that they would not be perverted to their detriment. Of the use they made of them the long list of official and unofficial representations to Augustus on every subject from the delinquencies of governors and disaster relief to the investigation of murder bears testimony.

How far these lines of communication protected the provincial depended largely on the provincial himself. It was up to him to initiate the approach to the emperor. Augustus had no thought of establishing a provincial police force or inspectorate. That lay quite outside the Roman tradition within which he worked. Above all he worked with the thoroughly Republican institution of *clientela,* concentrated and enhanced. The inhabitants of the empire were all clients of the emperor and a good emperor was he who best discharged the obligations of patronage. It was the emperor's duty to be personally concerned for every one of his subjects. A body of evidence attests Augustus' personal involvement in the details of administration, hearing petitions and giving judgement. A story told of the emperor Hadrian makes the point. When he was on a journey a woman approached him with a request. Hadrian replied that he had no time to attend to her and moved on. 'Then stop being emperor,' the woman shouted after him. The complex pattern of the ties of clientship which bound emperor and subjects in a nexus of mutual benefit was shattered in the military anarchy of the third century A.D. Its importance is indicated in that stability could be re-established only by a rigid social structure imposed by law and designed to replace the old informal patron-client relationship and to reproduce its benefits.

The Roman empire from the accession of Augustus to the death of Romulus Augustulus stands so solidly across the history of western Europe that it is easy to forget how nearly it did not happen. The ruling oligarchy of the Roman Republic pursued with explosive and destructive vitality their own power and glory, and if they had persisted in this attitude it would have caused the general disintegration of the Roman world, even if no external catastrophe had intervened to speed the process. But catastrophe was being prepared. In the last months of his life Julius Caesar, not knowing what to do with the power he had won, projected an invasion of Parthia. Had he lived to carry out this design, the result would almost certainly have been total defeat for the Roman army. That army, like all professional and highly trained forces, was progressively less effective as the conditions under which it had to fight and the enemy it faced departed from those for which it had been trained. Caught in the sands of the desert Caesar's army, like that of Crassus, would have been shot to pieces by the mounted archers of Parthia. The loss of the East would have followed and in the West civil war among the contenders for Caesar's power. Rome and all she stood for might well have gone down to chaos. That catastrophe Brutus and the Conspirators averted, but another appeared, less dramatic, more insidious, equally fatal: if the division of the Roman empire by Octavian and Antony, which corresponded to all the facts of geography and ethnology, language and culture, had been perpetuated, if the Roman world had split permanently into two exclusive parts, then the West would have died, cut off from the revenues of the East on which it depended for life. If Antony, not Octavian, had been victorious at Actium, the result would probably have been similar though slower. That this did not happen, that the Roman empire was not merely held together but fused into a new unity in which East and West supported each other in a relationship of mutual benefit, which endured to the foundation of Constantinople and beyond, was the greatest of all the achievements of Augustus. It is not a dim episode in the distant history of a remote people. The Age of Augustus forms a cardinal epoch in the history of all Europe and its effects and results are with us still today.

Fig. 33 The emperor Augustus from a contemporary cameo; *London, British Museum. Height* 12.5 cm.

Bibliography and Notes

The Ancient Sources: From all periods of the Augustan Age and from every part of the Roman empire there survives a mass of epigraphic material. The range of subject of these inscriptions is wide, from purely private dedications and epitaphs, among which must be mentioned the long and moving eulogy composed by a husband for his dead wife (sometimes known as the *Laudatio Turiae*), which incidentally reveals an act of cruelty by the Triumvir Lepidus, to the texts of laws, decrees of the Senate and edicts of Augustus. A wholly special place is occupied by the monumental record of his own achievements composed by Augustus himself and known as the *Res Gestae* or, more correctly, the *Index Rerum Gestarum.* This document has been known in some form since 1555 when the greater part of the text was discovered at Ankara on the walls of a mosque which had once been the temple of Rome and Augustus in the Roman town of Ancyra in the province of Galatia. The *Monumentum Ancyranum,* as this text is called, consists in the original Latin version with a Greek translation. Another copy, with both Latin and Greek texts, but in a much more fragmentary condition, was found at Apollonia in Pisidia and a third version of the Latin text only, again much damaged, was discovered in 1914 at Pisidian Antioch. Comparison of these three inscriptions and of the Greek and Latin texts has enabled the words of Augustus to be recovered in their entirety and with a high degree of certainty. According to the *Res Gestae* itself it was composed by Augustus between June 27, A.D. 14, and his death on August 19 of the same year. But this can refer only to a revision of an already existing text since Augustus' will, dated April 3, A.D. 13, already mentioned it. In his will Augustus directed that this record of his achievements should be engraved on two pillars of bronze set up at the entrance to his Mausoleum. Both the manuscript copy and the original inscription have long since perished. What we have are three examples of provincial copies which were set up in many, if not all, of the major cities of the empire. That the Greek texts from Ancyra and Apollonia are identical discloses an official translation and argues official inspiration in their erection. The inscription from Antioch probably never had a Greek version. The place was a colony of Roman citizens.

The most important epigraphic documents, including the *Res Gestae,* have been collected by V. Ehrenburg and A. H. M. Jones, *Documents Illustrating the Reigns of Augustus and Tiberius* (2nd ed., 1955). The *Res Gestae* has been elaborately edited by Jean Gagé (2nd ed., 1950) and with an introduction, commentary and English translation by P. A. Brunt and J. M. Moore (1967). The fragments of Augustus' other works will be found in H. Malcovati, *Caesaris Augusti Operum Fragmenta* (3rd ed., 1948). For the Augustan coinage, which is frequently historically illuminating, see H. Mattingly, *British Museum Catalogue of the Coins of the Roman Empire,* vol. I; H. Mattingly and others, *The Roman Imperial Coinage,* vol. I; M. Grant, *From Imperium to Auctoritas*; C. H. V. Sutherland, *Coinage in Roman Imperial Policy.*

The literary sources from which the history of the Age of Augustus is to be reconstructed are poor. They are most copious for the least important part, the period immediately after Caesar's death, and worst for the thirty-seven years that followed the constitutional settlement of 23 B.C. and which are most properly to be regarded as the Age of Augustus. For the twenty-one months between the death of Caesar in 44 B.C. and his own murder on December 7, 43 B.C. we have the evidence of Cicero. In the fourteen Philippic Orations, which he delivered or published in 44 and 43 B.C. and which are named after the speeches of the Athenian orator Demosthenes against the king of Macedon, Cicero mounted a massive attack upon Antony and his policies. In addition we have Cicero's letters to Atticus and other friends and a few of their replies. Neither the speeches nor the letters are works of sober history. They were produced by a man whose position in these months became increasingly isolated, his hopes increasingly forelorn, his ideals increasingly irrelevant. But they are invaluable not merely for the mass of detailed information they contain but also for the unique insight they give into the flavour and atmosphere of the period.

It was not only by his own words posthumously published in the *Res Gestae* that Augustus sought to mould and organize men's attitudes to himself and his regime. The name of Maecenas has come down to us as that of an ideal patron of the arts. But the patronage of that great connoisseur was not founded on disinterested love of literature. His task was to inculcate in the minds of the population of Rome and Italy correct attitudes and proper sentiments. To this end he gathered his famous circle of poets, in which he wrought better than he knew. It included Virgil and Horace. Horace was born on December 8, 65 B.C., of slave stock, his father being a freedman, at Venusia on the border of Apulia and Lucania. It is indicative of the growing importance and awareness of the class to which Horace's father belonged and which still lacked the secure place in society and administration that Augustus was to give it, that he was able to send his son to Rome to be educated by Orbilius, among whose pupils were the sons of senators and business magnates. Education, which at Rome was exclusively literary and rhetorical, was an avenue of advancement for the outsider, especially if he attracted the attention of a powerful patron. The great political figures of the Roman Republic practised literature themselves and encouraged it in others and to have his own circle of writers augmented a noble's prestige and could also be politically advantageous, publicity and propaganda being a large part of politics. Horace took his opportunities seriously and at the age of about twenty went to Athens, the centre of higher education in the Mediterranean world. Thither after the death of Caesar came M. Brutus to recruit the army that was soon to face Octavian and Antony. Horace took service as a junior officer and at Philippi saw the last desperate stand of the Republican oligarchy and the passing of a whole way of life. He threw away his shield and ran.

The years after Philippi were disastrous for Italy. When Horace returned in 42 B.C. his father was dead, his farm confiscated, but with what money he had he bought a clerkship in the treasury. Now in dire poverty he began to write verse and somehow he met Virgil and Varius Rufus who brought him to the notice of Maecenas, who recognized Horace's talent and his usefulness. For the next thirty years until his death on November 27, 8 B.C., a few months after that of his patron, Horace was able to devote himself without financial or material worries to the writing of poetry. The range of his poetic achievement was wide. His earliest work was the *Epodes*, a collection of seventeen poems written between 41 and 31 B.C. and published in 30 B.C. They fall into three main groups: bitter and venomous lampoons, erotic and miscellaneous verse and poems celebrating political events. Two of the last group are concerned with the battle of Actium, at which apparently Horace was present, and another graphically expresses the disillusion of Italy at the shattering of the precarious peace by the Perusine War, waged by L. Antonius against Octavian in 41 B.C. Concurrently with the *Epodes* Horace was working on poems of a different kind, the *Satires* in hexameter verse, of which the ten poems of Book I were published in about 35 B.C. and the eight poems of Book II about five years later. In subject matter they are extremely diverse, treating of matters of autobiography, gastronomy, moral philosophy and literary criticism among much else. Almost the only feature lacking is satire as we understand it, for the Latin word meant merely a miscellany. Between 31 and 23 B.C. Horace composed what he regarded as his greatest achievement, the first three books of the *Odes*. Then he returned to the type of poetry he had already attempted in the *Satires* and in 20 B.C. published the twenty poems which form Book I of the *Epistles*. In subject matter they are almost identical with the *Satires*, although perhaps more strongly philosophical in tone, while in metre they show a surer command and a subtler appreciation of the varied possibilities of the Latin hexameter. Horace was fond of the verse letter; he employed it later for three essays in literary criticism, the two poems addressed to Augustus and Florus, which together make up Book II of the *Epistles*, and the long hexameter letter to a certain Piso and his two young sons, which is erroneously called the *Ars Poetica* (it is not a systematic handbook of poetic technique). Having been a penniless deserter from the defeated army of Brutus Horace became the Poet Laureate of the Augustan regime. When in 17 B.C. Augustus celebrated the Secular Games inaugurating a new epoch in the history of Rome, it was Horace who composed the solemn hymn sung from the temples of Apollo and Diana. Augustus' command that he should celebrate the Alpine campaigns of Drusus and Tiberius in 15 B.C. produced the fourth Book of the *Odes*. The fourth and fourteenth poems of this collection are devoted to the achievements of Drusus and Tiberius respectively; odes five and fifteen praise the blessings of Augustus' rule. But Horace did not write to flatter. 'I will fear neither civil war nor violent death while Caesar rules the earth' (*Odes* III, 14, 14ff.). Again and again the theme returns in Horace's poems. He knew from harsh experience how narrow had been the escape from chaos.

Among the poets of the Augustan Age, or indeed among all the poets of Latin literature, Horace gives place to one and one only, namely Virgil. For in Virgil perfect mastery of poetic technique and complete control of language reacted with high seriousness of mind and profound and sensitive humanity to produce certainly the greatest poet of Classical civilization, whether Greek or Roman, and possibly the greatest poet in the whole of European literature. He came from Andes near Mantua in what was, when he was born on 15 October 70 B.C., not even part of Italy but a province of the empire, Cisalpine Gaul. His family was humble and he studied at Cremona and Milan before going south to Rome. There he studied rhetoric, medicine, astronomy and philosophy and at the same time began writing verse. In 42 B.C. Virgil, like so many other small Italian farmers, lost his land in the great demobilization after Philippi. It was then he began work on the earliest of the verses on which his fame rests, the *Eclogues*, a collection of ten pastoral poems which shows only rare glimpses of the splendour that Virgil was later to achieve. With two exceptions the *Eclogues* are modelled closely on the *Idylls* of the Greek Theocritus. But beside the full acceptance of the artificial conventions of the pastoral idiom the poems already display one of Virgil's strongest traits, a deep sense of Italy. Moreover, contemporary events and contemporary personages, the latter sometimes disguised as Greek shepherds, are introduced. The tenth *Eclogue* is concerned with a shepherd, certainly Virgil himself, who has been ejected from his farm near Mantua to provide land for discharged veterans and the first describes the joy of a dispossessed farmer restored to his land after an appeal to Octavian. The longing of Italy for peace and security comes clearly through the conventional form. 'A god has created these peaceful conditions for us', says Tityrus in *Eclogue* I. Like Horace, Virgil knew from experience the value of Augustus' gift to Italy. By 37 B.C. Maecenas' circle of poets had been formed. Horace describes how he and Virgil, Varius Rufus and Plotius Tucca travelled with Maecenas to Tarentum to negotiate one of several ephemeral pacts between Octavian and Antony. From that year Virgil was engaged on the composition of the four books of the *Georgics*. Again the basic form was Greek, the hexameter didactic poem. Virgil's subject was agriculture and husbandry, on which there was already a considerable prose literature in Latin. Largely written in honour of Maecenas and containing direct eulogies of Octavian, to whom Virgil recited the poem in 29 B.C., the *Georgics* have obvious reference to the establishment of peace and the revival of agriculture in Italy, but what in other hands might have become tedious pedantry or crude propaganda is transformed into grandeur by Virgil's passionate love of Italy and the sheer perfection of his verse. The *Georgics* were followed by the *Aeneid*, the writing of which occupied Virgil until his death on September 20, 19 B.C. The work was begun at the suggestion of Augustus, who wrote from Spain in 26 and 25 B.C. to urge Virgil to send him the draft or at least part of the poem. Virgil refused, but after the death of Marcellus in 23 B.C. he did recite Books II, IV and VI to Augustus and his sister Octavia. On Virgil's death the poem was complete but unfinished. He had instructed his literary executors Varius Rufus and Plotius Tucca that if he died before he had finished the work it should be destroyed, and Augustus himself intervened to save the *Aeneid*. Romantic preconceptions distort judgement and inhibit understanding of the *Aeneid* as of few other works of literature, for it is the least romantic of all poems. Its true subject, expressed through the story of the trials and wanderings of a minor Trojan hero to Italy where he is to found Rome, is the universal laws of human society by which man may live with man in peace and security and in which the unity and stability of the group take precedence over the desires and ambitions of the individual. Dido and Turnus, the leader of Italian resistance to Aeneas, command our sympathy falsely, for both typify in different ways the self-assertive and self-satisfying individualism which ends by destroying human society. Like all the greatest works of art the *Aeneid* exists at many levels and reveals itself, to use C. S. Lewis' striking image, 'like an onion: except that as you go in and in, each circle is larger than the last'. At one level the *Aeneid* is the story of the preliminaries to the foundation of Rome; at another, the epic of Rome herself, the glorification of all her past greatness; at yet another, the celebration of the new era inaugurated by Augustus. At its heart it is about the whole human condition everywhere and at every time as expressed in the establishment of ordered and civilized society; if the least romantic, the *Aeneid* is the most deeply human of all poems.

Horace and Virgil were the two poets of the age most engaged by the achievement of Augustus. Another of Maecenas' protégés, Sextus Propertius, again an Italian, from Umbrian Assisi, was, despite two elegies addressed to his patron and two in praise of Augustus, roused to passion only when he wrote of his love affair with Cynthia. There were, too, other literary circles than that of Augustus' minister. The Republican tradition survived, for instance, in the coterie of M. Valerius Messalla Corvinus, himself the author of treatises on grammar and style. Messalla's poets are represented by the body of verse which has come down to us under the name of Tibullus. Many of these poems are undoubtedly by Tibullus himself but others were composed by the pseudonymous Lygdamas, by Messalla's ward Sulpicia and by the unnamed perpetrator of the tasteless and bombastic Panegyric of Messalla. The concern of all the poems is personal and the standard of achievement varies from the exquisite artistry of Tibullus himself through the amateurishness of the learned lady Sulpicia to the bare competence of the Panegyric. Various details in the Tibullan corpus illuminate the social life of the Augustan Age, and more illumination comes from the verse of Ovid. Ovid, like most Roman poets, came from Italy, from Sulmo in the territory of the Paeligni, but unlike Horace and Virgil he was born in comfortable circumstances and into a family of some social consequence, a circumstance in which he took persistent and wholly unreasonable delight. Disdaining a career of public service, he maintained himself comfortably at Rome, marrying three times, enjoying fashionable society and writing verse, an idyllic existence which was rudely terminated when he was in some mysterious way implicated in the disgrace of Augustus' granddaughter Julia and peremptorily banished to Tomis on the Black Sea. It is difficult entirely to acquit Augustus of a certain malice in his choice of the place of exile for the sophisticated and worldly Ovid; Tomis was a place of disgusting climate inhabited by half-breed Greeks and barbarian Getae and constantly in danger from the wild tribes across the Danube. Despite this environment the verse still flowed from him. Ovid's was a small and shallow talent, remarkable only for the immense and dangerous facility of his versification, especially in the elegiac couplet. His output was enormous on such subjects as erotic technique (the *Ars Amatoria* contributed to his banishment: self-indulgent individualism was contrary to Augustus' image of the age), cosmetics, mythology, the calendar and religion of Rome and his own troubles in exile.

The Age of Augustus produced a large body of literature, of which only the merest fraction has survived. We have lost much that would have entertained and instructed: the *Histories* of C. Asinius Pollio, for instance, who abandoned Antony in the civil wars and retained until his death in A.D. 5 a detached and critical attitude to the regime established by Augustus; the poems of C. Cornelius Gallus, Augustus' first governor of Egypt until he suddenly fell from favour and committed suicide. Virgil knew him and admired his work, but only half a line now survives. There were the libellous lampoons of Cassius Severus, whose origin was low, whose life was evil, whose appearance was that of a gladiator, and who assailed without restraint or distinction the important and illustrious of both sexes. Of the great Augustan worthy Paullus Fabius Maximus he said, 'You are like a clever man, like a handsome man, like a rich man: only one thing you are not like but are in reality—dregs'. Paullus had his revenge and prosecuted Cassius at an inquiry ordered by Augustus, as a result of which Cassius was condemned and banished to Crete, which proved neither remote nor uncomfortable enough to abate the nuisance, and the emperor Tiberius removed him to the barren rock of Seriphus. Cassius' works were burned, as was the *History* of Aulus Cremutius Cordus, written under Augustus and Tiberius. Cremutius resolutely refused to glorify Augustus. Although he bewailed the civil wars, and, indeed, no man could avoid it, the authors of the proscription, Octavian, Antony and Lepidus, he proscribed in his pages to all eternity. His heroes were Cicero, Brutus and Cassius, whom he described as the last of the Romans. Sejanus, under Tiberius, had him prosecuted and Cremutius recognizing that conviction was inevitable, killed himself. His *History*, however, survived its author's death and the burning of his manuscript as his daughter preserved a copy. Had we these works today, and the list could be greatly extended, they might not have altered our judgement of the Augustan Age but they would certainly have added depth to our understanding. The memoirs of Q. Dellius ought to have been particularly fascinating reading. He was, before he deserted to Octavian, Antony's go-between with Cleopatra.

One loss especially tantalises, that of the later books of Livy's *History*. Livy came from the same part of the Roman world as Virgil, from Cisalpine Gaul from the town of Patavium, and from there he followed the regular path to Rome in pursuit of fame and fortune. We know little of his life. He seems to have established himself in the capital as a professor of rhetoric and at the age of thirty, in 29 B.C. he began the work which was to occupy him until his death in A.D. 17, a vast history of Rome from the foundation of the city to his own times in no fewer than 142 volumes. Of these only thirty-five now remain, the first ten and Books XXI–XLV which treat the war with Hannibal and the wars with Macedonia and Syria. The subject matter of the lost volumes is known, with the exceptions of Books CXXXVI and CXXXVII, from brief epitomes made in late antiquity from an already abridged text. These reveal the expected fact that the closer Livy came to his own times the fuller became his treatment. The first two and a half centuries, according to the traditional chronology, of Roman history filled only one book; the thirty-five years between the death of Caesar in 44 B.C. and that of Drusus in 9 B.C., where the work terminated whether by design or the accident of the author's death, required no less than twenty-six books. The loss of so detailed an account is greatly to be regretted. Livy's attitude to Augustus is a matter of speculation, though the extant books show him to be a traditionalist. As Professor R. S. Conway put it, 'It is to Livy more than any other writer that we owe our conception of the Roman national character'. The natural supposition is that Livy's general approach was that which Augustus himself publicized in his own Forum: the regime of Augustus formed the culmination and consummation of the achievements of the great heroes of the Republic. The writing of history at Rome was traditionally a political exercise by political men. Livy, however, stood outside this tradition of historiography, as he was a scholar, remote from and inexperienced in public affairs. Nor did he conform to the peculiar conventions of style and vocabulary which had evolved for senatorial history. He undertook his *History*, as the prologue makes clear, not as a contribution to politics, but as a refuge alike from political remedies as from political ills. Although he was familiar with the household of Augustus and encouraged the young Claudius to write history, Livy's attitude to the Augustan regime was one of detachment. The references to Augustus in the extant books of his *History* are factual and without flattery. On one occasion Augustus took the trouble personally to inform Livy of the official version of the story of Cornelius Cossus and the *spolia opima*, which had become a matter of contemporary relevance. Livy used the information in the most damaging and revealing manner; he recorded it, with due acknowledgement of its source, in a footnote and allowed his own account to stand unaltered. Augustus on another occasion called him a Pompeian, but the truth went deeper than mere praise of the great Pompey. As we have it, Livy's *History* is an implicit celebration of the ideal of the Republican aristocracy, which the Principate of Augustus had abolished.

Two contemporary Greek writers also provide valuable information. Strabo, an Asiatic Greek from Amassia in Pontus, was an independent spirit, admiring the Romans in a detached way for their empire but never entering Roman service, although he visited Rome at least three times, from 44 to 35 B.C., again four years later and lastly in 7 B.C. He wrote an historical work in forty-seven books, which is lost, and a *Geography* in seventeen books, which has survived. This work, after an introduction on geographical method and previous theory, consists in a survey of the Mediterranean world, country by country, from Spain in a clockwise direction round to North Africa. To the ancients geography was a difficult and rebellious subject in which theory and authority were considered surer guides than the uncertainties of personal observation. Strabo's *Geography* is a curious mixture, typical of the genre, of the opinions and observations of previous writers, some of which were clearly no longer valid when he wrote, but where he recorded what he himself had seen, his work is of great value.

Nicolaus of Damascus was born into a distinguished

Greek family about 64 B.C. He twice visited Rome with Herod the Great, at whose court he was an adviser from about 20 B.C. to 4 B.C. On Herod's death he retired into private life although he did represent Herod's successor, Archelaus, at Rome. His literary output was extremely varied, including tragedies and comedies, works on philosophy and natural science, a universal history in 144 books which went down to at least 4 B.C. and an autobiography. His importance for the historian of the Age of Augustus resides in his panegyrical biography of the early life of Augustus.

Only one Latin historian gives anything approaching a connected account of the whole of the Age of Augustus. C. Velleius Paterculus was from a Campanian military family; his paternal grandfather had served in Pompey's army, his father with the cavalry in Germany. Velleius himself saw service in the armies of Augustus in Thrace and Macedonia and in 1 B.C. was a member of the entourage of Gaius Caesar when the young prince visited the East. He then seems to have been taken up by the future emperor Tiberius, under whom he served for eight years in Germany and Pannonia. It was on Tiberius' recommendation that Velleius was elected to civil office, the quaestorship in A.D. 6, and in the first full year of Tiberius' reign, A.D. 15, he was praetor. Like many military men Velleius occupied his retirement with writing history. His work was dedicated to his friend M. Vinicius on his attaining the consulship for A.D. 30 and reviewed the history of Rome from its beginning to that year. The earliest part, from Romulus to the battle of Pydna in 167 B.C., has perished, but the remainder survives, becoming increasingly detailed as it approaches the author's own lifetime. Velleius was clearly impressed by his old commander, Tiberius, and highly sensible of the benefits of the Imperial system, but he was a serious writer, with pretentions to be a stylist, and his work is not to be dismissed as mere adulation.

The biographer Suetonius is, perhaps, the most famous of all the writers on Augustus. Almost alone of the authors we have considered he was probably born in Rome, in about A.D. 69, the son of an officer in a legion at Bedriacum. Although he practised law, he did not take the normal step from that profession into political life, nor were his inclinations military; when the younger Pliny secured for him an appointment as military tribune, Suetonius had the post transferred to a younger relative. In so far as Suetonius had any career, it seems to have been in the imperial civil service, for sometime between A.D. 119 and 122 he became secretary (*ab epistulis*) to the emperor Hadrian, but from this post he was dismissed, apparently for some breach of court etiquette, and seems to have retired into literature. Suetonius' literary production was exceedingly miscellaneous and has nearly all vanished, though we know by title works *On Famous Whores, On the Kings, On Public Offices, On Greek Terms of Abuse, On Critical Symbols in Books, On Cicero's De Re Publica,* and a *History of Public Games.* Beside these works, whose titles explain their subjects, we know also of a book called *Roma* and of another called *Pratum* (or *Prata,* apparently a miscellany in several volumes). There was also an historical work of doubtful scope and title and to catch any subject which had happened to escape Suetonius' wide-ranging pen a book entitled *On Sundry Things.* About his collection of lives of famous literary men we know rather more, since a few survive, variously abridged and interpolated by later writers, but it is on his *Lives of the Twelve Caesars,* from Caesar to Domitian, published in about A.D. 121 and complete apart from the loss of the first few chapters of the biography of Julius Caesar, that Suetonius' fame and influence rests. Biography was in antiquity a literary genre in its own right with its own rules of style and of selection and arrangement of subject matter, which had little in common with those prescribed for historiography. Suetonius was a scholar in the ancient sense (history was not then generally regarded as a scholarly activity), antiquarian and rhetorical. In his *Lives* he selected and arranged his information just as he would have done in a work on grammar. His purpose was to give a full picture of the personality of his subject, and consequently important historical and political events tend to be dismissed somewhat summarily. On the other hand, his interpretation was not distorted by any moralistic purpose: the *Lives of the Caesars* do not exist to point a moral or to inspire by imitation or revulsion the pursuit of an ideal life. That Suetonius was not confined by the strict restraints of ancient historiography can be valuable since it allowed him to quote verbatim on occasion the texts of documents and the words of individuals. For the composition of his *Lives* he had at his disposal a great mass of material now lost, especially literary compositions of history or biography and the imperial archives, to which as Hadrian's secretary he had easy access. His handling of this material was scholarly not critical. Although he examined conflicting statements carefully and although his information was based firmly on evidence, he had no conception of the proper and scientific evaluation of that evidence. Thus, while Suetonius himself was quite impartial, his estimate of the emperors is frequently biased. Moreover he earned for himself a quite unjustified reputation as a prurient scandalmonger. Nevertheless his *Lives* are among the most readable of all the products of ancient literature and preserve details of personality and character which no other source transmits. Not infrequently too, such is the deplorable state of our tradition, Suetonius is our only or our major authority for important historical events.

The Alexandrian Greek Appian, when an old man under the Roman emperor Antoninus Pius, wrote a military history of Rome, which is peculiar in that the wars are recounted not in a straightforward chronological fashion but by ethnographic and geographic divisions. The link between the wars of the Roman Republic and those of the Imperial period is provided by the five books of the *Civil Wars* which describe the progress of internal strife at Rome from 133 to 35 B.C. Although the tradition on which Appian drew went back ultimately to early or contemporary sources, notably for our period to the historians C. Asinius Pollio and Livy, and to the Memoirs of Augustus himself and those of Valerius Messalla, he did not consult them directly but employed a tendentious literary composition of late Augustan or Tiberian date which he adapted to his military preoccupation and geographical form. Interested solely in war and the horrors of war, Appian shares the general ignorance of imperial historians of Republican constitutional and political conditions. Nevertheless, that part of his *Civil Wars* which treats the period after the death of Julius Caesar is full, the rest of this section of his *History* being merely preliminary to it, and preserves much valuable material to supplement and sometimes to correct other writers on these years.

Cassius Dio came from Nicaea in Bithynia and enjoyed a distinguished career under the Severan dynasty. His father had been governor of Cilicia and of Dalmatia. Dio himself entered the Roman Senate under Commodus, became praetor in A.D. 193 and consul before A.D. 211, and he achieved the distinction of a second consulate in A.D. 229, when his colleague was none other than the emperor himself, Alexander Severus. Among many other works he composed a *Roman History* of fashionably vast extent from the beginning of the city to his own second consulship. Comparatively little survives, but Books XXXVI to LIV, which cover the period from 68 to 10 B.C., are fully preserved and Books LV to LX, from 9 B.C. to A.D. 46, exist in abbreviation. Dio's chief fault is that of Appian and all other imperial historians: he neither knew nor understood Republican political and constitutional conditions. Therefore he interpreted the events of the Augustan Age from his own experience of the developed imperial absolutism of the third century A.D. Moreover, his purpose was, of course, literary, not scientific; details and technicalities are, if possible, avoided and the style is highly rhetorical. His work is, however, of considerable importance, especially for the various Augustan constitutional settlements.

Such are the principal ancient sources for the Age of

Augustus. Many other writers provide additional information, e.g. Tacitus, Seneca, the elder Pliny, Plutarch in his *Lives* of late Republican personages.

Modern Treatments: The Age of Augustus is treated in all the general histories of Rome. The fullest treatment, although now outdated in detail, is in volume X of the *Cambridge Ancient History*. Monographs on Augustus are by Mason Hammond, *The Augustan Principate,* F. B. Marsh, *The Founding of the Roman Empire,* T. Rice Holmes, *The Architect of the Roman Empire.* All these, although they are still very useful and informative, have been to some extent superseded by Ronald Syme, *The Roman Revolution.*

Chapter I. On the Octavii see Suetonius, *Augustus,* 1ff; R. M. Geer, *American Journal of Philology,* 55, 1934, 337ff; D. C. Earl, *Latomus,* 19, 1960, 657ff. On Velitrae: Lily Ross Taylor, *The Voting Districts of the Roman Republic,* 54f; 66; 83; 214; 275; punishment in 338 B.C.: Livy, VIII, 14, 5–7; the Volscian inscription is published in E. Vetter, *Handbuch der italischen Dialekte,* no. 222, pp. 156f. Suetonius quotes from Augustus' *Autobiography, ipse Augustus nihil amplius quam equestri familia ortum se scribit vetere ac locuplete et in qua primus senator pater suus fuerit* (*Aug.* 2, 3). Mark Antony said that his great-grandfather was a freedman and a rope-maker from the area of Thurii and his grandfather was a money-changer (ibid). On the Octavii, Velitrae and Mars: Suetonius, *Aug.* 1. The classic studies of the Roman nobility are M. Gelzer, *Die Nobilität der Römischen Republik* and F. Münzer, *Römische Adelsparteien und Adelsfamilien.* The definition of *nobilitas* is Gelzer's. On the power of the nobility and *clientela*: H. H. Scullard, *Roman Politics 220–150 B.C.,* 8ff; G. de Sanctis, *Storia dei Romani,* IV, i, 489ff; Th. Mommsen, *Römische Forschungen,* I, 321ff; oversea *clientelae*: E. Badian, *Foreign Clientelae* (*264–70 B.C.*). The internal strife of the nobility: H. H. Scullard, *Roman Politics,* 8ff; R. Syme, *Roman Revolution,* 8ff; M. Gelzer, *Nobilität,* 50ff. On the ideology of the nobility: Donald Earl, *The Moral and Political Tradition of Rome,* 11ff. Pollution of the consulship: Sallust, *B.C.* 23, 6; *B.J.* 63, 7; D. C. Earl, *Historia,* 1966, 302ff; E. Badian, *Gnomon,* 1964, 384; *Durham University Journal,* 1964, 141ff. Ideology of the new men: J. Vogt, *Homo novus, ein Typus der Römischen Republik*; Donald Earl, *Moral and Political Tradition,* 13f; 44ff. The opportunities for advancement under Sulla became proverbial: cf. e.g. Sallust, *B.C.* 37, 6; similarly under Pompey, R. Syme, *Roman Revolution,* 32. Pompey and the oligarchy: cf. what Cicero said about Pompey's father: *hominem dis ac nobilitati perinvisum,* Asconius p. 79 (Clark); A. N. Sherwin-White, *Journal of Roman Studies,* 46, 1956, 1ff; On the Spanish Wars, in addition to the standard histories: H. Simon, *Roms Krieg im Spanien, 154–133 v. Chr.* and, briefly, D. C. Earl, *Tiberius Gracchus,* 109ff. On the political background and importance of the tribunate of Tiberius Gracchus: D. C. Earl, *Tiberius Gracchus, passim.* On the development of the client army: E. Badian, *Foreign Clientelae,* 272; 281; *Studies in Greek and Roman History,* 225. Catiline and *dignitas*: Sallust, *B.C.* 35; D. C. Earl, *The Political Thought of Sallust,* 94f; R. Syme, *Sallust,* 71f. Caesar and *dignitas:* cf. his own words, *B.C.* I, 9, 2: *Sibi semper primam fuisse dignitatem vitaque potiorem*; also, ibid, 7, 7; III, 91, 2; Cicero, *Pro Ligario* 18; *Pro Marcello,* 25; Hirtius, *B.G.* VIII, 52, 4; 53, 1. Cicero's exclamation: *Ad Att.* VII, 11, 1; Suetonius, *Caesar* 72, records Caesar's saying: 'If he had used the help of bandits and thugs in defending his *dignitas,* he would have given even them an appropriate reward.' Caesar's political alliance with men of the lowest sort was notorious to contemporaries: cf. e.g. Cicero, *Ad Fam.* VIII, 4, 2. On the marriage connections of Augustus' father: Suetonius, *Aug.* 4. On the family of Caesar: M. Gelzer, *Caesar, Politician and Statesman* (English translation, 1968) 19ff; R. Syme, *Journal of Roman Studies,* 34, 1944, 92ff. Crassus' remark is variously reported: e.g. Plutarch, *Crassus,* 2; Cicero, *De Officiis,* I, 25; the version in the text is that given by Pliny, *N.H.* XXXIII, 134, as being the most precise. For Crassus' actions in 55 B.C.: Plutarch, *Crassus,* 2. On this and Pompey's distributions: E. Badian, *Roman Imperialism in the Late Republic,* 72ff. For the attitude of the senator to the business man: Donald Earl, *Moral and Political Tradition,* 31. On *dignitas*: H. Wegehaupt, *Die Bedeutung und Anwendung von Dignitas in den Schriften der republikanischen Zeit*; R. Syme, *Roman Revolution,* 13ff and *passim.* On religion and politics Th. Mommsen: *Römisches Staatsrecht* (3rd ed. 1887) I, 76; L. R. Taylor, *Party Politics in the Age of Caesar,* chapter IV. Augustus' father in Macedonia: Suetonius, *Aug.* 3; Cicero's letter, *Ad Quintum Fratrem,* I, 1, 21. Augustus' boyhood: Suetonius, *Aug.* 5ff; myth and omens, ibid. 94ff. Caesar's will: Suetonius, *Caesar,* 83. Octavian's adoption must have been conditional on Calpurnia's not giving birth to a posthumous child. In view of this and doubts about the exact meaning of testamentary adoption W. Schmitthenner, *Oktavian und das Testament Cäsars,* argued that Octavian himself achieved his adoption after Caesar's death by political chicanery. But Caesar certainly intended Octavian to be his adopted son and Suetonius is probably right, cf. G. E. F. Chilver, *Journal of Roman Studies,* 44, 1954, 126ff.

Chapter II: Caesar on Sulla: Suetonius, *Caesar,* 77: *Sullam nescisse litteras qui dictaturam deposuerit.* Tyranny and clemency as political catchwords: C. Wirszubski, *Libertas as a Political Idea at Rome,* chapters II and III; R. Syme, *Roman Revolution,* 154ff; D. C. Earl, *The Political Thought of Sallust,* 54ff; 106ff; *Moral and Political Tradition,* 54ff; 59ff. On the *clementia Caesaris*: M. Treu, *Museum Helveticum,* 1948, 197ff. Decimus Brutus to M. Brutus and Cassius: Cicero, *Ad Fam.* XI, 1, 3–4. On Sextus Pompey: M. Hadas, *Sextus Pompey.* On the history of the Triumviral Period see, especially, T. Rice Holmes, *The Architect of the Roman Empire,* with full references to the ancient sources: M. A. Levi, *Ottaviano Capoparte*; R. Syme, *Roman Revolution,* chapters VII–XXI. Antony's funeral speech: Cicero, *Ad Att.* XIV, 10, 1; *Phil.* II, 90f. For Cicero's belief that Antony should have been killed with Caesar, see his letters to Cassius and Trebonius: *Ad Fam.* XII, 4; X, 28, and *Phil.* II, 34. Faberius and Antony's forgery: Cicero, *Phil.* I, 8ff; II, 36ff. Cicero's laments: *Ad Att.* XIV, 1, 1; 4, 1f; 13, 6; 6, 2; 11, 1; 20, 4. His fear of civil war: *Ad Att.* XIV 13, 2, cf. 22, 2; 14, 4; XV 4, 1. Cicero on Octavian's arrival in Italy: *Ad Att.* XIV, 5; 10; 11; 12. On the importance of Caesar's name to Octavian see Antony's words as reported by Cicero: *Phil.* XIII, 24: *et te, o puer, qui omnia nomini debes.* Cicero's witticism on Octavian: *Ad Fam.* XI, 20, 1: *laudandum adulescentum, ornandum, tollendum*; Cicero did not deny that he said it: ibid. 21, 1. On the provincial commands of Antony and Dolabella: W. Sternkopf, *Hermes,* 47, 1912, 357ff; Rice Holmes, *Architect,* I, 192ff; M. A. Levi, *Ottaviano Capoparte,* I, 76ff, who disputes the date 1 June. The conference at Antium: Cicero, *Ad Att.* XV, 11. Servilia snubbed Cicero when he began to deliver a speech on lost opportunities. On Octavian's sources of wealth at this time: Cicero, *Ad Att.* XV, 2, 3; R. Syme, *Roman Revolution,* 130ff; Pedius and Pinarius, ibid. 128f. On the comet: Pliny, *N.H.* II, 94, based on Augustus' *Autobiography.* On the alleged plot to murder Antony: Appian, *B.C.* III, 39, 158 acutely observes that to remove a rival was to remove a potential ally. Some Romans were not so acute: Cicero, *Ad Fam.* XII, 23, 2: *prudentes autem et boni viri et credunt factum et probant.* Octavian and the veterans in Campania: Nicolaus, *Vita Caesaris,* 31, 131ff; Cicero, *Ad Att.* XVI, 8, 1f; 11, 6. Octavian's correspondence with Cicero: Cicero, *Ad Att.* XVI, 8, 2. For Cicero's reaction to Octavian's speech: *Ad Att.* XVI, 15, 3, 6. Antony's pamphlets: Cicero, *Phil,* III, 15; 21; XIII, 19; Suetonius, *Aug.* 68. Antony's absence on November 24: Cicero, *Phil.* III, 20. On the redistribution of provinces: Cicero, *Phil.* III, 24–26; W. Sternkopf, *Hermes,* 47, 1912, 385ff; Rice Holmes, *Architect,* I, 33, 200f. Cicero's speeches: *Phil.* III–V; Cassius Dio, XLV, 18–47, has his own version of Cicero's Fifth Philippic. Octavian's attitude to being discarded: Cicero, *Ad Fam.* XI, 20, 1. Details of the military operations: Rice Holmes, *Architect,* I,

50ff. For a contemporary eyewitness report of the battle of Forum Gallorum: Ser. Sulpicius Galba's letter to Cicero, *Ad Fam.* X, 30. Cicero to M. Brutus on Octavian: *Ad M. Brutum,* I, 3, 1. For Brutus' reaction see his letters to Atticus: *Ad M. Brutum,* I, 17, and to Cicero, ibid. 4, 4; cf. Plutarch, *Brutus,* 22, 3. Antony's letter to Hirtius and Octavian: Cicero, *Phil.* XIII. Pollio's letter: Cicero, *Ad Fam.* X, 31, 4. Plancus and Octavian: Appian, *B.C.* III, 85, 352; Cassius Dio, XLVI, 42, 1; cf. Cicero, *Ad Fam.* X, 23, 6; 24, 4, 6. M. Brutus on Octavian: *Ad M. Brutum,* I, 16; 17. On the proscriptions: Ronald Syme, *Roman Revolution,* chapter XIV. Octavian's attitude: Suetonius, *Aug.* 27, 1. The figures of the proscribed: Livy, *Periocha,* 120; cf. Orosius, VI, 18, 10; Florus II, 16, 3; Appian, *B.C.* IV, 5, 20; 7, 28. For the surviving names: Drumann-Groebe, *Geschichte Roms* (2nd ed. 1899) I, 470ff; H. Kloevekorn, *De proscriptionibus a.a. Chr. 43 a M. Antonio, M. Aemilio Lepido, C. Iulio Octaviano triumviris factis* (Diss. Konigsberg, 1891). On the partisan nature of the proscriptions, probably exaggerated: M. A. Levi, *Ottaviano Capoparte,* I, 229ff. On the death of Cicero: Seneca, *Suasoriae,* VI, 17, quoting Livy; ibid. 24 gives Pollio's judgement on Cicero; see also Plutarch, *Cicero,* 47f; Appian, *B.C.* IV, 19, 73ff. The delegation of ladies and Hortensia: Appian, *B.C.* IV, 32, 136ff. The deification of Caesar: Cassius Dio, XLVII, 18, 3; H. Dessau, *Inscriptiones Latinae Selectae,* 73; 73a. The campaign of Philippi: Rice Holmes, *Architect,* 80ff. Octavian's movements: the dream, Velleius Paterculus, II, 70. 1; Suetonius, *Aug.* 91, 1; Agrippa and Maecenas on Octavian in the marsh: Pliny, *N.H.* VII, 148. M. Brutus on Antony: Plutarch, *Brutus,* 29. The war of Perusia: Rice Holmes, *Architect,* I, 92ff; R. Syme, *Roman Revolution,* 207ff. Sling bullets from Perusia survive, inscribed by the defenders with obscene abuse of Octavian: *Corpus Inscriptionum Latinarum,* XI, 6721, 1 and 11; Octavian's soldiers were similarly indecent about Fulvia, *Corpus Inscriptionum Latinarum,* XI, 6721, 5. The ritual slaughter at the altar of *Divus Iulius:* Suetonius, *Aug.* 15; Cassius Dio, XLVIII, 14, 4; Seneca, *De Clementia,* 1, 11. Antony and Cleopatra: Cassius Dio, XLVIII, 27, 1. Antony's failure to intervene in the Perusine war: E. Groag, *Klio,* 14, 1914, 43ff; R. Syme, *Roman Revolution,* 214f. The treaty of Brundisium and contemporary reaction: R. Syme, *Roman Revolution,* 216ff; Sextus Pompey, Rice Holmes, *Architect,* I, 106ff. Octavian's divorce of Scribonia: Suetonius, *Aug.* 62, 2. On the marriage to Livia Drusilla and its political consequences: R. Syme, *Roman Revolution,* 229; 234ff. Antony's mirth at Octavian's defeat: Suetonius, *Aug.* 16. Death of Sextus Pompey: Appian, *B.C.* V, 144, 598ff. The Roman People's rejection of Titius: Velleius Paterculus, II, 79, 5; Cassius Dio, XLVIII, 30, 5ff. Humiliation of Lepidus: Appian, *B.C.* V, 124, 513, suggests that his soldiers had already been won over; Dio, too, is cynical, XLIX, 12, 1; see also Velleius Paterculus, II, 80, who calls Lepidus *vir omnium vanissimus.* Honours paid to Octavian: Rice Holmes, *Architect,* 119f. with references to ancient sources. The golden statue and its inscription: Appian, *B.C.* V, 130, 541f. Octavian's Illyrian campaign: E. Swoboda, *Octavian und Illyricum*; R. Syme, *Journal of Roman Studies,* 23, 1933, 66; the political aspects have been discussed by W. Schmitthenner, *Historia,* 1958, 189ff; N. Vulic's arguments for vast conquests by Octavian are improbable and unsupported by evidence, *Journal of Roman Studies,* 24, 1934, 163ff. Agrippa and sewers etc.: Cassius Dio, XLIX, 42, 3; 43; 1ff; Frontinus, *De Aqueductis,* 9; Pliny, *N.H.* XXXVI, 121. On the pamphlet war before Actium: see K. Scott, *Mem. American Academy Rome,* 11, 1933, 7ff. Antony's letter: Suetonius, *Aug.* 69. The women named in this famous fragment are, presumably, the wives of members of Octavian's faction; at least, Terentilla seems to be Terentia, wife of Maecenas. Antony also defended himself against the other persistent charge, that of drunkenness, in a tract *De Sua Ebrietate,* Pliny, *N.H.* XIV, 148, who says of it *exiguo tempore ante proelium Actiacum id volumen evomuit,* cf. M. P. Charlesworth, *Classical Quarterly,* 27, 1933, 172ff. For Octavian's attacks: Suetonius, *Caesar,* 52, 2; Pliny, *N.H.* XXXIII, 50; Charisius, *Grammatici Latini,* 104, 18; 129, 7; 146, 34. On Antony's policies and attitudes: R. F. Rossi, *Marco Antonio, nelle lotta politica della tarda Repubblica Romana* ; H. Bucheim, *Die Orientpolitik des Triumvirs M. Antonius.* On Antony and Cleopatra and her historical importance: J. Kromayer, *Hermes,* 33, 1898, 50; A. E. Glauning, *Die Anhangerschaft des Antonius und des Octavian* (Diss. Leipzig, 1936), 31ff; R. Syme, *Roman Revolution,* 257ff; 270ff; Cassius Dio and Plutarch, *Antony,* the only full sources for the years 33 and 32 B.C. are not entirely satisfactory on chronology, which has been established by J. Kromayer, *Hermes,* 33, 1898, 37ff. Expiration of Triumviral powers: in *Res Gestae* 7 Augustus said that he had been Triumvir for ten years, but, as in 37 B.C., Antony continued to act as though still legally invested with power. Caesarion was probably not Caesar's son: J. Carcopino, *Ann. de l'Ecole des Hautes Etudes de Gand,* 1, 1937, 37ff. On Octavian's first sight of Antony's will alone; Plutarch, *Antony,* 58; see also Cassius Dio, L, 3, 5. The various rumours: Cassius Dio, L, 4; 5; Plutarch, *Antony,* 60. The oath of allegiance: Augustus, *Res Gestae,* 25; R. Syme, *Roman Revolution,* 284ff; A. von Premerstein, *Vom Werden und Wesen des Prinzipats,* 26ff. The battle of Actium: W. W. Tarn, *Journal of Roman Studies,* 21, 1931, 173ff; 28, 1938, 165ff; J. Kromayer, *Hermes,* 68, 1933, 361ff; G. W. Richardson, *Journal of Roman Studies,* 27, 1937, 153ff. Octavian's clemency: *Res Gestae,* 3; cf. Velleius Paterculus, II, 86, 2. Arius' observation: Plutarch, *Antony,* 81. Although Octavian kept Egypt as his own, he claimed to have added it to the Roman empire: *Res Gestae,* 27; *Inscriptiones Latinae Selectae,* 91 = Ehrenburg and Jones, *Documents,* no. 14, from the bases of obelisks set up at Rome, 10–9 B.C. The reconquest of the East for Rome: *Res Gestae,* 27; Virgil, *Georgics,* II, 171; III, 30; IV, 560ff.

Chapter III. The honours of Octavian after Actium: Rice Holmes, *Architect,* I, 171ff, with full references to the ancient sources; R. Syme, *Roman Revolution,* 303ff. M. Licinius Crassus and the *spolia opima:* H. Dessau, *Hermes,* 41, 1906, 142ff; R. Syme, *Roman Revolution,* 308ff; *Harvard Studies in Classical Philology,* 1959, 43ff; R. M. Ogilvie, *A Commentary on Livy Books 1–5,* 563f. C. Cornelius Gallus: Suetonius, *Aug.* 66, 2; Cassius Dio, LIII, 23, 5; the inscription, *Inscriptiones Latinae Selectae* 8995 = Ehrenburg and Jones, *Documents,* no. 21; R. Syme, *Roman Revolution,* 309f, who points out the barest possibility that Crassus and Gallus were related. Tacitus on military glory: *Agricola,* 39, 3; Donald Earl, *Moral and Political Tradition,* 89f. The settlement of 28–27 B.C.: *Res Gestae,* 34. The bibliography of the Augustan constitutional settlements is vast. Work on this subject between 1939 and 1950 is reviewed by G. E. F. Chilver, *Historia,* 1950, 408ff. See also: M. I. Henderson, *Journal of Roman Studies,* 44, 1954, 123ff; E. T. Salmon, *Historia,* 1956, 456ff; P. A. Brunt, *Journal of Roman Studies,* 51, 1961, 236ff; P. Grenade, *Essai sur les origines du Principat.* R. Syme, *Roman Revolution,* chapters XXII and XXIII, will be consulted with profit. I have here followed closely A. H. M. Jones, *Studies in Roman Government and Law,* chapters I and II. On the various censorial powers of Augustus: A. H. M. Jones, *Studies,* chapter II. Caesar's new senators: Suetonius, *Caesar,* 80, 2; R. Syme, *Papers of the British School at Rome,* 1938, 1ff; *Roman Revolution,* 78ff. Senatorial accretions under the Triumvirs: Cassius Dio, XLVIII, 34, 5; Jerome, *Chron.* p. 158 H; *Digest,* I, 14, 3 (Barbarius Philippus). Purge of Senate: Cassius Dio, LII, 42, 1ff; Velleius Paterculus, II, 89, 4. Census of 28 B.C.: Cassius Dio, LIII, 1; *Res Gestae,* 8. On Augustus' *provincia*: Cassius Dio, LIII, 12–13; Strabo, p. 840; R. Syme, *Roman Revolution,* 326ff. Honours voted to Augustus: *Res Gestae,* 34. The name Augustus: Suetonius, *Aug.* 7, 2; cf. Cassius Dio, LIII, 16, 8; Ovid, *Fasti,* I, 609ff. Augustus' own desire for Romulus: Cassius Dio, LIII, 16, 7. On *respublica*: C. Wirszubski, *Libertas,* 121; Donald Earl, *Moral and Political Tradition,* 63ff. Horace on Augustus: *Epist.* II, 1, 1ff. Augustus' censorial powers in 19 B.C.: Cassius Dio, LIV, 10; 30; *Res Gestae* 6; A. H. M. Jones, *Studies,* 24f. Moral and social legislation: *Res Gestae,* 6; H. Last, *Cambridge Ancient History,* X, 441ff. On Papius and Poppaeus: Cassius Dio, LVI, 10, 3. Augustus pressed his point by reciting to the Senate the speech of the Republican Q. Caecilius Metellus 'On Increasing the Birth-rate': Suetonius, *Aug.* 89, 2; Livy, *Periocha,* 59. On the reaction of Virgil, Horace and Livy to the establishment of the Principate: Donald Earl, *Moral and Political Tradition,* chapter III. Cassius Dio, LIII, 11 suggests that the Senate did not know that Augustus intended to hold the consulship every year after 27 B.C. Augustus and the senatorial provinces: the inscription is published by H. Pleket, *The Greek Inscriptions in the Rijksmuseum Van Oudheden at Leyden,* pp. 49ff. The fullest account of the trial of Primus is Cassius Dio, LIV, 3, but he misdates it and the conspiracy of Varro Murena to 22 B.C. See also Velleius Paterculus, II, 91; Suetonius, *Aug.* 19, 1; 56, 4; 66, 3; *Tib.* 8; R. Syme, *Roman Revolution,* 333f. K. M. T. Atkinson, *Historia,* 1960, 440ff has followed Dio in dating the trial and conspiracy to 22 B.C., arguing that the conspirator Varro was not the consul of 23 but his cousin L. Murena, in which case neither event influenced the settlement of 23. Velleius Paterculus, II, 91, 2, mentions L. Murena and Fannius Caepio; the latter he describes as *et ante hoc . . . pessimus.* Maecenas' breach of confidence: Suetonius, *Aug.* 66, 3. Augustus' illness and his dispositions: Cassius Dio, LIII, 30, 1–2; Suetonius, *Aug.* 28, 1. The settlement of 23 B.C.: A. H. M. Jones, *Studies,* 7ff. The situation after 23 B.C.: Cassius Dio, LIV, 6, 1–2; 10, 1–3; *Res Gestae,* 11 and 12 (the altar of Fortuna Redux and the reception in Campania). For the arguments and evidence which indicate a settlement in 19–18 B.C., see A. H. M. Jones, *Studies,* 13ff. Augustus' *auctoritas*: *Res Gestae,* 34, 3; G. E. F. Chilver, *Historia,* 1950, 420ff. A number of surviving inscriptions bear on the celebration of the Secular Games: two decrees of the Senate, an edict of the *XVviri sacris faciundis,* charged with the actual arrangements, which ordered public joy and diminution of feminine grief, and the *Acta sacrorum saecularium* which record the composition of the solemn hymn by Horace and its performance by two choirs of twenty-seven boys and twenty-seven girls respectively. They are collected in Ehrenburg and Jones, *Documents,* nos. 30–32. H. Mattingly, *Classical Review,* 48, 1934, 161ff has argued that Augustus originally intended the celebration for 22 B.C.; compare the postponement of the moral and social legislation from 28 to 18 B.C. The restoration of the Republic took much longer and was more difficult than Augustus originally envisaged.

Chapter IV: Salvidienus, Agrippa and Octavian: Velleius Paterculus, II, 59, 5. Distribution of names ending in *-ienus* in Italy: W. Schulze, *Zur Geschichte lateinischer Eigennamen,* 104ff. Note the excellent C. Billienus who almost became consul 105–100 B.C.: Cicero, *Brutus,* 175. Coins of Salvidienus with inscription *Q. Salvius imp. cos. desig.*: *British Museum Catalogue of Coins of the Roman Republic,* II, 407. It may possibly have been a cognomen: R. Syme, *Roman Revolution,* 129. Obscurity of Agrippa's family: Seneca, *De Ben.* III, 32, 4. His preference to forget that he was Vipsanius: Seneca, *Controv.* II, 4, 13. It is exceedingly rare and its origin untraceable: W. Schulze, *Lateinischer Eigennamen,* 531ff. Cilnius Maecenas: Tacitus, *Ann.* VI, 11. Maecenas' royal ancestry: e.g. Horace, *Odes,* I, 1, 1. Cilnius may have been adopted as a cognomen and Tacitus' notice an example of the not uncommon practice of inverting nomen and cognomen. Brutus' abuse of Salvidienus: Cicero, *Ad M. Brutum,* I, 17, 4. Cassius Dio, XLVIII, 33, 1 records an alleged portent of future greatness from Salvidienus' boyhood. Agrippa a coeval of Octavian: Nicolaus, *Vita Caesaris,* 7, 16. Agrippa's character: Pliny *N.H.* XXXV, 26, *vir rusticitati propior quam deliciis.* His short temper: Suetonius, *Aug.* 66, 3. His ambition: Velleius Paterculus, II, 79, 1; cf. 93, 1; Pliny, *N.H.* VII, 46. Nobles' refusal to attend his funeral: Cassius Dio, LIV, 29, 6. Advocates confiscation of art treasures: Pliny, *N.H.* XXXV, 26. Constitutional powers: R. Syme, *Roman Revolution,* 306; 337; 345ff; 389. His marriages: ibid. 238; 379; 416. Maecenas on Agrippa: Cassius Dio, LIV, 6, 5. For a biography of Agrippa: M. Reinhold, *Marcus Agrippa*; R. Syme, *Roman Revolution, passim.* Maecenas' grandfather: Cicero, *Pro Cluentio,* 153. His father: *Inscriptiones Latinae Selectae,* 7848 = Ehrenburg and Jones, *Documents,* no. 219. A Maecenas is also mentioned by Sallust, *Hist.* III, 83, Maurenbrecher; presumably a member of the same family; R. Syme, *Roman Revolution,* 129f. Maecenas' character: Velleius Paterculus, II, 88, 2: *otio ac mollitiis paene ultra feminam fluens*; Seneca, *Epp.* 114, 4ff. Bathyllus: Tacitus, *Ann.* I, 54. Young donkeys: Pliny, *N.H.* VIII, 170. His loquacity: Suetonius, *Aug.* 66, 3. His attitude to death: Seneca, *Epp.* 101, 10ff. C. Sallustius Crispus: R. Syme, *Roman Revolution,* 267; 384f; 410; 412; 439. Tacitus' assessment: *Ann.* III, 3, 30. M. Lollius: R. Syme, *Roman Revolution,* 338; 391; 398; 406; 428ff. Sulpicius Quirinius: ibid. 399; 435; 429. Tiberius' funeral speech: Tacitus, *Ann.* III, 48. Augustus' legates 27–23 B.C.: R. Syme, *Roman Revolution,* 329f; consuls, ibid. 327f; 242; 325; 372. On the *ordo Equester*: R. Syme, *Roman Revolution,* 352ff; A. N. Sherwin-White, *Papers of the British School at Rome,* 1939, 11ff; A. H. M. Jones, *Studies,* chapter VII; H. G. Pflaum, *Les procurateurs équestres sous le haut empire* and *Les carrières procuratoriennes équestres.* Wealth of Isidorus: Pliny, *N.H.* XXXIII, 135. Claudius' speech: *Inscriptiones Latinae Selectae,* 212; cf. Tacitus, *Ann.* XI, 23ff; R. Syme, *Tacitus,* 317ff and Appendix 40. Vedius Pollio and his lampreys: Cassius Dio, LIV, 23; Pliny, *N.H.* IX, 77; Seneca, *De Ira,* III, 40, 2; *De Clementia,* I, 18, 2. Otho, Vitellius, Vespasius: R. Syme, *Roman Revolution,* 361. Augustus' senatorial committee: Cassius Dio, LIII, 21, 4; Suetonius, *Aug.* 35, 3. Tiberius' practice: Suetonius, *Tib.* 55. Augustus and the Senate: P. Sattler, *Augustus und der Senat.* Augustus and the *nobiles*: R. Syme, *Roman Revolution,* 368; 379; 419ff; 479ff; 490ff. Conspiracies: of the younger Lepidus, Velleius Paterculus, II, 88; Cinna, Cassius Dio LV, 14ff (dating it to A.D. 4); Seneca, *De Clementia,* I, 9 (apparently dating it to the period 16–13 B.C.). Both reproduce a rhetorical exercise. Neither Suetonius nor Tacitus mention Cinna's conspiracy. Julia and the five nobles: R. Syme, *Roman Revolution,* 426f; the younger Julia, Tacitus, *Ann.* III, 24; IV, 71; Suetonius, *Aug.* 19, 1; Scholiast on Juvenal VI, 158; the affair is highly obscure, see E. Hohl, *Klio,* 30, 1937, 337ff; R. Syme, *Roman Revolution,* 432. Juvenal on pedigrees: *Satire* VIII. Tacitus on the nobles after Actium, *Ann.* I, 2. Hadrian executed C. Calpurnius Piso Frugi Licinianus and a member of another branch of the same family was consul in A.D. 111. The Acilii Glabriones survived even into the next century with consuls in the direct line in A.D. 210 and 256. The interpretation of the consular lists and of election results for the reign of Augustus present difficult problems. A. H. M. Jones, *Studies,* chapter III has argued persuasively that there was no systematic gerrymandering of the elections by Augustus and collects evidence to show that elections for the higher offices were genuine contests; the lower posts frequently suffered a dearth of candidates. For the interpretation of the consular lists, with special reference to the proportion of *nobiles* to new men: P. A. Brunt, *Journal of Roman Studies,* 1961, 71ff. On senators in the emperor's service: E. Birley, *Proceedings of the British Academy,* 1953, 197ff; A. McAlindon, *Journal of Roman Studies,* 1957, 191ff. On the rise of the provincials: R. Syme, *Tacitus,* 585ff; P. Lambrechts, *La Composition du sénat romain de l'accession au trône d'Hadrien a la mort de Commode*; Donald Earl, *Moral and Political Tradition,* 86ff; 97ff. It is this development which conditions the essential nature of the Roman Imperial Period. Under the Republic Rome held down an empire, sending out Romans to govern it. From Augustus onwards the whole empire becomes more and more a self-governing organism with the provinces themselves providing their own rulers. This with the formation of a truly integrated multi-racial ruling class is one of the more remarkable achievements of human history.

Chapter V: It is impossible to arrive at an accurate figure for the population of ancient Rome, but approximately 1,000,000 seems the likeliest figure for the end of the Republic. For various theories and calculations: W. J. Oates, *Classical Philology*, 29, 1943, 101ff: Z. Yavetz, *Latomus*, 17, 1958, 500ff; J. E. Parker, *Journal of Roman Studies*, 57, 1967, 80ff. On the living conditions of the urban plebs: Z. Yavetz, *Latomus*, 17, 1958, 500ff. Yavetz has collected the ancient material with especial regard to housing conditions, particularly that of Cicero and Vitruvius. Cicero's annual rent income: *Ad Att.* XVI, 1, 5; XV, 17, 1; 20, 4. Cicero's manoeuvre: *Ad Att.* XIV, 9, 1. *Ad Att.* XII, 32, 3 throws interesting light on Cicero as a landlord. Fires and natural disasters: Z. Yavetz, *Latomus*, 17, 1958, 510ff; 516. Augustus' rebuilding of dwellings destroyed in 50 B.C.: Orosius, VII, 2, 1. Regulations on height of buildings: Strabo, V, 7, 3. On Roman building laws in general: M. Voigt, *Römische Baugesetze*, in *Ber. Ges. Wiss. Leipzig*, Phil-Hist. Klasse, 55. Augustus' recitation of Rutilius' speech: Suetonius, *Aug.* 89, 2. The *Vigiles*; P. K. Baillie-Reynolds, *The Vigiles of Imperial Rome.* Egnatius Rufus and his fire-brigade: Cassius Dio, LIII, 24; Velleius Paterculus, II, 91, 2. Augustus and the food supply: *Res Gestae*, 5. The *Annona*: Tenney Frank, *An Economic Survey of Ancient Rome*, V, 139f; 218ff. Wealth of Chrysogonus: Cicero, *Pro Roscio Amerino*, 133; see also *Phil.* III, 30; V, 11 on the house of Mark Antony. Caesar's plans for Rome: Cicero, *Ad Att.* XIII, 33a, 1; 35, 1. These plans made Cicero very angry. Roman demagogues in poor quarters: C. Gracchus moved house from the Palatine to the neighbourhood of the Forum, in an effort to shore up his collapsing popularity, Plutarch, *C. Gracchus*, 12; Pompey lived in Carinae, Cicero, *De Haruspicum Responso*, 49; Velleius Paterculus, II, 77; Suetonius, *Tiberius*, 15; Julius Caesar, before becoming Pontifex Maximus, lived in Subura, Suetonius, *Caesar*, 46; a similar tale is told of Sulla, Plutarch, *Sulla*, 1. Augustus' house near the Forum: Suetonius, *Aug.* 72. The description of his house on the Palatine: Suetonius, *Aug.* 72–73. See also: Velleius Paterculus, II, 81, 3; Ovid, *Fasti*, IV 951ff; Suetonius, *Aug.* 57; *Res Gestae*, 35; Ehrenburg and Jones, *Documents*, p. 45 (Calendar of Praeneste for 13 January). The Augustan building: *Res Gestae*, 19–21; cf. Suetonius, *Aug.* 28, 3; 30, 1. On these and other buildings in Rome: G. Lugli, *Roma Antica: Il centro Monumentale*; T. Ashby and S. B. Platner, *Topographical Dictionary of Ancient Rome*; E. Nash, *Pictorial Dictionary of Ancient Rome*; D. R. Dudley, *Urbs Roma*, which collects the ancient literary evidence. Agrippa's Campus: Strabo, V, 3, 8. Agrippa's Pantheon: Cassius Dio, LIII, 27; Pliny, *N.H.* IX, 121; XXXVI, 38; D. R. Dudley, *Urbs Roma*, 187ff. Pliny's list of architectural marvels is in *N.H.* XXXVI. The temple of Apollo: Suetonius, *Aug.* 29; Cassius Dio, LIII, 13; Virgil, *Aeneid*, VIII, 704ff; 720ff on which see Servius' comment; Propertius, II, 31; Horace, *Odes*, I, 31, 1ff. The Palatine library; Ovid, *Tristia*, III, 1, 63ff. The temple was destroyed on March 18, A.D. 363: Ammianus Marcellinus, XXIII, 33. For detailed studies of various Augustan buildings: E. B. van Deman, *The Building of the Roman Aqueducts*; T. Ashby, *Aqueducts of Ancient Rome*; the Senate House, A. Bartoli, *I lavori della Curia* and *Studi Romani*, 1954, 129ff; the temple of Magna Mater, K. Esdaile, *Mitteilungen des Deutschen Archäologischen Instituts, Römische Abteilung*, 23, 1908, 368ff; G. Carettoni, *Journal of Roman Studies*, 50, 1960, 200ff; temple of Apollo, G. Lugli, *Comptes-rendus des séances de l'Academie des Inscriptions et Belles-Lettres*, Paris, 1950, 276ff; Palatine library and Roman libraries in general, L. Crema, *L'Architettura Romana*, 376f; House of Augustus, G. Carettoni, *Journal of Roman Studies*, 50, 1960, 201; G. E. Rizzo, *Monumenti della Pittura Antica*, Roma III, *Le pitture della Casa di Livia*; Theatre of Marcellus, A. Calza Bini, *Boll. del centro per la storia dell'architettura*, 7, 1953; the Pantheon, R. Vighi, *Il Pantheon*; W. MacDonald, *Architecture of the Roman Empire*, I, chapter V; Agrippa, F. W. Shipley, *Agrippa's Building Activities in Rome*, Washington University Studies, language and literature, no. 4, 1933; the Forum of Augustus, Suetonius, *Aug.* 29; 31; Ovid, *Fasti*, V, 551ff; 563ff; Horace, *Odes* IV, 8, 13ff; C. Ricci, *Capitolium*, 6, 1930, 157ff; H. T. Rowell, *Memoirs of the American Academy in Rome*, 1940, 132ff; the surviving inscriptions can be found in A. DeGrassi, *Inscriptiones Italiae*, XIII, 3; D. R. Dudley, *Urbs Roma*, 125ff. Virgil's parade of heroes; *Aeneid* VI, 825ff. The Ara Pacis: *Res Gestae*, 12; the constitution of the altar on July 4, 13 B.C., Ehrenburg and Jones, *Documents*, p. 49 (Calendars of Amiternum and Antium); its consecration on January 30, 9 B.C., ibid. p. 46 (Calendars of Cumae, Caere, Praeneste). The most comprehensive study is G. Moretti, *Ara Pacis Augustae.* I have here followed closely the description and interpretation of J. M. C. Toynbee, *Proceedings of the British Academy*, 1953, 67ff. S. Weinstock, *Journal of Roman Studies*, 50, 1960, 44ff. has challenged the identification of the monument as the Ara Pacis Augustae, but see J. M. C. Toynbee, *Journal of Roman Studies*, 51, 1961, 153ff. Virgil on the landing of Aeneas: *Aeneid*, VIII, 81ff. Praise of Italy, *Georgics*, II, 143ff; Horace, *Odes*, IV, 15. The quotation from Professor D. R. Dudley is from *Urbs Roma*, 195. The decree of Jupiter: Virgil, *Aeneid*, I, 278f; the Sybil, *Aeneid*, VI, 851ff. The Mausoleum of Augustus: Strabo, V, 3, 8; R. A. Cordingley and I. A. Richmond, *Papers of the British School at Rome*, 1927, 23ff; A. Munoz, *Capitolium*, 13, 1938, 491ff. Commerce and industry in Rome: Tenney Frank, *Economic Survey*, V, 218ff. Public works in Italy: ibid. 95ff. Augustus' repair of Via Flaminia: *Res Gestae*, 20. The Golden Milestone: Cassius Dio, LIV, 8; M. E. Blake, *Ancient Roman Construction in Italy*, I, 340. The Post: Suetonius, *Aug.* 49, 3. Claudius attempted to lighten the burden by edict: *Corpus Inscriptionum Latinarum*, III, 7251. Purchase of land for veterans: *Res Gestae*, 16. Italian agriculture: Tenney Frank, *Economic Survey*, V, 139ff (cereals); 146ff. (wine. Augustus' taste for Rhaetic wine, Suetonius, *Aug.* 77; cf. Strabo, IV, 6, 8); 153ff. (olives. See Pliny, *N.H.* XV, 3); 161ff. (orchards. Augustus' taste for green figs, Suetonius, *Aug.* 76, 1). Live stock: Tenney Frank, *Economic Survey*, V, 162f. (cattle); 163ff (sheep. Strabo, VI, 3, 5; 6; 9; V, 1, 7, 12; Horace *Odes* II, 6, 10); 167f. (swine. Strabo, V, 1, 12; Polybius, II, 15; XII, 4, 8) 168 (poultry). Italian industry: Tenney Frank, *Economic Survey*, V, 185ff. (ironware); 194ff. (glassware); 197ff. (copper and bronzeware); 199ff. (clothing and woollen industry); 207ff. (brickmaking); 210ff. (jewelry and silverware); 188ff. (Arretine ware). The Portland Vase, being a specially made object, is not typical of mass produced glassware. The basic technique in its making was to cover a blue glass body with opaque white glass which was then carved away, as in a cameo, to produce the decoration. E. Simon, *Die Portlandvase*, has attempted to connect the figures on the vase closely with Augustus, cf. L. Polacco, *Athenaeum* (Pavia), n.s. 36, 1958, 123ff. The most recent discussion of the vase is B. Ashmole, *Journal of Hellenic Studies*, 87, 1967, 1ff. Bronze table-ware etc.: E. Pernice, *Gefässe und Geräte aus Bronze in Pompeji.* Jewelry: R. A. Higgens, *Greek and Roman Jewellery.* Gold and Silver-plate: D. E. Strong, *Greek and Roman Gold and Silver Plate.* The Boscoreale treasure consists of over 100 pieces hidden in a wine vat below a house and buried by lava and ash which suffocated its guardian. The Augustus cup and its companion depicting Tiberius were perhaps produced by court silversmiths as pieces of official propaganda for distribution as gifts on special imperial occasions (Strong, 136). The treasure is published by H. de Villefosse, 'Le Trésor de Boscoreale', *Monuments Piot*, V, 1899–1902, pp. 7–279, plates 1–36. The Hildesheim treasure: E. Pernice and F. Winter, *Der Hildesheimer Silberfund.* Gems and cameos: M. L. Vollenweider, *Die Steinschneidekunst und ihre Künstler in spätrepublikanischer und augusteischer Zeit.* Augustus and Dioscurides: Suetonius, *Aug.* 50; Pliny, *N.H.* XXXVII, 8 and 10. Arretine ware: H. Dragendorff and C. Watzinger, *Arretinische Reliefkeramik*; R. J. Charleston, *Roman Pottery.* Roman and Italian trade: Tenney Frank, *Economic Survey*, V, 267ff. Augustus and 'pirates': *Res Gestae*, 25; Ostia, Strabo, V, 3, 5. The Claudian reconstruction: Suetonius, *Claudius*, 20, 3; Cassius Dio, LX, 11, 1ff. Even after this, lack of return cargoes from Ostia caused ships to put in first at Puteoli, Pliny, *N.H.* XIX, 3. Virgil, Horace and the unity of Italy: Donald Earl, *Moral and Political Tradition,* chapter III, *passim.* The quotations from Virgil are *Aeneid,* I, 33; XII, 826; VIII, 678f.

Chapter VI: Roman provincial government in the Late Republic: E. Badian, *Roman Imperialism in the Late Republic.* Transalpine Gaul: ibid. 23ff. The date of the foundation of Narbo: H. B. Mattingly, *Mélanges Grenier,* 1962, 1159ff. Cyrene: S. I. Oost, *Classical Philology,* 1963, 11ff; E. Badian, *Journal of Roman Studies,* 55, 1965, 110ff; *Roman Imperialism,* 29f. Egypt: E. Badian, *Roman Imperialism,* 30; 65. Asia: ibid. 22f; 43ff. On the financial importance of Asia: Cicero, *De Imperio Cn. Pompeii,* 14. In cc. 18f. of the same speech Cicero alleges as an accepted fact that even a threat to Asia inevitably produced collapse of credit at Rome. Pompey: E. Badian, *Roman Imperialism,* 70ff. Badian's judgement on Republican provincial administration is from *Roman Imperialism,* 77. For examples of exploitation, known mainly from Cicero, *ibid.* 73ff. The evidence for the relations of the emperor and the Senate in the government of the provinces is collected and discussed by F. Millar, *Journal of Roman Studies,* 56, 1966, 156ff. On the Greek East: A. H. M. Jones, *Cities of the Eastern Roman Provinces*; D. Magie, *Roman Rule in Asia Minor*; G. W. Bowersock, *Augustus and the Greek World.* The Augustan governors of the Eastern provinces are discussed by G. Bowersock, *Augustus and the Greek World,* chapter II. Cyme inscription: H. W. Pleket, *The Greek Inscriptions in the Rijksmuseum van Oudheden at Leyden,* no. 57; F. Millar, *Journal of Roman Studies,* 56, 1966, 161. Edict of Augustus concerning the Jews: Josephus, *Ant. Jud.* XVI, 160–5; 162–5 = Ehrenburg and Jones, *Documents,* no. 314. Cyrene edicts: Ehrenburg and Jones, *Documents,* no. 311; F. de Visscher, *Les Edits d'Auguste decouverts à Cyrene*; F. Millar, *Journal of Roman Studies,* 56, 1966, 162. Details of the embassies to Augustus are collected by Millar, ibid. 163f. Senatorial decree of 4 B.C., the *senatus consultum Calvisianum* preserved with the Cyrene edicts: Ehrenburg and Jones, *Documents,* no. 311. Provincial censuses: Livy *Periocha,* 134; 138–9; Cassius Dio, LIII, 22, 5; *Inscriptiones Latinae Selectae,* 212, 35ff (Gaul); Josephus, *Ant. Jud.* XVII, 355; XVIII, 2; 26; *Inscriptiones Latinae Selectae,* 2683 (Syria and Judaea); *Corpus Inscriptionum Latinarum,* X, 680 (Lusitania). *I.L.S.* 2683 = Ehrenburg and Jones, *Documents,* no. 231. P. Sulpicius Quirinius is the Cyrenius of Luke II, 2. Spread of citizenship in the provinces: A. N. Sherwin-White, *The Roman Citizenship.* Colonization: F. Vittinghoff, *Römische Kolonisation und Burgerrechtspolitik unter Caesar und Augustus.* Spain: Strabo, III, 2, 15. Gades and its *Equites* and Cornelius Balbus: Strabo, III, 5, 3. Narbonese Gaul: Strabo, IV, 1, 12. Eastern colonies: G. W. Bowersock, *Augustus and the Greek World,* chapter V. Tarentum, Rhegium and Naples: Strabo, V, 4, 7; cf. Livy, XXXV, 16, 3. Naples' reluctance to accept Roman citizenship: Cicero, *Pro Balbo,* 8, 21. Greek inscriptions from Naples: *Inscriptiones Graecae,* XIV, 714–828. *Graeca urbs*: Tacitus, *Ann.* XV, 33. The chief local magistrate, demarchos, *Scriptores Historiae Augustae, Hadrian,* 19, 1. One inscription, *Corpus Inscriptionum Latinarum,* X, 1491, exhibits an incredible mixture of Latin and Greek. Virgil on the arts: *Aeneid,* VI, 847ff. Strabo's description of Neapolitan life: V, 4, 7. The Neapolitan Games: Cassius Dio, LV, 10, 9 (wrongly dated to 2 B.C.); R. M. Geer, *Transactions of the American Philological Association,* 66, 1935, 208ff. Advertisement at Olympia: *Inschriften von Olympia,* no. 56. Augustus and Naples: Velleius Paterculus, II, 123; Suetonius, *Aug.* 98, 5; Cassius Dio, LVI, 29, 2. Capri: Strabo, V, 4, 9; Suetonius *Aug.* 92, 2; Cassius Dio, LII, 43, 2. On Augustus' philhellenism and the attitude of the Romans to Hellenic life: G. W. Bowersock, *Augustus and the Greek World,* chapter VI. The cities of the Eastern empire: ibid, chapter VII. Greeks in the imperial service: ibid. chapter III. Spanish wars: R. Syme, *American Journal of Philology,* 1934, 293ff; W. Schmitthenner, *Historia,* 1962, 29ff; Velleius Paterculus, II, 90, 4. The Augustan reorganization of Spain: C. H. V. Sutherland, *The Romans in Spain,* chapter VIII; J. M. Blaquez, *Emerita,* 1962, 71ff. Gaul: N. J. de Witt, *Urbanisation and the Franchise in Roman Gaul*; J. J. Hatt, *Histoire de la Gaule romaine.* On the northern frontier and Augustus' campaigns in Illyricum and Germany: J. J. Wilkes, *University of Birmingham Historical Journal,* 1965, 1ff. The inscription on the trophy of Augustus: Ehrenburg and Jones, *Documents,* no. 40. The subjection of Pannonia: *Res Gestae,* 30. Augustus' reaction to the Varian disaster: Suetonius, *Aug.* 23, 2. The effect of the disaster on Augustus' policy: J. Morris, *Acta Universitatis Carolinae, Phil. et Hist.* (Prague), 1963, 157f. Augustus' organization of the East: G. W. Bowersock, *Augustus and the Greek World,* chapter IV. Parthia: N. C. Debevoise, *A Political History of Parthia.* Armenia: *Res Gestae,* 27, where Augustus claims to have acted magnanimously in not annexing the country. Recovery of standards: *Res Gestae,* 29. The Roman army: R. E. Smith, *Service in the Post-Marian Roman Army*; H. M. D. Parker, *The Roman Legions* (2nd ed. 1958); G. L. Cheeseman, *The Auxilia of the Roman Imperial Army.* The navy: C. G. Starr, *The Roman Imperial Navy* (2nd ed. 1960). The praetorian guard: M. Durry, *Les Cohortes prétoriennes*; A. Passerini, *Le coorti pretorie. Aerarium militare*: *Res Gestae,* 17; Cassius Dio, LV, 25, 2ff. In A.D. 6 there was the prospect of unusually large numbers of soldiers being discharged. Augustus' substitution of a cash bounty for land: Cassius Dio, LIV, 25, 5f. Between 7 and 2 B.C. Augustus spent no less than 400,000,000 sesterces in providing gratuities for demobilized soldiers: *Res Gestae,* 16.

Chapter VII: The imperial cult under Augustus: L. R. Taylor, *The Divinity of the Roman Emperor*; K. Latte, *Römische Religionsgeschichte,* chapter XI. On the Greek cults of mortals: U. Wilcken, *Sitzungsberichte der preussischen Akademie,* Phil-Hist. Klasse, 28, 1938, 298ff; C. Habicht, *Gottmenschentum und griechische Städte*; E. Bikerman, *Institutions des Séleucides,* 236ff. Imperial cult in the Greek East: G. W. Bowersock, *Augustus and the Greek World,* chapter IX. Cult of Roma at Smyrna: Tacitus, *Ann.* IV, 56. For a list of cults of Roma: D. Magie, *Roman Rule in Asia Minor,* II, 1613. Cult of Sulla at Athens: *Inscriptiones Graecae,* II (2nd ed.), 1039; *Supplementum Epigraphicum Graecum,* 13, 279; A. E. Raubitschek, *Studies in Honour of A. C. Johnson,* 29ff. Cicero's anger with Pelops: Plutarch, *Cicero,* 24, 7. Persistence of cult of Flamininus: Plutarch *Flamininus,* 16. Dedications to Augustus, lists in L. R. Taylor, *The Divinity of the Roman Emperor,* 270ff; cf. K. Latte, *Römische Religionsgeschichte,* 312ff. Joint cult with Roma: Suetonius, *Aug.* 52; cf. Tacitus, *Ann.* IV, 37. Continuance of cults of Augustus alone in some eastern cities: D. Magie, *Roman Rule in Asia Minor,* II, 1294, n.52; list, 1614. Leagues and associations: G. W. Bowersock, *Augustus and the Greek World,* 115f. Cult of Augustan dynasty: L. R. Taylor, *The Divinity of the Roman Emperor,* 270ff. for dedications to members of the imperial family. Cult of C. Marcius Censorinus: *Supplementum Epigraphicum Graecum,* 2, 549. Augustus' prohibition honours to provincial governors: Cassius Dio LVI, 25, 6. Language of honorific inscriptions: G. W. Bowersock, *Augustus and the Greek World,* 119; C. Julius Eurycles, *L'Année Epigraphique,* 1929, no. 99, 11, 19f. C. Iulius Xenon: G. W. Bowersock, *Augustus and the Greek World,* 120. The imperial cult in Rome, Italy and the West: L. R. Taylor, *The Divinity of the Roman Emperor,* 181ff. Augustus' attitude to Caesar: R. Syme, *Roman Revolution,* 317ff. Caesar's funeral and deification: Suetonius, *Caesar,* 84; 88. Livy on Caesar: Seneca, *N.Q.* V, 18, 4. Virgil, *Aeneid,* VI, 834ff. Horace, *Odes,* I, 12, 47 (the comet). Augustus' election as Pontifex Maximus: *Res Gestae,* 10; Ehrenburg and Jones, *Documents,* p. 47 (calendars of Maffei, Cumae, Praeneste); Ovid, *Fasti,* III, 419ff. Shrines of Lares and Genius at the crossroads in Rome and Italy: L. R. Taylor, *The Divinity of the Roman Emperor,* 181ff; 215ff.

Chapter VIII: The fullest discussion of the problems of the succession is R. Syme, *Roman Revolution,* chapters XXIII, XXVII, XXVIII, which is here followed closely. Inscription from Acerrae: *Inscriptiones Latinae Selectae,* 137. Augustus' letter to Gaius and Lucius: Gellius, *N.A.* XV, 7, 3. On the conspiracy of Julia: E. Groag, *Wiener Studien,* 41, 1919, 79ff. The divorce decree: Suetonius, *Tiberius,* 11, 4. Tiberius' avoidance of attention: ibid. 12. His visit to Samos: ibid. 13. Lollius and Sulpicius: R. Syme, *Roman Revolution,* 429ff. Preamble to Augustus' will: Suetonius, *Tib.* 23. Augustus' prayer: Suetonius, *Aug.* 28, 2. Augustus' last days: Suetonius, *Aug.* 97–99. His funeral: ibid. 100. The oath to Tiberius: Tacitus, *Ann.* I, 7. Augustus' will: Suetonius, *Aug.* 101; E. Hohl, *Klio,* 30, 1937, 323ff. On the imperial wealth: P. A. Brunt, *Journal of Roman Studies,* 56, 1966, 75ff. Murder of Agrippa Postumus: Tacitus, *Ann.* I, 6.

Epilogue: Suetonius on Augustus' appearance: *Aug.* 79; Augustus' sexual tastes: Suetonius, *Aug.* 68–71. Fear of thunder and lightning: ibid. 90. On the immunity of seals and laurels: Pliny, *N.H.* II, 55. His health and hypochondria: Suetonius, *Aug.* 81–82. *Laudatio Turiae,* date between 8 and 2 B.C.: Ehrenburg and Jones, *Documents,* no. 357. Hadrian and the woman: Cassius Dio, LXIX, 6, 3. Augustus often personally administered justice into the night even when ill: Suetonius, *Aug.* 33, and Maecenas once had to fight his way through the crowd surrounding Augustus as he gave judgement: Cassius Dio, LV, 7, 2. In the early imperial period, at least, the administration of the emperor was a very personal thing and conscientious emperors worked very hard indeed, see F. Millar, *Journal of Roman Studies,* 57, 1967, 9ff.

Acknowledgements

The Publishers would like to thank all those organizations and individuals who have helped in the collection of the illustrations for this volume and would like to acknowledge the following sources: Reproductions by courtesy of the Trustees of the British Museum, London: front of jacket, plates 1, 8, 9, 54, 58, 80; figures 1, 2, 3, 4, 5, 6, 7, 8, 9, 10, 12, 13, 15, 18, 20, 21, 22, 23, 24, 25, 26, 27, 28, 29, 30, 31, 32, 33; Soprintendenza alle Antichità del Piemonte, Turin: plates 6, 57, 64; Palais des Archevêques, Narbonne: plate 7; Metropolitan Museum of Art, Rogers Fund, 1919, New York: plates 10, 39; Villa Torlonia, Avezzano: plate 11; Museo Nazionale, Naples: plates 17, 18, 19, 20, 23, 49, 50, 60, 65, 66, 73, 74, 79; Biblioteca Apostolica Vaticana: plate 24; Glyptotheque Ny Carlsberg, Copenhagen: plate 25; Musée du Louvre, Paris: plates 26, 41, 71; Cherchel Museum, Algeria: plate 27; Museo delle Terme, Rome: plates 30, 76; Monumenti Musei e Gallerie Pontificie, Vatican: plates 37, 55; Musée Lapidaire d'Art Païen, Arles: plate 38; Sabratha Museum, Libya: plates 42, 43; Musée du Bardo, Tunis: plate 56; Staatliche Museen, Berlin: plates 59, 75, 77, 78, back of jacket; figure 11; Wellington Museum, London: plate 70; Kunsthistorisches Museum, Vienna: plate 81; Académie de France à Rome: plate 33; reproduction by permission of the Trustees of the Chatsworth Settlement: figure 19.

In addition the Publishers would like to thank everyone who assisted Mario Carrieri while he was photographing on their behalf in Rome and acknowledge the photographs to the following sources: Mario Carrieri: plates 2, 3, 4, 5, 12, 13, 14, 15, 16, 21, 28, 29, 30, 31, 32, 34, 35, 36, 48, 51, 52, 53, 57, 61, 62, 63, 64, 67, 68, 69, 72, 82; Roger Wood: plates 1, 27, 42, 43, 44, 45, 47; John R. Freeman: front of jacket, plates 8, 9, 58, 80; figures 1, 2, 3, 4, 5, 6, 7, 8, 9, 10, 12, 13, 15, 18, 19, 20, 21, 22, 23, 24, 25, 26, 27, 28, 29, 31; The Mansell Collection, London: plate 11; Edwin Smith: plates 17, 18, 19, 20, 23, 49, 50, 60, 65, 66, 73, 74, 79; Giraudon, Paris: plates 22, 41, 46; Thames and Hudson Ltd, London: plate 24; Oscar Savio Fotografo, Rome: plate 33; French Government Tourist Office, London: plate 40; Victoria and Albert Museum, London; Crown Copyright: plate 70; Service Photographique, Palais Royal, Paris: plates 26, 71; Scala Istituto Fotografico Editoriale, Florence: plate 76; Fototeca Unione, Rome: plates 83, 84; figures 14, 16; Italian Government Tourist Office, London: figure 17.

Index

Roman names, except those of emperors and certain members of the imperial family, are entered under *nomina*.

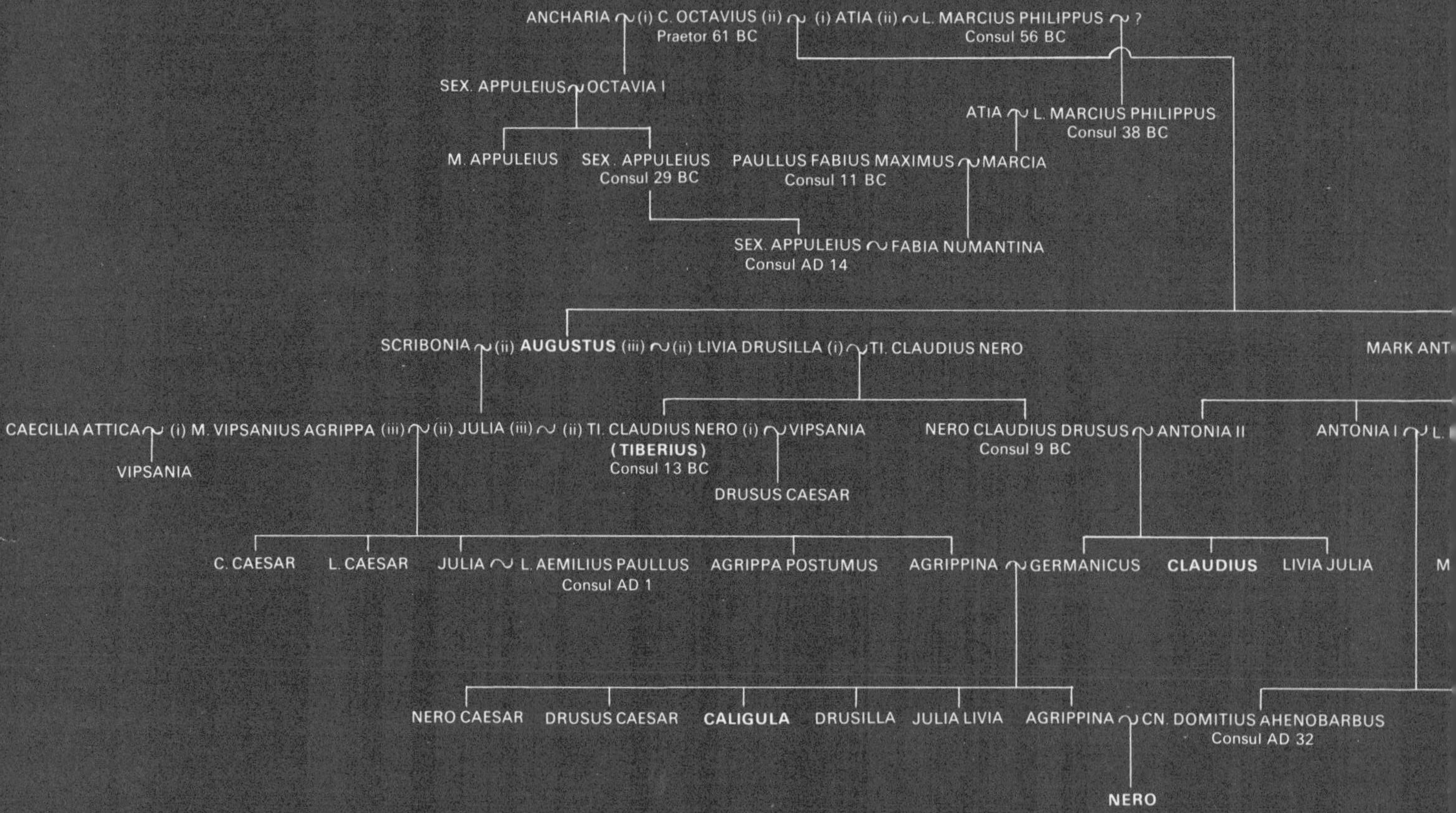
ANCHARIA
(i) C. OCTAVIUS (ii)
Praetor 61 BC
(i) ATIA (ii)
L. MARCIUS PHILIPPUS
Consul 56 BC
?
SEX. APPULEIUS
OCTAVIA I
ATIA
L. MARCIUS PHILIPPUS
Consul 38 BC
M. APPULEIUS
SEX. APPULEIUS
Consul 29 BC
PAULLUS FABIUS MAXIMUS
Consul 11 BC
MARCIA
SEX. APPULEIUS
Consul AD 14
FABIA NUMANTINA
SCRIBONIA
(ii) AUGUSTUS (iii)
(ii) LIVIA DRUSILLA (i)
TI. CLAUDIUS NERO
MARK ANT
CAECILIA ATTICA
(i) M. VIPSANIUS AGRIPPA (iii)
(ii) JULIA (iii)
(ii) TI. CLAUDIUS NERO (i)
(TIBERIUS)
Consul 13 BC
VIPSANIA
NERO CLAUDIUS DRUSUS
Consul 9 BC
ANTONIA II
ANTONIA I
L.
VIPSANIA
DRUSUS CAESAR
C. CAESAR
L. CAESAR
JULIA
L. AEMILIUS PAULLUS
Consul AD 1
AGRIPPA POSTUMUS
AGRIPPINA
GERMANICUS
CLAUDIUS
LIVIA JULIA
M
NERO CAESAR
DRUSUS CAESAR
CALIGULA
DRUSILLA
JULIA LIVIA
AGRIPPINA
CN. DOMITIUS AHENOBARBUS
Consul AD 32
NERO